The Federal Courts

The Federal Courts

FOURTH EDITION

Robert A. Carp, *University of Houston*

Ronald Stidham, *Appalachian State University*

CQ PRESS A Division of Congressional Quarterly Inc.

Washington, D.C.

CQ Press
A Division of Congressional Quarterly Inc.
1414 22nd Street, N.W.
Washington, D.C. 20037

(202) 822-1475; (800) 638-1710

www.cqpress.com

Printed in the United States of America

05   04   03   02   01   5   4   3   2   1

Grateful acknowledgment is made to the following publishers for granting permission to reprint from copyrighted material: Princeton University Press, from J. Woodford Howard, Jr., *Courts of Appeals in the Federal Judicial System: A Study of the Second, Fifth, and District of Columbia Circuits,* copyright © 1981; University of Chicago Press, from Walter F. Murphy, *Elements of Judicial Strategy,* copyright © 1964; University of Tennessee Press, from Robert A. Carp and C. K. Rowland, *Policymaking and Politics in the Federal District Courts,* copyright © 1983; the Law and Society Association.

Photo credits: 1, Administrative Office of the U.S. Courts; 41, 122, 168, Reuters; 68, *The Informer* (Houston, Texas); 199, AFP Photos; 227, Library of Congress.

Cover design: Chiquita Babb, Septima Design
Text design: Kachergis Book Design, Pittsboro, North Carolina

♾ The paper used in this publication meets the minimum requirements of the American National Standard for Information Sciences—Permanence of Paper for Printed Library Materials, ANSI Z39.48-1992.

LIBRARY OF CONGRESS CATALOGING-IN-PUBLICATION DATA

Carp, Robert A., 1943–
    The federal courts / Robert A. Carp, Ronald Stidham.--4th ed.
        p.   cm.
    Includes bibliographical references and index.
    ISBN 1-56802-591-2 (alk. paper)
        1. Courts—United States. 2. Judges—United States. 3. Judicial process—United States. I. Stidham, Ronald, 1940– II. Title.

    KF8719.C33 2001
    347.73'2--dc21   2001023139

To Joan Novak, my longtime and much-valued friend
R. A. C.

To my daughter, Heather; my daughter-in-law, Kim;
and my sons, Tony, Todd, and Sam
R. S.

Contents

Tables and Figures

Preface

In the time since the third edition of *The Federal Courts* appeared in 1998, the United States has witnessed a number of changes. A new chief executive occupies the White House, and the nation awaits the impact that President George W. Bush will have on the federal judiciary. Supreme Court watchers are particularly attentive because the Court's ideological balance now teeters between conservatives and moderates. With at least three justices leaning toward retirement, the president will be in a position to affect the Court's ideological stance for years to come. Scholars are also beginning to assess the overall impact that former president Bill Clinton has had on the federal courts. At the end of his second term, almost half of all U.S. trial and appellate judges bore the Clinton label. His commitment to making federal judges "look like America" seems to have been realized, with half of his judges being either women or minorities—a radical departure from the virtually all-male, all-white judiciaries of the past. Court watchers are also able to assess whether the Clinton judicial team is deciding cases differently than did previous presidential cohorts, a subject that we address in Chapters 3 and 4.

We have made several changes, both in substance and in style, in this fourth edition. First, we have incorporated a large number of comparative references and examples. While we make no pretense that this is a true comparative judicial text, we did highlight with some frequency those aspects of our judicial system that are uniquely American and those that are comparable with other nations. We also sought to include a variety of countries as the sources of our comparisons and not focus just on Canada and England, which have judiciaries most similar to the U.S. system. We have also provided many comparisons with state judicial systems where such juxtapositions seem appropriate to put the federal court system into better perspective. This is particularly true for Chapters 2, 4, and 5. A second substantive change is that we have begun each chapter with several provocative questions that we hope will capture students' attention and generate class discussion. These queries focus on key or unifying themes that are addressed in the substance of the chapter. Third, we have added a glossary at the end of the text to provide elaboration on important concepts or words that are used in the book. Fourth, we have created two indexes, one for concepts and court cases and another for names. Finally, we have provided students with the Cornell University Web page (supct.law. cornell.edu/supct/), from which they can obtain summaries of Supreme Court decisions immediately after decisions are handed down by the justices—and at no cost to the students.

We have sought to prepare a readable, comprehensive textbook about the federal judiciary and its effect on the daily lives of Americans. It is designed primarily for students in courses on judicial process and behavior, constitutional law, American government, and law and society. We have written the book with minimal resort to the jargon and theoretical vocabulary of political science and the law. Although at times it is necessary and useful to include some technical terms and evoke some theoretical concepts in our look at U.S. courts, we address the basic questions on a level that is meaningful to an educated layperson. For those who may desire more specialized explanations or who wish to explore more deeply some of the issues we touch on, the footnotes and selected bibliography contain ample resources for such quests. Readers will find the contributions of historians, political scientists, legal scholars, court administrators, journalists, and psychologists in the pages that follow. Those interested in behavioralism will find much material of interest to them, and so will those who favor a more traditional approach to studying the federal judiciary.

Throughout the text we are constantly mindful of the interrelation between the courts and public policy. We have worked from the premise that significant portions of our lives—as individuals and as a nation—are affected by what our federal judges choose to do and refrain from doing. We reject the often held assumption that only liberals make public policy while conservatives practice restraint; rather, we believe that to some degree all judges engage in this normal and inevitable activity. Liberals on the bench may well hand down rulings that advance the policy goals of their particular interests (civil rights or environmental protections, for example), and conservatives can be expected to act in ways consistent with their policy interests, such as taking a tough stand on law and order or advancing the cause of states' rights. The question then, as we see it, is not whether U.S. courts make policy, but rather, which direction the policy decisions will take. In the chapters that follow we will explain why this has come to be, how it works, and what the consequences are for the United States today.

Chapter 1 provides a brief sketch of the organizational structure of the federal judiciary, placed in historical perspective. As we will see, much of the reason why our judges have the powers they do is a function of historical quirks, pragmatic compromises made during now-forgotten political duels, and haphazard factors quite unintended by the founders of the Republic. Our federal judicial system did not appear one day out of whole cloth but is the product of two centuries of evolution, trial and error, and a pinch of serendipity. The distinction between routine norm enforcement and policy making by federal judges is first addressed in this chapter, and we also provide data on the workload of the federal courts.

Chapter 2 outlines the jurisdiction of the three levels of the U.S. courts. Besides a discussion of what judges are authorized to do in the federal system, there is an in-depth look at judicial self-restraint. We believe that a full understanding of how judges affect our daily lives also requires us to outline those many substantive areas into which the federal jurists may *not* roam and where they are *not* free to make public policy.

In Chapter 3 we take a close look at the men and women who wear the black robe in the United States. What are their background characteristics and their qualifications for office? What are their values, and how do these values manifest themselves in the subsequent behavior of the judges and justices? In this chapter we also explore the process of judicial selection and look at the major participants. We strongly emphasize that there is a discernible policy link between the values of a majority of voters in a presidential election, the values of the appointing president, and the subsequent policy content of decisions made by judges nominated by the chief executive.

Chapter 4 is the first of two on judicial decision making. Here we outline those aspects of the decision-making process that are characteristic of *all* judges, and we do this in the context of the "legal subculture" and the "democratic subculture." Under the former we emphasize the importance of the traditional legal reasoning model for explaining judges' decisions—a model that still accounts for the lion's share of most routine, norm-enforcement decision making. Using the lens of the democratic subculture, we look at a number of extralegal factors that appear to be associated with judges' policy decisions: political party affiliation, local customs and traditions, environmental influences such as public opinion, and pressures from Congress and the president. We also take a look at role theory.

Chapter 5 examines the special case of decision making in collegial, appellate courts. We explore the assumptions and contributions of small-group theory, attitude theory, and rational choice theory to our understanding of the behavior of multijudge tribunals.

Chapter 6 explores the policy impact of federal court decisions and discusses the process by which judicial rulings are implemented—or why some are *not* implemented. We look at the conditions that must prevail if court decisions are to be carried out efficiently and meaningfully, and we also examine the various individuals and institutions that play such a vital role in this process.

In the final chapter we discuss some factors that determine whether judges will engage in policy making and that also predict the substantive direction of policy decisions.

Many people contributed to the writing of this book, and to all of them we offer sincere thanks. At CQ Press, we would like to thank Brenda Carter, Gwenda Larsen, Rita Matyi, and Talia Greenberg. We also would like to express our gratitude to Colleen McGuiness for the excellent job she did in copyediting the final version of the text. Several anonymous adopters of the previous edition offered helpful suggestions for updating and improving the text, and we appreciate their assistance. For any errors that remain, we assume responsibility.

Robert A. Carp thanks two of his research assistants, Bruce Carroll and John Dorris. Each was enormously helpful in coding the decisions of the federal district judges, which served as the basis for Figure 3-1 and Table 3-3.

Ronald Stidham would like to express his gratitude to his colleagues in the Political Science/Criminal Justice Department at Appalachian State University. Their friendship and support made the process of writing this new edition much easier than it might have been.

Both authors are grateful to Kenneth Manning, at the University of Massachusetts at Dartmouth, for his considerable help in the preparation and analysis of the data on the district court judges' voting behavior that appear in Chapters 3 and 4. During the past several years Professor Manning has spent countless hours working on the development of the district court data set. He has been immensely helpful in analyzing the data, and he has worked to upgrade the process of data collection and coding. His contributions have been substantial, and we look forward to working with him again in the future.

Robert A. Carp
Ronald Stidham

CHAPTER 1

History and Organization of the Federal Judicial System

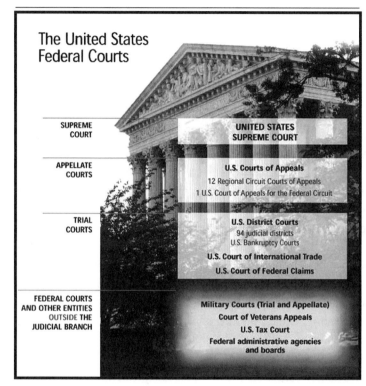

The United States Federal Courts

SUPREME COURT	**UNITED STATES SUPREME COURT**
APPELLATE COURTS	**U.S. Courts of Appeals** 12 Regional Circuit Courts of Appeals 1 U.S. Court of Appeals for the Federal Circuit
TRIAL COURTS	**U.S. District Courts** 94 judicial districts U.S. Bankruptcy Courts **U.S. Court of International Trade** **U.S. Court of Federal Claims**
FEDERAL COURTS AND OTHER ENTITIES OUTSIDE THE JUDICIAL BRANCH	**Military Courts (Trial and Appellate)** **Court of Veterans Appeals** **U.S. Tax Court** Federal administrative agencies and boards

Article III of the Constitution begins, "The judicial Power of the United States, shall be vested in one supreme Court, and in such inferior Courts as the Congress may from time to time ordain and establish"—securing for the first time a judicial branch in American government.

✎ Under the Articles of Confederation there was no national judiciary in the United States. However, this was remedied when the Founding Fathers set up a national court system in Article III of the U.S. Constitution. But if Article III established a national court system, why then was Congress obliged to pass the massive Judiciary Act of 1789 within months after the Constitution was adopted?

✎ Why is the U.S. Supreme Court described as "distinctly American in conception and function"?

✎ How can a democracy justify the fact that federal judges appointed for life possess the power to nullify federal and state laws that were enacted by elected representatives?

✎ Because Article III judges are appointed for life and are independent of one another, what guarantees exist that justice is consistently and equitably dispensed?

ONE OF THE MOST IMPORTANT, most interesting, and most confusing features of the judiciary in the United States is the dual court system; that is, each level of government (state and national) has its own set of courts. Thus, there is a separate court system for each state, one for the District of Columbia, and one for the federal government. Some legal problems are resolved entirely in the state courts, whereas others are handled entirely in the federal courts. Still others may receive attention from both sets of tribunals, which sometimes causes friction. This dissension is undoubtedly most evident when persons convicted of a crime by a state court seek relief in a federal court by means of a writ of habeas corpus—an order issued by a judge to determine whether a person has been lawfully imprisoned. The controversy over the use of this writ increased with the rise during the latter half of the twentieth century in the number of habeas corpus petitions filed in federal district courts by persons convicted in state courts. In 1941 there were 127 habeas petitions filed; in 1942, 130. The number began to rise sharply in 1962. By 1990 the number of habeas petitions filed had reached 11,000.[1]

Proponents of the use of the writ of habeas corpus point out that it is a right protected by the U.S. Constitution and thus argue that the federal courts should be widely accessible to state prisoners. Opponents, however, feel that habeas corpus proceedings allow federal judges to interfere unduly in state legal matters.

Another complaint stems from the fact that state prisoners have traditionally been free to file a seemingly endless number of petitions in a variety of courts. Consequently, death row inmates have been able to postpone their executions for years by a series of petitions filed in various courts.

The debate over habeas corpus relief led to calls for extensive study of the uses and abuses of the process. Both a special ad hoc committee of the Judicial Conference (chaired by former U.S. Supreme Court justice Lewis F. Powell Jr.) and the Federal Courts Study Committee looked at the problem. These efforts eventually bore fruit when in April 1996 President Bill Clinton signed into law the Antiterrorism and Effective Death Penalty Act. This law's habeas corpus provisions create one-year deadlines for filing habeas petitions, limit successive petitions, and restrict the review of state prisoner petitions if the claims were adjudicated on the merits in state courts. Furthermore, in capital cases the law establishes, among other things, a 180-day time frame for filing a habeas petition.[2]

To simplify matters, we will discuss the federal courts in this chapter and the state courts in Chapter 3. Because knowledge of the historical events that helped shape the national court system can shed light on the present judicial structure, our study of the federal judiciary begins with a description of the court system as it has evolved over more than two centuries. We will first examine the three levels of the federal court system in the order in which they were established: the Supreme Court, the courts of appeals, and the district courts. The emphasis in our discussion of each level will be on historical development, policy-making roles, and decision-making procedures.

In a brief look at other federal courts we will focus on the distinction between constitutional and legislative courts, using the example of bankruptcy courts to illustrate a major difference in the two types. Next, we will discuss the individuals and organizations that provide staff support and administrative assistance in the daily operations of the courts. Our overview discussion will then conclude with a brief look at the workload of the federal courts.

The Historical Context

Prior to the ratification of the Constitution, the country was governed by the Articles of Confederation. Under the Articles, practically all functions of the national government were vested in a single-chamber legislature called Congress. There was no separation of executive and legislative powers.

The absence of a national judiciary was considered a major weakness of the Articles of Confederation. Both James Madison and Alexander Hamilton, for example, saw a need for a separate judicial branch. Consequently, the delegates gathered at the Constitutional Convention in Philadelphia in 1787 expressed widespread agreement that a national judiciary should be established. A good deal of disagreement arose, however, on the specific form that the judicial branch should take.

The Constitutional Convention and Article III

The first proposal presented to the Constitutional Convention was the Randolph, or Virginia, Plan, which would have set up both a Supreme Court and inferior federal courts. Opponents of the Virginia Plan responded with the Paterson, or New Jersey, Plan, which called for the creation of a single federal supreme tribunal. Supporters of the New Jersey Plan were especially disturbed by the idea of lower federal courts. They argued that the state courts could hear all cases in the first instance and that a right of appeal to the Supreme Court would be sufficient to protect national rights and provide uniform judgments throughout the country.

The conflict between the states' rights advocates and the nationalists was resolved by one of the many compromises that characterized the Constitutional Convention. The compromise is found in Article III of the Constitution, which begins,

"The judicial Power of the United States, shall be vested in one supreme Court, and in such inferior Courts as the Congress may from time to time ordain and establish." Thus the conflict would be postponed until the new government was in operation.

The Judiciary Act of 1789

Once the Constitution was ratified, action on the federal judiciary came quickly. When the new Congress convened in 1789, its first major concern was judicial organization. Discussions of Senate Bill 1 involved many of the same participants and arguments as were involved in the Constitutional Convention's debates on the judiciary. Once again, the question was whether lower federal courts should be created at all or whether federal claims should first be heard in state courts. Attempts to resolve this controversy split Congress into two distinct groups.

One group, which believed that federal law should be adjudicated in the state courts first and by the United States Supreme Court only on appeal, expressed the fear that the new government would destroy the rights of the states. The other group of legislators, suspicious of the parochial prejudice of state courts, feared that litigants from other states and other countries would be dealt with unjustly. This latter group naturally favored a judicial system that included lower federal courts. The law that emerged from the debate, the Judiciary Act of 1789, set up a judicial system composed of a Supreme Court, consisting of a chief justice and five associate justices; three circuit courts, each comprising two justices of the Supreme Court and a district judge; and thirteen district courts, each presided over by one district judge. The power to create inferior federal courts, then, was immediately exercised. Congress created not one but two sets of lower courts.

The U.S. Supreme Court

A famous jurist once said, "The Supreme Court of the United States is distinctly American in conception and function, and owes little to prior judicial institutions."[3] To understand what the framers of the Constitution envisioned for the Court, another American concept must be considered: the federal form of government. The founders provided for both a national government and state governments; the courts of the states were to be bound by federal laws. However, final interpretation of federal laws simply could not be left to a state court and certainly not to several state tribunals, whose judgments might disagree. Thus, the Supreme Court must interpret federal legislation. Another of the founders' intentions was for the federal government to act directly upon individual citizens as well as upon the states. The Supreme Court's function in the federal system may be summarized as follows:

In the most natural way, as the result of the creation of Federal law under a written constitution conferring limited powers, the Supreme Court of the United States came into being with its unique function. That court maintains the balance between State and Nation through the maintenance of the rights and duties of individuals.[4]

Given the High Court's importance to the U.S. system of government, it was perhaps inevitable that the Court would evoke great controversy. A leading student of the Supreme Court says:

Nothing in the Court's history is more striking than the fact that, while its significant and necessary place in the Federal form of Government has always been recognized by thoughtful and patriotic men, nevertheless, no branch of the Government and no institution under the Constitution has sustained more continuous attack or reached its present position after more vigorous opposition.[5]

The Court's First Decade

George Washington, in appointing the first Supreme Court justices, established two important traditions. First, he began the practice of naming to the Court those with whom he was politically compatible. Washington, the only president ever to have an opportunity to appoint the entire federal judiciary, did a good job of filling federal judgeships with party bedfellows. Without exception, the federal judgeships went to faithful Federalists.

Second, Washington's appointees offered roughly equal geographic representation on the federal courts. His first six appointees to the Supreme Court included three Northerners and three Southerners. On the basis of ability and legal reputation, only three or four of Washington's original appointees merited their justiceships. Many able men were either passed over or declined to serve.

The chief justiceship was the most important appointment Washington made. The president felt that the man to head the first Supreme Court should be an eminent lawyer, statesman, executive, and leader. Many names were presented to Washington, and at least one person, James Wilson, formally applied for the position. Ultimately, Washington settled upon John Jay of New York. Although only forty-four years old, Jay had experience as a lawyer, a judge, and a diplomat. In addition, he was the main drafter of his state's first constitution. Concerning the selection of Jay as chief justice, it has been said:

That Washington picked Jay over his top two rivals for the post, James Wilson and John Rutledge, was either fortuitous or inspired—for it would scarcely have added to the fledgling Supreme Court's popular prestige to have its Chief Justice go insane, as Rutledge later did, or spend his last days jumping from one state to another to avoid being arrested for a debt, as did Wilson.[6]

Washington, however, appointed both Rutledge and Wilson to the Court as associate justices. Neither man contributed significantly to the Court as a government institution. Thus Washington became the first of many presidents to misjudge an appointee to the Court.

The remaining three associate justices who served on the original Supreme Court were William Cushing, John Blair, and James Iredell. Cushing remained on the Court for twenty years, more than twice as long as any of the other original justices, although senility affected his competency in later years. Blair was a close personal friend of Washington's, and Iredell was a strong Federalist from North Carolina who was instrumental in getting that state to join the union. The appointments of Blair and Iredell, then, have been seen as sheer political reward. Despite the generally mediocre quality of the original six appointees, they were held in somewhat higher esteem by their contemporaries, according to studies of early letters and correspondence.[7]

The Supreme Court met for the first time on Monday, February 1, 1790, in the Royal Exchange, a building located in the Wall Street section of New York City. Compared with today's Supreme Court sessions, that first session was unimpressive. Tongue in cheek, one Court historian noted: "The first President immediately on taking office settled down to the pressing business of being President. The first Congress enacted the first laws. The first Supreme Court adjourned."[8]

Only Jay, Wilson, and Cushing, the three Northern justices, were present on opening day. Justice Blair arrived from Virginia for the second day; Rutledge and Iredell, the other Southerners, did not appear at all during the opening session.

The Supreme Court's first session lasted just ten days. During this period the Court selected a clerk, chose a seal, and admitted several lawyers to practice before it in the future. There were no cases to be decided; the Court did not rule on a single case during its first three years. In spite of this insignificant and abbreviated beginning,

the New York and the Philadelphia newspapers described the proceedings of this first session of the Court more fully than any other event connected with the new Government; and their accounts were reproduced in the leading papers of all the States.[9]

The minor role the Supreme Court played continued throughout its first decade of existence. The period 1790–1799 saw several individuals decline their nomination to the Court and one, Robert H. Harrison, chose to accept a state position instead of a Supreme Court justiceship.

During its first decade the Court decided only about fifty cases. However, one of these, *Chisholm v. Georgia*, involved the Court in considerable controversy.[10] In *Chisholm* the justices held that a citizen of one state could sue another state in a federal court. That decision was vigorously attacked by states' rights forces and was ultimately overturned by ratification of the Eleventh Amendment in 1798.

Given the scarcity of Supreme Court business in the early days, Chief Justice Jay's contributions may be traced primarily to his circuit court decisions and his judicial conduct. In one circuit court opinion Jay and his colleagues, Justice Cushing and district judge Henry Marchant, unanimously held that Rhode Island could not permit a debtor to extend his obligations for three years and grant him immunity from arrest and penalties during that time.[11] Jay viewed such an action as a violation of the contract clause contained in Article I, Section 10. His view, a clear affirmation of national supremacy and federal judicial authority, may have set the stage for John Marshall's later opinions along these lines.

In another circuit court case, Jay held that Congress had no authority to assign nonjudicial functions to the courts.[12] Congress had attempted to give the courts the duty of approving applications for military pensions, subject to suspension by the secretary of war and revision by Congress.

Perhaps the most important of Jay's contributions, however, was his insistence that the Supreme Court could not provide legal advice for the executive branch in the form of an advisory opinion. Jay was asked by Treasury Secretary Alexander Hamilton to issue an opinion on the constitutionality of a resolution passed by the Virginia House of Representatives that declared that a congressional bill for the assumption of the state debts was unconstitutional. President Washington also asked Jay for advice on questions relating to Washington's Neutrality Proclamation. In both instances, Jay's response was a firm no because he believed that Article III of the Constitution provides that the Court is to decide only cases pertaining to actual controversies. On balance, "despite his lack of judicial craftsmanship and the brief time in which he might display his personal talents, Jay was successful in establishing the dignity of the office and the independence of the Supreme Court."[13]

The Impact of Chief Justice Marshall

John Marshall served as chief justice from 1801 to 1835 and dominated the Court to a degree unmatched by any other justice. In effect, Marshall was the Court—perhaps because, in the words of one scholar, he "brought a first-class mind and a thoroughly engaging personality into second-class company."[14]

Marshall's dominance of the Court enabled him to initiate some major changes in the way opinions were presented. Prior to his tenure, the justices ordinarily wrote separate opinions (called seriatim opinions) in major cases. Under Marshall's stewardship, the Court adopted the practice of handing down a single opinion. As one might expect, the evidence shows that from 1801 to 1835 Marshall himself wrote almost half the opinions.[15]

Marshall's goal was to keep dissension to a minimum. Arguing that dissent undermined the Court's authority, he tried to persuade the justices to settle their differences privately and then present a united front to the public. No doubt his first-class mind and engaging personality aided him in this endeavor. As strange as it may sound, so did the cozy living arrangements of the time. The justices lived in the same Washington, D.C., boardinghouse while the Court was in session. Thus, they were together before, during, and after work in a pleasant, comfortable routine that discouraged deep disagreements. Can you imagine having breakfast, lunch, and dinner every day with a fellow justice whom you have sharply criticized in a public opinion? Human nature, it would seem, was on Marshall's side in keeping dissension at a low level.

In addition to bringing about changes in opinion-writing practices, Marshall used his powers to involve the Court in the policy-making process. Early in his tenure as chief justice, the Court asserted its power to declare an act of Congress unconstitutional, in *Marbury v. Madison* (1803).[16]

This case had its beginnings in the presidential election of 1800, when Thomas Jefferson defeated John Adams in his bid for reelection. Before leaving office in March 1801, however, Adams and the lame-duck Federalist Congress combined efforts to create several new federal judgeships. To fill these new positions Adams nominated, and the Senate confirmed, loyal Federalists. In addition, Adams named his outgoing secretary of state, John Marshall, to be the new chief justice of the Supreme Court.

As secretary of state it had been Marshall's job to deliver the commissions of the newly appointed judges. Time ran out, however, and seventeen of the commissions were not delivered before Jefferson's inauguration. The new president ordered his secretary of state, James Madison, not to deliver the remaining commissions.

One of the disappointed nominees was William Marbury. He and three of his colleagues, all confirmed as justices of the peace for the District of Columbia, decided to ask the Supreme Court to force Madison to deliver their commissions. They relied upon Section 13 of the Judiciary Act of 1789, which granted the Supreme Court the authority to issue writs of mandamus—court orders commanding a public official to perform an official, nondiscretionary duty.

The case placed Marshall in an uncomfortable predicament. Some suggested that he disqualify himself because of his earlier involvement as secretary of state. There was also the question of the Court's power. If Marshall were to grant the writ, Madison (under Jefferson's orders) would be almost certain to refuse to deliver the commissions. The Supreme Court would then be powerless to enforce its order. However, if Marshall refused to grant the writ, Jefferson would win by default.

The decision Marshall fashioned from this seemingly impossible predicament was evidence of sheer genius. He declared Section 13 of the Judiciary Act of 1789 unconstitutional because it granted original jurisdiction to the Supreme Court in excess of that specified in Article III of the Constitution. Thus the Court's power to review and determine the constitutionality of acts of Congress was established. This decision is rightly seen as one of the single most important decisions the Supreme Court has ever handed down. A few years later the Court also claimed the right of judicial review over actions of state legislatures. During Marshall's tenure it overturned more than a dozen state laws on constitutional grounds.[17]

Inferior federal and state courts also exercise the power to review the constitutionality of legislation. Judicial review is one of the features that sets American courts apart from those in other countries. Herbert Jacob says that "the United States is the outlier in the extraordinary power that its ordinary courts exercise in reviewing the constitutionality of legislation; France and Germany occupy intermediate positions, and the Japanese courts are the least active."[18] Constitutional challenges to legislation do occur in France and Germany, but ordinary judges sitting in ordinary courts do not exercise these powers. In Japan, the Supreme Court, although possessing the power of constitutional review, rarely exercises it. Judicial review in England is basically of administrative actions.[19]

The Changing Issue Emphasis of the Supreme Court

Until approximately 1865 the legal relationship between the national and state governments, or cases of federalism, dominated the Court's docket. John Marshall believed in a strong national government and was not hesitant to restrict state policies that interfered with its activities. A case in point is *Gibbons v. Ogden* (1824), in which the Court overturned a state monopoly over steamboat transportation on the ground that it interfered with national control over interstate commerce.[20] Another good example of Marshall's use of the Court to expand the federal government's powers came in *McCulloch v. Maryland* (1819), in which the chief justice held that the necessary-and-proper clause of the Constitution permitted Congress to establish a national bank.[21] The Court also ruled that the state could not tax a nationally chartered bank. The Court's insistence on a strong government in Washington did not significantly diminish after Marshall's death. Roger Taney, who succeeded Marshall as chief justice, served from 1836 to 1864. Although the Court's position during this period was not as uniformly favorable to the federal government, the Taney Court did not reverse the Marshall Court's direction.

During the period 1865–1937 issues of economic regulation dominated the Court's docket. The shift in emphasis from federalism to economic regulation was brought on by a growing number of national and state laws aimed at monitoring business activities. As such laws increased, so did the number of cases challenging their constitutionality. Early in this period the Court's position on regulation was mixed, but by the 1920s the bench had become hostile toward government regulatory policy. Federal regulations were generally overturned on the ground that they were unsupported by constitutional grants of power to Congress, whereas state laws were thrown out mainly as violations of economic rights protected by the Fourteenth Amendment.

Matters came to a head in the mid-1930s as a result of the Court's conflict with President Franklin D. Roosevelt (FDR), whose New Deal program to combat the effects of the Great Depression included broad measures to control the economy. "In the 16 months starting in January 1935, the Supreme Court heard cases involving ten major New Deal measures or actions; eight of them were declared unconstitutional by the Court."[22] Following his overwhelming reelection in 1936, Roosevelt fought back against the Court. On February 5, 1937, he proposed a plan whereby an additional justice could be added to the Court for each sitting justice over the age of seventy. The result of FDR's "Court-packing" plan would have been to increase the Court's size temporarily to fifteen justices.

While Roosevelt's proposal was being debated in Congress, the Court made an about-face and began to uphold New Deal legislation and similar state legislation.[23] This "switch in time that saved nine," as it has been called, came about because Chief Justice Charles Evans Hughes and Justice Owen Roberts changed their votes to establish majority support for the New Deal legislation. As a result, the Court-packing plan became a moot issue and quietly died in Congress.

Since 1937 the Supreme Court has focused on civil liberties concerns—in particular, the constitutional guarantees of freedom of expression and freedom of religion. In addition, an increasing number of cases have dealt with procedural rights of criminal defendants. Finally, the Court has decided a great number of cases concerning equal treatment by the government of racial minorities and other disadvantaged groups.

The Supreme Court's position on civil liberties and civil rights has varied a good deal over the years. Without doubt, it gave its strongest and most active support for civil liberties and civil rights during the period 1953–1969, when Earl Warren served as chief justice. Perhaps the best-known decision of the period was *Brown v. Board of Education* (1954), which ordered desegregation of the public schools.[24] Other notable decisions guaranteed the right to counsel in state trials, limited police search and seizure practices, required that police inform suspects of their rights, mandated legislatures to be apportioned according to population, and prohibited state-written and state-required prayer in public schools.[25] These and many other controversial decisions led to heavy criticism of the Warren Court.

Although the Court has dealt with a large number of civil rights and civil liberties claims since 1937 and still continues to do so, one recent term may be best remembered for decisions concerning federalism and separation of powers. As one observer put it,

The Court, proclaiming its primacy in deciding what the Constitution means, scolded Congress for infringing on state powers in the Brady handgun law, for enforcing religious freedom in ways that usurped the power of the courts and the states and for restricting the Internet in a law that violates the First Amendment.[26]

The Supreme Court as a Policy Maker

The Supreme Court's role as a policy maker derives from the fact that it interprets the law. Public policy issues come before the Court in the form of legal disputes that must be resolved.

Courts in any political system participate to some degree in the policymaking process because it is their job. Any judge faced with a choice between two or more interpretations and applications of a legislative act, executive order, or constitutional provision must choose among them because the controversy must be decided. And when the judge chooses, his or her interpretation becomes policy for the specific litigants. If the interpretation is accepted by the other judges, the judge has made policy for all jurisdictions in which that view prevails.[27]

In a recent article about the European Court of Justice, which serves the fifteen member states of the European Union, Sally J. Kenney said that this court, like the U.S. Supreme Court, "is grappling with the most important policy matters of our time—separation of powers, the environment, communications, labor policy, affirmative action, sex discrimination, and human rights issues."[28] Fundamental human rights issues in the European Court of Justice are typically raised in the context of trade, however.[29]

An excellent example of U.S. Supreme Court policy making may be found in the area of racial equality. In the late 1880s many states enacted laws requiring the separation of blacks and whites in public facilities. In 1890, for instance, Louisiana enacted a law requiring separate but equal railroad accommodations for blacks and whites. A challenge came two years later. Homer Plessy, who was one-eighth black, protested against the Louisiana law by refusing to move from a seat in the white car of a train traveling from New Orleans to Covington, Louisiana. Arrested and charged with violating the statute, Plessy contended that the law was unconstitutional. The U.S. Supreme Court, in *Plessy v. Ferguson* (1896), upheld the Louisiana statute.[30] Thus the Court established the separate-but-equal policy that was to reign for about sixty years. During this period many states required that the races sit in different areas of buses, trains, terminals, and theaters; use different restrooms; and drink from different water fountains. Blacks were sometimes excluded from restaurants and public libraries. Perhaps most important, black students often had to attend inferior schools.

Separation of the races in public schools was contested in the famous *Brown v. Board of Education* case. Parents of black schoolchildren claimed that state laws requiring or permitting segregation deprived them of equal protection of the laws under the Fourteenth Amendment. The Supreme Court ruled that separate educational facilities are inherently unequal and, therefore, segregation constitutes a denial of equal protection. In the *Brown* decision the Court laid to rest the separate-but-equal doctrine and established a policy of desegregated public schools.

In an average year the Court decides, with signed opinions, between eighty and ninety cases. Thousands of other cases are disposed of with less than the full treatment. Thus the Court deals at length with a very select set of policy issues that have varied throughout the Court's history.

In a democracy broad matters of public policy are, in theory at least, presumed to be left to the elected representatives of the people—not to judicial appointees with life terms. Thus, in principle, U.S. judges are not supposed to make policy. However, in practice judges cannot help but make policy to some extent.

The Supreme Court, however, differs from legislative and executive policy makers. Especially important is the fact that the Court has no self-starting device. The justices must wait for problems to be brought to them; there can be no judicial policy making if there is no litigation. The president and members of Congress have no such constraints. Moreover, even the most assertive Supreme Court is limited to some extent by the actions of other policy makers, such as lower-court judges, Congress, and the president. The Court depends upon others to implement or carry out its decisions.

The Supreme Court as Final Arbiter

The Supreme Court has both original and appellate jurisdiction. Original jurisdiction means that a court has the power to hear a case for the first time. Appellate jurisdiction means that a higher court has the authority to review cases originally decided by a lower court.

The Supreme Court is overwhelmingly an appellate court because most of its time is devoted to reviewing decisions of lower courts. Regardless of whether its decisions are seen as correct, it is the highest appellate tribunal in the country. As such, it has the final word in the interpretation of the Constitution, acts of legislative bodies, and treaties—unless the Court's decision is altered by a constitutional amendment or, in some instances, by an act of Congress.

Since 1925 a device known as certiorari has allowed the High Court to exercise discretion in deciding which cases it should review. Under this method a person may request Supreme Court review of a lower-court decision; then the justices determine whether the request should be granted. In the term concluded in the summer of 1999, the Court handed down decisions with full opinions in eighty-four cases.[31] If review is granted, the Court issues a writ of certiorari, which is an order to the lower court to send up a complete record of the case. When certiorari is denied, the decision of the lower court stands.

The Supreme Court at Work

The formal session of the Supreme Court lasts from the first Monday in October until the business of the term is completed, usually in late June or July. Since 1935 the Supreme Court has had its own building in Washington, D.C. The imposing five-story marble building has the words "Equal Justice Under Law" carved above the entrance. It stands across from the Capitol. Formal sessions of the Court are held in a large courtroom that seats three hundred people. At the front of the courtroom is the bench where the justices are seated. When the Court is in session, the chief justice, followed by the eight associate justices in order of seniority (length of continuous service on the Court), enters through the purple draperies behind the bench and takes a seat. Seats are arranged according to seniority, with the chief justice in the center, the senior associate justice on the chief justice's right, the second-ranking associate justice on the left, and continuing alternately in declining order of seniority. Near the courtroom are the conference room, where the justices decide cases, and the chambers that contain offices for the justices and their staffs.

The Court's term is divided into sittings, of approximately two weeks each, during which the justices meet in open session and hold internal conferences, and recesses, during which the justices work behind closed doors as they consider cases and write opinions. The eighty to ninety cases per term that receive the Court's full treatment follow a fairly routine pattern, which is described below.

Oral Argument. Oral arguments are generally scheduled on Monday through Wednesday during the sittings. The sessions run from 10:00 a.m. until noon and from 1:00 until 3:00 p.m. Because the procedure is not a trial or the original hearing of a case, no jury is assembled and no witnesses are called. Instead, the two opposing attorneys present their arguments to the justices. The general practice is to allow thirty minutes for each side, although the Court may decide that additional time is necessary. The Court can normally hear four cases in one day. Attorneys presenting oral arguments are frequently interrupted with probing questions from the justices. The oral argument is considered very important by both attorneys and justices because it is the only stage in the process that allows such personal exchanges.

The Conference. On Fridays preceding the two-week sittings the Court holds conferences; during sittings it holds conferences on Wednesday afternoon and all day Friday. At the Wednesday meeting the justices discuss the cases argued on Monday. At the longer conference on Friday they discuss the cases that were argued on Tuesday and Wednesday, plus any other matters that need to be considered. The most important of these other matters are the certiorari petitions.

Prior to the Friday conference each justice is given a list of the cases that will be discussed. The conference begins at about 9:30 or 10:00 a.m. and runs until 5:30 or 6:00 p.m. As the justices enter the conference room they shake hands with each other and take their seats around a rectangular table. They meet behind locked doors, and no official record is kept of the discussions. The chief justice presides over the conference and offers an opinion first in each case. The other justices follow in descending order of seniority. At one time a formal vote was then taken in reverse order (with the junior justice voting first); however, today the justices usually indicate their view during the discussion, making a formal vote unnecessary.

A quorum for a decision on a case is six members; obtaining a quorum is seldom difficult. Cases are sometimes decided by fewer than nine justices because of vacancies, illnesses, or nonparticipation resulting from possible conflicts of interest. Supreme Court decisions are made by a majority vote. In case of a tie the lower-court decision is upheld.

Opinion Writing. After a tentative decision has been reached in conference, the next step is to assign the Court's opinion to an individual justice to write. The chief justice, if voting with the majority, either writes the opinion or assigns it to another justice who voted with the majority. When the chief justice votes with the minority, then the most senior justice in the majority makes the assignment.

After the conference the justice who will write the Court's opinion begins work on an initial draft. Other justices may work on the case by writing alternative opinions. The completed opinion is circulated to justices in both the majority and the minority groups. The writer seeks to persuade justices originally in the minority to change their votes and to keep his or her majority group intact. A bargaining process occurs and the wording of the opinion may be changed to satisfy other justices or obtain their support. A deep division in the Court makes it difficult to achieve a clear, coherent opinion and may even result in a shift in votes or in another justice's opinion becoming the Court's official ruling.

In most cases a single opinion does obtain majority support, although few rulings are unanimous. Those who disagree with the opinion of the Court are said to dissent. A dissent does not have to be accompanied by an opinion. In recent years, however, it usually has been. Whenever more than one justice dissents, each may write an opinion or all may join in a single opinion.

On occasion a justice will agree with the Court's decision but differ in his or her reason for reaching that conclusion. Such a justice may write what is called a concurring opinion. A good example may be found in Justice Potter Stewart's concurring opinion in *Stanley v. Georgia* (1969).[32] In that case an investigation of Robert Eli Stanley's alleged bookmaking activities led to the issuance of a search warrant for his home. Federal and state agents conducting the search found three reels of film, a projector, and a screen. After viewing the films, the state officers seized them as pornographic. Stanley was convicted of "knowingly having possession of obscene matter" in violation of Georgia law. The Supreme Court overturned the Georgia trial court's decision on the ground that mere private possession of lewd material could not constitutionally be made a crime. Justice Stewart agreed that the lower-court decision should be overturned, but he did so for a different reason: He felt that the films had been seized unlawfully in violation of the Fourth and Fourteenth Amendments.

An opinion labeled "concurring and dissenting" agrees with part of a Court ruling but disagrees with other parts. Finally, the Court occasionally issues a per curiam opinion—an unsigned opinion that is usually brief. Such opinions are often used when the Court accepts the case for review but gives it less than full treatment. For example, it may decide the case without benefit of oral argument and issue a per curiam opinion to explain the disposition of the case.

The procedures followed in the U.S. Supreme Court are not common to high courts everywhere. For example, the European Court of Justice differs from the U.S. Supreme Court in two important respects. First, it has no mechanism for denying certiorari; it must hear all cases referred to it regardless of their importance. Second, it issues only one judgment; there are no concurring or dissenting opinions.[33]

The U.S. Courts of Appeals

The courts of appeals have been described as "perhaps the least noticed of the regular constitutional courts."[34] They receive less media coverage than the Supreme Court, in part because their activities are simply not as dramatic. However, one should not assume that the courts of appeals are unimportant to the judicial system. Recall that in its 1998 term the Supreme Court handed down decisions with full opinions in only eighty-four cases, which means that the courts of appeals are the courts of last resort for most appeals in the federal court system.

Circuit Courts: 1789–1801

The Judiciary Act of 1789 created three circuit courts—the southern, middle, and eastern circuits—each composed of two justices of the Supreme Court and a district judge. The circuit court was to hold two sessions each year in each district within the circuit.

The district judge became primarily responsible for establishing the circuit court's workload. The two Supreme Court justices then came into the local area and participated in the cases. This practice tended to give a local rather than national focus to the circuit courts.

The circuit court system was regarded from the beginning as unsatisfactory, especially by Supreme Court justices, who objected to the traveling imposed upon them. As early as September 1790, Chief Justice Jay wrote to the president urging changes in the circuit-riding duties prescribed by the Judiciary Act of 1789. Justice Iredell, who resided in North Carolina, was particularly hard-pressed. In addition to traveling some one thousand miles between his home and Philadelphia (where Supreme Court sessions were held), he was required to tour the states of Georgia, North Carolina, and South Carolina twice annually. It is no wonder Iredell referred to his life as that of a "travelling postboy."[35]

Supreme Court justices were not the only ones who objected to the circuit-riding duties. Attorney General Edmund Randolph and President Washington also urged relief for the Supreme Court justices. Congress made a slight change in 1793 by altering the circuit court organization to include only one Supreme Court justice and one district judge. The Randolph proposal for separate circuit court judgeships to replace Supreme Court participation was not implemented, however. The circuit courts had become the center of a political controversy. The Federalists urged passage of Randolph's proposal for separate circuit judges; the Anti-Federalist leaders saw the Randolph proposal as an attempt to enlarge the federal judiciary and remove it from state surveillance.

Circuit Courts: 1801–1891

In the closing days of President John Adams's administration in 1801, Congress passed the "midnight judges" act, which eliminated circuit riding by the Supreme Court justices, authorized the appointment of sixteen new circuit judges, and greatly extended the jurisdiction of the lower courts.

Some saw the Judiciary Act of 1801 as the Federalists' last-ditch effort to prolong their domination of government, whereas others viewed it as an extension of federal jurisdiction to suits that previously had been tried only in state courts. Certainly the Federalists were interested in federal judgeships, and they wanted to protect the judiciary from Anti-Federalists. The act of 1801, however, was not a last-minute effort. Efforts to change the circuit courts had been ongoing for more than ten years.

The new administration of Thomas Jefferson strongly opposed the "midnight judges" act, and Congress wasted little time in repealing it. The Circuit Court Act of 1802 restored circuit riding by Supreme Court justices and expanded the number of circuits. However, the 1802 legislation allowed the circuit court to be presided over by a single district judge. At first glance, such a change may seem slight, but it proved to be of great importance. Increasingly, the district judges began to assume responsibility for both district and circuit courts. In practice, then, original and appellate jurisdiction were both in the hands of the district judges.

The next major step in the development of the courts of appeals did not come until 1869, although there had been a growing recognition that some form of judicial reorganization was necessary. The pro-state and pro-nationalist interests disagreed on the exact form of judicial relief that should be enacted. The pro-nationalists did not want a plan that would transfer power from the national government to the states. They favored shifting many conflicts to the lower federal courts under the supervision of the Supreme Court. Thus, "reorganization of the circuit courts continued to be the key to the nationalists' strategy."[36]

Expansion of the circuit courts, allowing them greater control over appeals, would free the Supreme Court to concentrate on the key cases as well as to formulate policy. The pro-state interests also wanted to lessen the High Court's burden, but by reducing its power. Unable to do so, they were willing to accept only minor changes in the basic judicial structure established in 1789.

The political stalemate prevented any major reorganization between 1802 and 1869. Consequently, the courts simply were unable to handle the flood of litigation. Then, in 1869, Congress approved a measure that authorized the appointment of nine new circuit judges and reduced the Supreme Court justices' circuit court duty to one term every two years. Still, the High Court was flooded with cases because no limitations were placed on the right of appeal to the Supreme Court. Six years later Congress broadened the jurisdiction of the circuit courts. The workload of the Supreme Court was not significantly decreased, however, because an automatic right of appeal to the High Court still existed. A more drastic revision of the federal judicial system was to come in 1891.

The Courts of Appeals: 1891 to the Present

On March 3, 1891, the Evarts Act was signed into law, creating new courts known as circuit courts of appeals. These new tribunals were to hear most of the appeals from district courts. The old circuit courts, which had existed since 1789, also remained—a situation surely confusing to all but the most serious students of the judicial system. The new circuit court of appeals was to consist of one circuit judge, one circuit court of appeals judge, one district judge, and a Supreme Court justice. Two judges constituted a quorum in these new courts.

Following passage of the Evarts Act, the federal judiciary had two trial tribunals: district courts and circuit courts. It also had two appellate tribunals: circuit courts of appeals and the Supreme Court. Most appeals of trial decisions were to go to the circuit court of appeals, although the act also allowed direct review in some instances by the Supreme Court. In short, creation of the circuit courts of appeals released the Supreme Court from many petty types of cases. Appeals could still be made, but the High Court would now have much greater control over its own workload. Much of its former caseload was thus shifted to the two lower levels of the federal judiciary.

The next step in the evolution of the courts of appeals came in 1911. In that year Congress passed legislation abolishing the old circuit courts, which had no appellate jurisdiction and frequently duplicated the functions of district courts.

Today, as a result of a name change implemented in the 1948 Judicial Code, the intermediate appellate tribunals are officially known as courts of appeals. Despite their official name, they continue to be referred to colloquially as circuit courts. Although these intermediate appellate courts have been manned at one time or another by circuit judges, courts of appeals judges, district judges, and Supreme Court justices, they now are staffed by 179 authorized courts of appeals judges.

Nine regional courts of appeals, each covering several states, were created in 1891. Another, covering the District of Columbia, was absorbed into the system after 1893. Next came the Court of Appeals for the Tenth Circuit, which was carved from the Eighth Circuit in 1929. In 1981, following a long battle during which many civil rights activists expressed the fear that a split might negate gains they had made acting through the courts, the Court of Appeals for the Eleventh Circuit was carved from the Fifth Circuit.[37]

For several years the heavy caseload and geographical expanse of the Ninth Circuit have prompted discussions of a split in that circuit. A number of bills to accomplish that purpose have been introduced in Congress since 1990 but none has passed.

The courts of appeals in each of the twelve regional circuits are responsible for reviewing cases appealed from federal district courts (and in some cases from administrative agencies) within the boundaries of the circuit. Figure 2-1 depicts the appellate and district court boundaries and indicates the states contained in each.

A specialized appellate court came into existence in 1982 when Congress established the Federal Circuit, a jurisdictional instead of a geographic circuit. The United States Court of Appeals for the Federal Circuit was created by consolidating the Court of Claims and the Court of Customs and Patent Appeals.

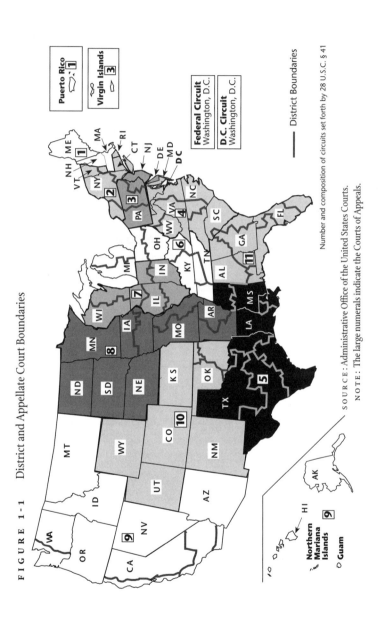

FIGURE 1-1 District and Appellate Court Boundaries

SOURCE: Administrative Office of the United States Courts.

NOTE: The large numerals indicate the Courts of Appeals.

Number and composition of circuits set forth by 28 U.S.C. § 41

Puerto Rico [1]

Virgin Islands [3]

Federal Circuit
Washington, D.C.

D.C. Circuit
Washington, D.C.

—— District Boundaries

Northern Mariana Islands [9]

Guam

The Review Function of the Courts of Appeals

As one modern-day student of the judiciary has noted:

The distribution of labor among the Supreme Court and the Courts of Appeals, implicit in the Judiciary Act of 1925, has matured into fully differentiated functions for federal appellate courts. Substantively, the Supreme Court has become more and more a constitutional tribunal. Courts of Appeals concentrate on statutory interpretation, administrative review, and error correction in masses of routine adjudications.[38]

Although the Supreme Court has had discretionary control of its docket since 1925, the courts of appeals still have no such luxury. Instead, their docket depends on how many and what types of cases are appealed to them.

Most of the cases reviewed by the courts of appeals originate in the federal district courts. Litigants disappointed with the lower-court decision may appeal the case to the court of appeals of the circuit in which the federal district court is located. The appellate courts have also been given authority to review the decisions of certain administrative agencies. This type of case enters the federal judicial system at the court of appeals level instead of at the federal district court level.

Because the courts of appeals have no control over which cases are brought to them, they deal with both routine and highly important matters. At one end of the spectrum are frivolous appeals or claims that have no substance and little or no chance for success. Such appeals are no doubt encouraged by the fact that the Supreme Court has ruled that assistance of counsel for first appeals should be granted to all indigents who have been convicted of a crime.[39] Occasionally a claim is successful, which then motivates other prisoners to appeal.

At the other end of the spectrum are the cases that raise major questions of public policy and evoke strong disagreement. Decisions by the courts of appeals in such cases are likely to establish policy for society as a whole, not just for the specific litigants. Civil liberties, reapportionment, religion, and education cases provide good examples of the kinds of disputes that may affect all citizens.

There are two purposes of review in the courts of appeals. The first is error correction. Judges in the various circuits are called upon to monitor the performance of federal district courts and federal agencies and to supervise their application and interpretation of national and state laws. In doing so, the courts of appeals do not seek out new factual evidence, but instead examine the record of the lower court for errors. In the process of correcting errors the courts of appeals also settle disputes and enforce national law.

The second function is sorting out and developing those few cases worthy of Supreme Court review. The circuit judges tackle the legal issues earlier than the Supreme Court justices and may help shape what they consider review-worthy claims. Judicial scholars have found that appealed cases sometimes differ in their second hearing from their first.

The Courts of Appeals as Policy Makers

The Supreme Court's role as a policy maker derives from the fact that it interprets the law; the same holds true for the courts of appeals. The scope of the courts of appeals' policy-making role takes on added importance given that they are the courts of last resort in the vast majority of cases. A study of three circuits, for example, found that the U.S. Supreme Court reviewed only nineteen of the nearly four thousand decisions of those tribunals.[40]

As an illustration of the far-reaching impact of circuit court judges, consider the recent decision in a case involving the Fifth Circuit. For several years the University of Texas Law School (as well as many other law schools across the country) had been granting preference to black and Mexican American applicants to increase the enrollment of these classes of minority students. This practice was challenged in a federal district court on the ground that it discriminated against white and nonpreferred minority applicants in violation of the Fourteenth Amendment. On March 18, 1996, a panel of Fifth Circuit judges ruled in *Hopwood v. Texas* that the Fourteenth Amendment does not permit the school to discriminate in this way and that the law school may not use race as a factor in law school admissions.[41] The U.S. Supreme Court denied a petition for a writ of certiorari in the case, thus leaving it the law of the land in Texas, Louisiana, and Mississippi, the states comprising the Fifth Circuit.[42] Although it may technically be true that only schools in the Fifth Circuit are affected by the ruling, an editorial in the *National Law Journal* indicates otherwise, noting that

while cockeyed optimists might argue that *Hopwood*'s impact is limited to three states in the South . . . , the truth is that across the country law school (and other) deans, fearing similar litigation, are scrambling to come up with an alternative to affirmative action.[43]

A major difference in policy making by the Supreme Court and by the courts of appeals should be noted. Whereas there is one High Court for the entire country, each court of appeals covers only a specific region. Thus, the courts of appeals are more likely to make policy on a regional basis. Still, as evidenced by the *Hopwood* case, they are a part of the federal judicial system and "participate in both national and local policy networks, their decisions becoming regional law unless intolerable to the Justices."[44]

The Courts of Appeals at Work

The courts of appeals do not have the same degree of discretion as the Supreme Court to decide whether to accept a case for review. Still, circuit judges have developed methods for using their time as efficiently as possible.

Screening. During the screening stage the judges decide whether to give an appeal a full review or to dispose of it in some other way. The docket may be reduced to some extent by consolidating similar claims into single cases, a process that also results in a uniform decision. In deciding which cases can be disposed of without oral argument, the courts of appeals increasingly rely on law clerks or staff attorneys. These court personnel read petitions and briefs and then submit recommendations to the judges. As a result, many cases are disposed of without reaching the oral argument stage. One recent study noted that prior to 1970 procedural terminations (terminations without a hearing) averaged 27 percent of the cases commenced in the courts of appeals. From 1970 through 1990 the average increased to 46 percent.[45]

Three-Judge Panels. Those cases given the full treatment are normally considered by panels of three judges rather than by all the judges in the circuit. This means that several cases can be heard at the same time by different three-judge panels, often sitting in different cities throughout the circuit.

Panel assignments are typically made by the circuit executive or someone else and then a clerk assigns cases blindly to the panels. Because all the circuits now contain more than three judges, the panels change frequently so that the same three judges do not sit together permanently. Regardless of the method used to determine panel assignments, one fact remains clear: A decision reached by a majority of a three-judge panel does not necessarily reflect the views of a majority of the judges in the circuit.

En Banc Proceedings. Occasionally, different three-judge panels within the same circuit may reach conflicting decisions in similar cases. To resolve such conflicts and to promote circuit unanimity, federal statutes provide for an en banc procedure, in which all the circuit's judges sit together on a panel and decide a case. The exception to this general rule occurs in the large Ninth Circuit, where assembling all the judges becomes too cumbersome. There, en banc panels normally consist of eleven judges. The en banc procedure may also be used when the case concerns an issue of extraordinary importance, as in the famous *Tinker v. Des Moines Inde-*

pendent Community School District decision.[46] That case raised the question of whether high school students wearing black armbands in the classroom to protest the Vietnam War should be protected by the First Amendment. When the Court of Appeals for the Eighth Circuit heard that case in 1967, the en banc procedure was used.

The en banc procedure may be requested by the litigants or by the judges of the court. The circuits themselves have discretion to decide if and how the procedure will be used. Clearly, its use is the exception, not the rule.

Oral Argument. Cases that have survived the screening process and have not been settled by the litigants are scheduled for oral argument. Attorneys for each side are given a short amount of time (in some cases no more than ten minutes) to discuss the points made in their written briefs and to answer questions from the judges.

The Decision. Following the oral argument the judges may confer briefly and, if they are in agreement, may announce their decision immediately. Otherwise, a decision will be announced only after the judges confer at greater length. Following the conference some decisions will be announced with a brief order or per curiam opinion of the court. A small portion of decisions will be accompanied by a longer, signed opinion and perhaps even dissenting and concurring opinions. Recent years have seen a general decrease in the number of published opinions, although circuits vary in their practices.

U.S. District Courts

The U.S. district courts represent the basic point of input for the federal judicial system. Although some cases are later taken to a court of appeals or perhaps even to the Supreme Court, most federal cases never move beyond the U.S. trial courts. In terms of sheer numbers of cases handled, the district courts are the workhorses of the federal judiciary. However, their importance extends beyond simply disposing of a large number of cases.

The First District Courts

Congress made the decision to create a national network of federal trial courts when it passed the Judiciary Act of 1789. Section 2 of the act established thirteen district courts by (1) making each of the eleven states then in the union a district and (2) making the parts of Massachusetts and Virginia that were to become Maine and Kentucky into separate districts. That organizational scheme established the practice, which still exists, of honoring state boundary lines in drawing districts. Thus, from the very beginning "the federal judiciary was state-contained, with the administrative and political structure of the states becoming the organizational structure of the federal courts."[47]

The First District Judges

Each federal district court was to be presided over by a single judge who resided in the district. As soon as this became known, President Washington began receiving letters from individuals desiring appointment to the various judgeships. Many asked members of Congress or Vice President Adams to recommend them to President Washington. Personal applications were not necessarily successful and were not the only way in which names came to the president's attention. Harry Innes, for example, was not an applicant for the Kentucky judgeship but received it after being recommended by a member of Congress from his state.[48]

Not everyone nominated was willing to serve as a district judge, however. Three of the thirteen whose names were originally submitted to the Senate for confirmation declined the appointment—perhaps because the nominating process "did not permit consultation either with the individuals concerned or representatives of the 'neighborhood' who might know if the office would be accepted."[49] The rejections were somewhat embarrassing, and Washington resorted to careful preliminary screening of future appointments and relied more heavily on his secretary of state for recommendations.

Many of the early prospective Supreme Court nominees preferred state-level appointments. The same held true for district court appointments. Some declined federal district judgeships to pursue other federal or state positions. Still others simply held a district judgeship and a state office simultaneously.[50] Eventually, states began to pass laws prohibiting state officeholders from accepting federal positions.

As new states came into the union, additional district courts were created. The additions, along with resignations, gave Washington an opportunity to offer judgeships to thirty-three people, twenty-eight of whom accepted. A student of the early courts offers a profile of the judges Washington appointed. Their average age at appointment was forty-six. All but three were born in the United States, and sixteen had received college educations. All were members of the bar, and all but seven had state or local legal experience as judges, prosecutors, or attorneys general.[51] Presidents have continued to appoint lawyers with public service backgrounds to the federal bench.

Present Organization of the District Courts

The practice of respecting state boundaries in establishing district court jurisdictions began in 1789 and has been periodically reaffirmed by statutes ever since. As the country grew, new district courts were created. Eventually, Congress began to divide some states into more than one district. California, New York, and Texas have the most, with four each. Other than consistently honoring state lines, the organization of district constituencies appears to follow no rational plan. Size and population vary widely from district to district. Over the years, a court was added for the District of Columbia, and several territories have been served by district courts. U.S. district courts now serve the fifty states, the District of Columbia, Guam, Puerto Rico, the Virgin Islands, and the Northern Mariana Islands.

Congress often provides further organizational detail by creating divisions within a district. In doing this, the national legislature precisely lists the counties included in a particular division as well as the cities in which court will be held.

As indicated, the original district courts were each assigned one judge. With the growth in population and litigation, Congress has periodically had to add judges to most of the districts. The Federal Judgeship Act of 1990 created seventy-four new district judgeships, bringing the current total to 649. Today all districts have more than one judge; the Southern District of New York, which includes Manhattan and the Bronx, currently has twenty-eight judges and is thus the largest. Because each federal district court is normally presided over by a single judge, several trials may be in session at various cities within the district at any given time.

The District Courts as Trial Courts

Congress established the district courts as the trial courts of the federal judicial system and gave them original jurisdiction over virtually all cases. They are the only federal courts in which attorneys examine and cross-examine witnesses. The factual record is thus established at this level. Subsequent appeals of the trial court decision will focus on correcting errors, not on reconstructing the facts. The task of determining the facts in a case often falls to a jury, a group of citizens from the community who serve as impartial arbiters of the facts and apply the law to the facts.

The Constitution guarantees the right to a jury trial in criminal cases in the Sixth Amendment and the same right in civil cases in the Seventh Amendment. The right can be waived, however, in which case the judge becomes the arbiter both of questions of fact and of matters of law. Such trials are referred to as bench trials. Two types of juries are associated with federal district courts. The grand jury is a group of men and women convened to determine whether probable cause exists to believe that a person has committed the federal crime of which he or she has been accused. Grand jurors meet periodically to hear charges brought by the U.S. attorney. Petit jurors are chosen at random from the community to hear evidence and determine whether a defendant in a civil trial has liability or whether a defendant in a criminal trial is guilty or not guilty. Federal rules call for twelve jurors in criminal cases but permit fewer in civil cases. The federal district courts generally use six-person juries in civil cases.

Norm Enforcement by the District Courts

Some students of the judiciary make a distinction between norm enforcement and policy making by the courts.[52] Trial courts are viewed as engaging primarily in norm enforcement, whereas appellate courts are seen as having greater opportunity to make policy.

Norm enforcement is closely tied to the administration of justice, because all nations develop standards considered essential to a just and orderly society. Societal norms are embodied in statutes, administrative regulations, prior court decisions, and community traditions. Criminal statutes, for example, incorporate concepts of acceptable and unacceptable behavior into law. A judge deciding a case concerning an alleged violation of that law is basically practicing norm enforcement. Because cases of this type rarely allow the judge to escape the strict restraints of legal and procedural requirements, he or she has little chance to make new law or develop new policy. In civil cases, too, judges are often confined to norm enforcement; opportunities for policy making are infrequent. Rather, such litigation generally arises from a private dispute whose outcome is of interest only to the parties in the suit.

Policy Making by the District Courts

The district courts also play a policy-making role. One leading judicial scholar explains how this function differs from norm enforcement:

When they make policy, the courts do not exercise more discretion than when they enforce community norms. The difference lies in the intended impact of the decision. Policy decisions are intended to be guideposts for future actions; norm-enforcement decisions are aimed at the particular case at hand.[53]

The discretion that a federal trial judge exercises should not be overlooked, however. As Americans have become more litigation-conscious, disputes that were once resolved informally are now more likely to be decided in a court of law. The courts find themselves increasingly involved in domains once considered private. What does this mean for the federal district courts? According to one study, "These new areas of judicial involvement tend to be relatively free of clear, precise appellate court and legislative guidelines; and as a consequence the opportunity for trial court jurists to write on a clean slate, that is, to make policy, is formidable."[54] In other words, when the guidelines are not well established, district judges have a great deal of discretion to set policy. In fact, some district judges have gained considerable notoriety because of their policy-making activities. One well-known example is Judge William Wayne Justice of the Eastern District of Texas. For more than two decades his orders dealing with the standards to be maintained in the state's prison system to comply with the Eighth Amendment's prohibition against cruel and unusual punishment affected state appropriations. Justice's far-reaching criminal justice, public education, and legislative redistricting decisions prompted the suggestion that if he were "in the legislature he would never be able to legislate as effectively as he does from the bench."[55]

Three-Judge District Courts

In 1903 Congress passed legislation providing for the use of special three-judge district courts in certain types of cases. Such courts are created on an ad hoc basis; the panels are disbanded when a case has been decided. Each panel must include at least one judge from the federal district court and at least one judge from the court of appeals. Normally, two district judges and one appellate judge constitute the panel. Appeals of decisions of three-judge district courts go directly to the Supreme Court.

The earliest types of cases to be heard by three-judge district courts were suits filed by the attorney general under the Sherman Antitrust Act or the Interstate Commerce Act. Congress later provided that these special courts could decide suits brought by private citizens challenging the constitutionality of state or federal statutes and seeking injunctions to prevent enforcement of the challenged statutes.

An example of the use of a three-judge district court is provided by the abortion case of *Roe v. Wade*.[56] Jane Roe (a pseudonym), a single, pregnant woman, challenged the constitutionality of the Texas anti-abortion statute and sought an injunction to prohibit further enforcement of the law. The case was initially heard by a three-judge court consisting of district judges Sarah T. Hughes and W. N. Taylor and Fifth Circuit Court of Appeals Judge Irving L. Goldberg. The three-judge district court held the Texas abortion statute invalid but declined to issue an injunction against its enforcement on the ground that a federal intrusion into the state's affairs was not warranted. Roe then appealed the denial of the injunction directly to the Supreme Court.

Over the years congressional statutes, such as the Civil Rights Act of 1964, the Voting Rights Act of 1965, and the Presidential Election Campaign Fund Act of 1974, have specified the use of three-judge district courts. However, increases in the number of cases decided by such courts led to complaints about caseload problems, because appeals from the three-judge panels go directly to the Supreme Court. Thus, in 1976 Congress virtually eliminated three-judge district courts except in cases concerning reapportionment of state legislatures and congressional redistricting and in some cases under the Civil Rights Acts.

Constitutional Courts and Legislative Courts

The Judiciary Act of 1789 established the three levels of the federal court system in existence today. Periodically, however, Congress has exercised its power, based on Article III and Article I of the Constitution, to create other federal courts. Courts established under Article III are known as constitutional courts, and those created under Article I are called legislative courts. The former handles the bulk of litigation in the system and, for this reason, will remain the focus of discussion here. The Supreme Court, courts of appeals, and federal district courts are constitutional courts. The U.S. Court of Military Appeals is one example of a legislative court. It was created in 1950 under authority found in Article I, Section 8 of the Constitution, "To constitute Tribunals inferior to the supreme Court," and "To make Rules for the Government and Regulation of the land and naval Forces." Another important legislative court currently in existence is the United States Tax Court (formerly an administrative agency called the Tax Court of the United States, its name was changed by a 1969 statute). Another Article I court is the Court of Veterans Appeals, which was established by legislation signed by President Ronald Reagan on November 18, 1988. This court has exclusive jurisdiction to review decisions of the Board of Veterans Appeals. Judges on this court serve fifteen-year terms of office.

The two types of courts may be further distinguished by their functions. Legislative courts, unlike their constitutional counterparts, often have administrative and quasi-legislative as well as judicial duties. Another difference is that legislative courts are often created to help administer a specific congressional statute. Constitutional courts, however, are tribunals established to handle litigation.

Finally, the constitutional and legislative courts vary in their degree of independence from the other two branches of government. Article III (constitutional court) judges serve during a period of good behavior, or what amounts to life tenure. Because Article I (legislative court) judges have no constitutional guarantee of good-behavior tenure, Congress may set specific terms of office for them. Judges of Article III courts are also constitutionally protected against salary reductions while in office. Those who serve as judges of legislative courts have no such protection. In sum, the constitutional courts have a greater degree of independence from the other two branches of government than the legislative courts. How important is such independence? Events surrounding the fate of federal bankruptcy courts reveal independence to be a major consideration.

On November 6, 1978, President Jimmy Carter signed into law the Bankruptcy Reform Act. That legislation (1) required that bankruptcy cases be filed in bankruptcy courts, not district courts; (2) extended the terms of current bankruptcy judges through March 1984; (3) provided that after March 3, 1984, bankruptcy judges were to be appointed by the president, with Senate confirmation, for fourteen-year terms; (4) simplified existing bankruptcy law; and (5) expanded the jurisdiction of bankruptcy judges. A system of bankruptcy courts was seemingly in place.

Trouble began, however, less than three years later. In a brief order issued on April 23, 1981, and a supplemental memorandum issued on July 24, 1981, U.S. District Judge Miles W. Lord of Minnesota held that the Bankruptcy Reform Act's delegation of Article III authority to bankruptcy judges was unconstitutional.[57] Judge Lord argued that Congress had exceeded its constitutional power when it authorized bankruptcy judges to exercise the jurisdiction and duties of district judges without at the same time vesting them with the tenure and salary protections given Article III judges. The independence question was at the heart of Judge Lord's decision.

The case was appealed to the Supreme Court, which, in a June 1982 decision, agreed that portions of the Bankruptcy Reform Act were unconstitutional. The Court held that certain powers granted by the act to bankruptcy judges could be exercised only by Article III judges, who are insulated from political pressures by life tenure and protection from pay cuts.[58] The Supreme Court asked Congress to pass remedial legislation aimed at handling the bankruptcy problem. After several failures on Congress's part, the federal district courts in September 1982 put into operation a contingency plan recommended by the Judicial Conference of the United States.[59] Among other things, the Judicial Conference's emergency rule removed contested matters from bankruptcy judges to district court judges.

After several unsuccessful attempts Congress passed a law in July 1984 to correct the problem. The new legislation provided for the creation of bankruptcy courts as units of the district courts. Bankruptcy judges are now appointed for fourteen-year terms by the court of appeals for the circuit in which the district is located. Most bankruptcy cases can now be handled entirely by the bankruptcy judge.

Administrative and Staff Support in the Federal Judiciary

The daily operation of federal courts requires a myriad of personnel. Although judges are the most visible actors in the judicial system, a large supporting cast is also at work. Their efforts are necessary to perform the tasks for which judges are unskilled or unsuited, or for which they simply do not have adequate time. Some members of the support team, such as law clerks, may work specifically for one judge. Others—for example, U.S. magistrate judges—are assigned to a particular court. Still others may be employees of an agency, such as the Administrative Office of the United States Courts, that serves the entire judicial system.

United States Magistrate Judges

In an effort to help federal district judges deal with increased workloads, Congress passed the Federal Magistrates Act in 1968. This legislation created the office of U.S. magistrate to replace the U.S. commissioners, who had performed limited duties for the federal trial courts for a number of years. In 1990, with passage of the Judicial Improvements Act, their title was changed to U.S. magistrate judge. Magistrate judges are formally appointed by the judges of the district court for eight-year terms of office, although they can be removed before the expiration of the term for "good cause." As of 1999, these officials were paid $125,764 per year.[60]

The magistrate judge system constitutes a structure that responds to each district court's specific needs and circumstances. Within guidelines set by the Federal Magistrates Acts of 1968, 1976, and 1979, the judges in each district court establish the duties and responsibilities of their magistrate judges. Most significantly, the 1979 legislation permits a magistrate judge, with the consent of the involved parties, to conduct all proceedings in a jury or nonjury civil matter and enter a judgment in the case and to conduct a trial of persons accused of misdemeanors (less serious offenses than felonies) committed within the district, provided the defendants consent.

In other words, Congress has given federal district judges the authority to expand the scope of magistrate judges' participation in the judicial process. However, because each district has its own particular needs, a magistrate judge's specific duties may vary from one district to the next and from one judge to another. Because the decision to delegate responsibilities to a magistrate judge is still made by the district judge, a magistrate judge's participation in the processing of cases may be more narrow than that permitted by statute.

Law Clerks

The first use of law clerks by an American judge is generally traced to Horace Gray of Massachusetts. In the summer of 1875, while serving as chief justice of the Massachusetts Supreme Court, he employed, at his own expense, a highly ranked new graduate of the Harvard Law School.[61] Each year, he would employ a new clerk from Harvard. When Gray was appointed to the U.S. Supreme Court in 1882, he brought a law clerk with him to the nation's highest court.

Justice Gray's successor on the High Court was Oliver Wendell Holmes, like Gray a former chief justice of the Massachusetts Supreme Court. Holmes also adopted the practice of annually hiring honor graduates of Harvard Law School as his clerks. At first, Holmes's clerks were selected by Professor John Chipman Gray. Upon Gray's death in 1915, Holmes asked a young Harvard Law School professor named Felix Frankfurter (later a Supreme Court justice himself) to serve as procurer of law clerks. When he joined the Court in 1916, Louis Brandeis made the same request of Frankfurter. Professor Frankfurter, whose protégés were known as the "happy hot dogs," thus supplied clerks for Holmes, Brandeis, and Holmes's successor, Benjamin Cardozo.

When William Howard Taft, a former law professor at Yale, became chief justice, he secured a new law clerk annually from the dean of the Yale Law School. Harlan Fiske Stone, former dean of the Columbia Law School, joined the Court in 1925 and made it his practice to hire a Columbia graduate each year. Over time, then, the short-term law professor protégé became the typical Supreme Court law clerk.

Since these early beginnings there has been a steady growth in the use of law clerks by all federal courts. More than two thousand law clerks now work for federal judges and more than six hundred serve bankruptcy judges and U.S. magistrate judges.[62] In addition to the law clerks hired by individual judges, all appellate courts and some district courts hire staff law clerks who serve the entire court.

A law clerk's duties vary according to the preferences of the judge for whom he or she works. They also vary according to the type of court. Law clerks for federal district judges often serve primarily as research assistants. They spend a good deal of time examining the various motions filed in civil and criminal cases. They review each motion, noting the issues and the positions of the parties involved, then research important points raised in the motions and prepare written memorandums for the judges. Because their work is devoted to the earliest stages of the litigation process, they may have a substantial amount of contact with attorneys and witnesses. Law clerks at this level may also be involved in the initial drafting of opinions. As one federal district judge said, "I even allow my law clerks to write memorandum opinions. I first tell him what I want and then he writes it up. Sometimes I sign it without changing a word." [63]

At the appellate level, the law clerk becomes involved in a case first by researching the issues of law and fact presented by an appeal. Saving the judge's time is important. Consider the courts of appeals. These courts do not have the same discretion to accept or reject a case that the Supreme Court has. Nevertheless, the courts of appeals now use certain screening devices to differentiate between cases that can be handled quickly and those that require more time and effort. Law clerks are an integral part of this screening process.

Beginning around 1960 some courts of appeals began to utilize a new concept: the staff law clerk. The staff clerk, who works for the entire court as opposed to a particular justice, began to be used primarily because of the rapid increase in the number of pro se matters (generally speaking, those involving indigents) coming before the courts of appeals. Today, some district courts also have pro se law clerks for handling prisoner petitions. In some circuits the staff law clerks deal only with pro se matters; in others they review nearly all cases on the court's docket. As a result of their review, a truncated process may be followed; that is, no oral argument or full briefing is made.

A number of cases are scheduled for oral argument, and the clerk may be called upon to assist the judge in preparing for it. Intensive analysis of the record by judges prior to oral argument is not always possible. They seldom have time to do more than scan pertinent portions of the record called to their attention by law clerks. As one judicial scholar aptly noted, "To prepare for oral argument, all but a handful of circuit judges rely upon bench memoranda prepared by their law clerks, plus their own notes from reading briefs." [64]

Once a decision has been reached by an appellate court, the law clerk frequently participates in writing the order that accompanies the decision. The clerk's participation generally consists of drafting a preliminary opinion or order pursuant to the judge's directions. A law clerk may also be asked to edit or check citations in an opinion written by the judge.

Because the work of the law clerk for a Supreme Court justice roughly parallels that of a clerk in the other appellate courts, all aspects of their responsibility do not need to be restated here. However, a few important points about Supreme Court law clerks deserve mention. Clerks play an indispensable role in helping justices decide which cases should be heard. At the suggestion of Justice Lewis Powell in 1972, a majority of the Court's members began to participate in a "certpool"; the justices pool their clerks, divide up all filings, and circulate a single clerk's certiorari memo to all those participating in the pool.[65] The memo summarizes the facts of the case, the questions of law presented, and the recommended course of action—whether the case should be granted a full hearing, denied, or dismissed. Justice John Paul Stevens, who does not participate in the certpool, nonetheless finds this initial reading of certiorari petitions by the law clerks invaluable. "They examine them all and select a small minority that they believe I should read myself. As a result, I do not even look at the papers in over 80 percent of the cases that are filed."[66]

Once the justices have voted to hear a case, the law clerks, like their counterparts in the courts of appeals, prepare bench memoranda that the justices may use during oral argument. Finally, law clerks for Supreme Court justices, like those who serve courts of appeals judges, help to draft opinions.

Administrative Office of the U.S. Courts

The administration of the federal judicial system as a whole is managed by the Administrative Office of the U.S. Courts, which essentially functions as "the judiciary's housekeeping agency."[67] Since its creation in 1939 it has handled everything from distributing supplies to negotiating with other government agencies for court accommodations in federal buildings to maintaining judicial personnel records to collecting data on cases in the federal courts.

The Administrative Office also serves a staff function for the Judicial Conference of the United States, the central administrative policy-making organization of the federal judicial system. In addition to providing statistical information to the conference's many committees, the Administrative Office acts as a reception center and clearinghouse for information and proposals directed to the Judicial Conference.

Closely related to this staff function is the Administrative Office's role as liaison for both the federal judicial system and the Judicial Conference. The Administrative Office serves as advocate for the judiciary in its dealings with Congress, the executive branch, professional groups, and the general public. Especially important is its representative role before Congress where, along with concerned judges, it presents the judiciary's budget proposals, requests for additional judgeships, suggestions for changes in court rules, and other key measures.

The Federal Judicial Center

The Federal Judicial Center, created in 1967, is the federal courts' agency for continuing education and research. Its duties fall generally into three categories: (1) conducting research on the federal courts, (2) making recommendations to improve the administration and management of the federal courts, and (3) developing educational and training programs for personnel of the judicial branch.

Since its inception, judges have benefited from orientation sessions and other educational programs put on by the Federal Judicial Center. In recent years, magistrate judges, bankruptcy judges, and administrative personnel have also been the recipients of educational programs. The Federal Judicial Center's extensive use of videos and satellite technology allows it to reach large numbers of people. Chief Justice William H. Rehnquist, in a recent year-end report, noted that a video seminar on new developments in federal habeas corpus law broadcast from the center's studio in Washington reached approximately seventeen hundred judges, judicial staff members, and others.[68]

Federal Court Workload

The workload of the courts is heavy for all three levels of the federal judiciary— U.S. district courts, courts of appeal, and the Supreme Court.

For fiscal year 1999 slightly more than 320,000 cases were commenced in the federal district courts. This figure has fluctuated somewhat over the past five years, ranging from a high of 322,390 cases in 1997 to a low of 294,123 cases in 1995 (see Table 2-1).

Criminal cases accounted for nearly 19 percent of the district courts' docket in 1999. As with the total docket, the number of criminal cases has increased steadily

TABLE 1-1   Cases Commenced in U.S. District Courts, Fiscal Years 1995–1999

Cases	1995	1996	1997	1998	1999
Civil cases	248,335	269,132	272,027	256,787	260,271
Criminal cases	45,788	47,889	50,363	57,691	59,923
Total	294,123	317,021	322,390	314,478	320,194

SOURCE: Compiled from data in *1999 Judicial Business of the U.S. Courts*, 23, 25; available online at *http://www. uscourts.gov/judbus1999/index.html*.

TABLE 1-2   Appeals Filed and Terminated in U.S. Courts of Appeals, Fiscal Years 1995–1999

Appeals	1995	1996	1997	1998	1999
Filed	50,072	51,991	52,319	53,805	54,693
Terminated	49,805	50,413	51,194	52,002	54,088

SOURCE: Compiled from data in *1999 Judicial Business of the U.S. Courts*, 18; available online at *http://www.uscourts.gov/judbus1999/index.html*.

NOTE: Data for the U.S. Court of Appeals for the Federal Circuit are not included.

over the past five years, from 45,788 cases in 1995 to 59,923 cases in 1999. Criminal cases, while fewer in number than civil cases, are often very time consuming for the courts. Drug cases, which abound in some of the federal district courts in states bordering international boundaries, are especially complex and often involve multiple defendants.

Civil cases far outnumber criminal cases in the federal trial courts, making up 81 percent of the docket in 1999. Civil case filings have fluctuated over the years. From 248,335 in 1995, they increased to a high of 272,027 in 1997 before declining to 256,787 in 1998. They again increased to 260,271 in 1999.

In 1995, 50,072 appeals were filed in one of the regional circuit courts (see Table 2-2). This figure increased every year, to a high of 54,693 appeals in 1999. Fortunately, the number of appeals terminated by the courts of appeals has also been steadily increasing over the past five years. In 1995, 49,805 appeals were terminated and by 1999 the number of terminations had risen to 54,088.

The overall caseload of the Supreme Court is large by historical standards. However, it fluctuated only slightly between the 1994 and 1998 terms (see Table 2-3). The total number of paid cases, pauper cases, and original jurisdiction cases on the High Court's docket stood at 8,100 for the 1994 term, declined slightly to 7,565 cases for the 1995 term, and declined slightly again to 7,602 cases for the 1996 term. The number of cases on the High Court's docket then increased slightly to 7,692 cases for the 1997 term. A much larger increase occurred the next year, however, as there were 8,083 cases on the docket for the 1998 term.

Perhaps the key point to remember about the workload of the Supreme Court is that it has discretion to decide which cases merit its full attention. As a result, the number of cases argued before the Court has declined rather dramatically over the years. In the 1998 term only ninety cases were argued and eighty-four were disposed of by full opinions.

TABLE 1-3   Cases on the Docket, Argued, and Disposed of by Full Opinions in the U.S. Supreme Court, October Terms 1994–1998

Cases	1994	1995	1996	1997	1998
Paid cases	2,515	2,456	2,430	2,432	2,387
Pauper cases	5,574	5,098	5,165	5,253	5,689
Original cases	11	11	7	7	7
Total	8,100	7,565	7,602	7,692	8,083
Cases argued	94	90	90	96	90
Cases disposed of by full opinions	91	87	87	93	84

SOURCE: Compiled from data in *1999 Judicial Business of the U.S. Courts,* 83; available online at http://www. uscourts.gov/judbus1999/index.html.

Summary

In this chapter we offered a brief historical review of the development of the federal judiciary. A perennial concern has existed since preconstitutional times for independent court systems.

We focused on the three basic levels created by the Judiciary Act of 1789, noting, however, that Congress has periodically created both constitutional and legislative courts. The bulk of federal litigation is handled by U.S. district courts, courts of appeals, and the Supreme Court. We also briefly examined the role of bankruptcy judges, magistrate judges, and law clerks associated with the federal judiciary.

In terms of administrative assistance for the federal courts, our discussion centered on the Administrative Office of the U.S. Courts and the Federal Judicial Center. A brief look at the workload of each of the three levels of the federal judiciary concluded the chapter.

NOTES

1. See Victor E. Flango, *Habeas Corpus in State and Federal Courts* (Williamsburg, Va.: National Center for State Courts and State Justice Institute, 1994), 9–10.

2. This summary is drawn from *The Third Branch* 28 (November 1996): 1–2.

3. Charles Evans Hughes, *The Supreme Court of the United States* (New York: Columbia University Press, 1966), 1.

4. Ibid., 2.

5. Charles Warren, *The Supreme Court in United States History,* vol. 1 (Boston: Little, Brown, 1924), 4.

6. Fred Rodell, *Nine Men* (New York: Random House, 1955), 47.

7. See Warren, *The Supreme Court in United States History,* 44.

8. John P. Frank, *Marble Palace* (New York: Knopf, 1958), 9.

9. Warren, *The Supreme Court in United States History*, 51.

10. *Chisholm v. Georgia*, 2 Dallas 419 (1793).

11. *Champion and Dickason v. Casey*, U.S. District Court for the District of Rhode Island, June 2, 1792.

12. *Hayburn's Case*, 2 Dallas 409 (1792).

13. Robert J. Steamer, *Chief Justice: Leadership and the Supreme Court* (Columbia: University of South Carolina Press, 1986), 232.

14. Frank, *Marble Palace*, 79.

15. See Sheldon Goldman, *Constitutional Law and Supreme Court Decision-Making* (New York: Harper and Row, 1982), 41.

16. *Marbury v. Madison*, 1 Cranch 137 (1803).

17. See Lawrence Baum, *The Supreme Court*, 5th ed. (Washington, D.C.: CQ Press, 1995), 22.

18. Herbert Jacob, "Conclusion," in Herbert Jacob, Herbert M. Kritzer, Doris Marie Provine, Erhard Blankenburg, and Joseph Sanders, *Courts, Law, and Politics in Comparative Perspective* (New Haven, Conn.: Yale University Press, 1996), 394.

19. Ibid.

20. *Gibbons v. Ogden*, 9 Wheaton 1 (1824).

21. *McCulloch v. Maryland*, 4 Wheaton 316 (1819).

22. Goldman, *Constitutional Law and Supreme Court Decision-Making*, 249.

23. See *National Labor Relations Board v. Jones and Laughlin Steel Corp.*, 301 U.S. 1 (1937); *Steward Machine Co. v. Davis*, 301 U.S. 548 (1937); and *West Coast Hotel Co. v. Parrish*, 300 U.S. 379 (1937).

24. *Brown v. Board of Education*, 347 U.S. 483 (1954).

25. See *Gideon v. Wainwright*, 372 U.S. 335 (1963); *Mapp v. Ohio*, 367 U.S. 643 (1961); *Miranda v. Arizona*, 384 U.S. 436 (1966); *Baker v. Carr*, 369 U.S. 186 (1962); and *Engel v. Vitale*, 370 U.S. 421 (1962), respectively.

26. Tony Mauro, "Supreme Court Term: A Showcase of Power," *USA Today*, June 30, 1997, 3A. Two other interesting accounts of the Supreme Court's term may be found in Harvey Berkman, "Court Declares 'No Trespass,' " *National Law Journal*, July 14, 1997, A1, A26; and Steven G. Calabresi, "A Constitutional Revolution," *Wall Street Journal*, July 10, 1997, A14. The cases are *Printz v. United States*, 95-1478 (June 27, 1997); *City of Boerne v. Flores*, 95-2074 (June 25, 1997); and *Reno v. ACLU*, 96-511 (June 26, 1997), respectively.

27. Robert H. Birkby, *The Court and Public Policy* (Washington, D.C.: CQ Press, 1983), 1.

28. Sally J. Kenney, "The European Court of Justice: Integrating Europe through Law," *Judicature* 81 (1998): 250.

29. Ibid., 251.

30. *Plessy v. Ferguson*, 163 U.S. 537 (1896).

31. Administrative Office of U.S. Courts, http://www.uscourts.gov/judbus1999/index.html.

32. *Stanley v. Georgia*, 394 U.S. 557 (1969).

33. See Kenney, "The European Court of Justice," 252, 255.

34. Stephen T. Early Jr., *Constitutional Courts of the United States* (Totowa, N.J.: Littlefield, Adams, 1977), 100.

35. See Warren, *The Supreme Court in United States History*, 85, 86.

36. Richard J. Richardson and Kenneth N. Vines, *The Politics of Federal Courts* (Boston: Little, Brown, 1970), 27.

37. For a thorough account of the Fifth Circuit split, see Deborah J. Barrow and Thomas G. Walker, *A Court Divided: The Fifth Circuit Court of Appeals and the Politics of Judicial Reform* (New Haven, Conn.: Yale University Press, 1988).

38. J. Woodford Howard Jr., *Courts of Appeals in the Federal Judicial System: A Study of the Second, Fifth, and District of Columbia Circuits* (Princeton, N.J.: Princeton University Press, 1981), 75–76.

39. See *Douglas v. California*, 372 U.S. 353 (1963).

40. See Donald R. Songer, "The Circuit Courts of Appeals," in *The American Courts: A Critical Assessment*, ed. John B. Gates and Charles A. Johnson (Washington, D.C.: CQ Press, 1991), 47.

41. *Hopwood v. Texas*, No. 94-50664, Fifth Circuit, March 18, 1996.

42. *Hopwood v. Texas*, 116 S. Ct. 2581 (1996).

43. "Hopwood's Shadow," *National Law Journal*, January 27, 1997, A22.

44. Howard, *Courts of Appeals in the Federal Judicial System*, 79.

45. Christine B. Harrington and Daniel S. Ward, "Patterns of Appellate Litigation, 1945–1990," in *Contemplating Courts*, ed. Lee Epstein (Washington, D.C.: CQ Press, 1995), 211.

46. *Tinker v. Des Moines Independent Community School District*, 393 U.S. 503 (1969).

47. Richardson and Vines, *The Politics of Federal Courts*, 21.

48. Dwight F. Henderson, *Courts for a New Nation* (Washington, D.C.: Public Affairs Press, 1971), 27.

49. Ibid., 28.

50. Ibid., 29–30.

51. Ibid., 30–31.

52. See Herbert Jacob, *Justice in America*, 4th ed. (Boston: Little, Brown, 1984), chap. 2.

53. Ibid., 37.

54. Robert A. Carp and C. K. Rowland, *Policymaking and Politics in the Federal District Courts* (Knoxville: University of Tennessee Press, 1983), 3.

55. Quoted in C. K. Rowland and Robert A. Carp, *Politics and Judgment in Federal District Courts* (Lawrence: University Press of Kansas, 1996), 2.

56. The decision of the three-judge district court may be found in *Roe v. Wade*, 314 F. Supp. 1217 (1970), and the Supreme Court decision in *Roe v. Wade*, 410 U.S. 113 (1973).

57. See *Northern Pipeline Construction Co. v. Marathon Pipe Line Company*, 6 B.R. 928 (1981) and 12 B.R. 946 (1981).

58. *Northern Pipeline Construction Co. v. Marathon Pipe Line Company*, 458 U.S. 50 (1982).

59. See *The Third Branch* 15 (January 1983): 1 and 8, for a chronology of events in this matter.

60. *National Law Journal*, http://www.nlj.com/1999/get_paid0614/75.html.

61. Our discussion of the historical evolution of law clerks is drawn from John Bilyeu Oakley and Robert S. Thompson, *Law Clerks and the Judicial Process* (Berkeley: University of California Press, 1980), 10–22.

62. Frank M. Coffin, *On Appeal: Courts, Lawyering, and Judging* (New York: W. W. Norton, 1994), 72.

63. Quoted in Robert A. Carp and Russell R. Wheeler, "Sink or Swim: The Socialization of a Federal District Judge," *Journal of Public Law* 21 (1972): 379.

64. Howard, *Courts of Appeals in the Federal Judicial System*, 198.

65. See David M. O'Brien, *Storm Center: The Supreme Court in American Politics*, 2d ed. (New York: W. W. Norton, 1990), 165.

66. J. P. Stevens, "Some Thoughts on Judicial Restraint," *Judicature* 66 (1982): 179.

67. Peter G. Fish, *The Politics of Federal Judicial Administration* (Princeton, N.J.: Princeton University Press, 1973), 124, 166.

68. William Rehnquist, "1996 Year-End Report on the Federal Judiciary," *The Third Branch* 29 (January 1997): 1–8.

SUGGESTED READINGS

Barrow, Deborah J., and Thomas G. Walker. *A Court Divided: The Fifth Circuit Court of Appeals and the Politics of Judicial Reform.* New Haven, Conn.: Yale University Press, 1988. An excellent study of the politics involved in the splitting of the Fifth Circuit Court of Appeals.

Baum, Lawrence. *The Supreme Court*, 6th ed. Washington, D.C.: CQ Press, 1998. A brief look at all aspects of the U.S. Supreme Court.

Federal Judiciary Homepage. Available online at http://www.uscourts.gov. An excellent source of information about all aspects of the federal judiciary. Also provides links to other useful Internet sites.

Gates, John B., and Charles A. Johnson, eds. *The American Courts: A Critical Assessment*. Washington, D.C.: CQ Press, 1991. A collection of readings about state and federal trial and appellate courts, judicial selection, and judicial decision making.

Howard, J. Woodford Jr. *Courts of Appeals in the Federal Judicial System*. Princeton, N.J.: Princeton University Press, 1981. A good study of federal courts of appeals in the Second, Fifth, and District of Columbia circuits.

Richardson, Richard J., and Kenneth N. Vines. *The Politics of Federal Courts*. Boston: Little, Brown, 1970. An excellent study of the politics involved in the creation of the federal judicial system.

Rowland, C. K., and Robert A. Carp. *Politics and Judgment in Federal District Courts*. Lawrence, Kan.: University Press of Kansas, 1996. A thorough study of the various factors that influence the decisions of federal district judges.

Steamer, Robert J. *Chief Justice: Leadership and the Supreme Court*. Columbia: University of South Carolina Press, 1986. A thorough study of the leadership styles of the men who have served as chief justice.

CHAPTER 2

Jurisdiction and Policy-Making Boundaries

With the denial of constitutional protection to same-sex marriages in Congress's Defense of Marriage Act of 1996, the arena now shifts back to the states, where laws on the subject are unclear or nonexistent.

What would happen if Congress did not like the decisions the federal courts were handing down in a particular policy area and it passed a law that removed the subject matter from the courts' jurisdiction? Would the action be constitutional? It has happened in the past. In what realms might Congress act in a similar manner again?

Are "activist" judges as out of control as some say? Are judges limited in what they can do? Who or what establishes those boundaries, and should they be changed?

Would it be a good idea if the president, Congress, and other governmental agencies could get the courts to rule on the constitutionality of proposed governmental actions before such actions were put into place? Wouldn't considerable time and trouble be saved if courts were allowed to nip unconstitutional acts in the bud before they did any harm? Courts in other nations have this authority.

IN SETTING THE JURISDICTIONS of courts, Congress and the U.S. Constitution—and their state counterparts—mandate the types of cases each court can hear. Because the role of legislative bodies in setting courts' jurisdictions is an ongoing one, we will consider how Congress in particular can influence judicial behavior by redefining the types of cases judges can hear. We will also provide a detailed discussion of judicial self-restraint, examining ten principles, derived from legal tradition and constitutional and statutory law, that govern a judge's decision about whether to review a case.

Federal Courts

The federal court system is divided into three separate levels: the trial courts, the appellate tribunals, and the U.S. Supreme Court.

U.S. District Courts

In the United States Code, Congress has set forth the jurisdiction of the federal district courts. These tribunals have original jurisdiction in federal criminal and civil cases; that is, by law, the cases must be heard first in these courts, no matter who the parties are or how significant the issues.

Criminal Cases. These cases commence when the local U.S. attorneys have reason to believe that a violation of the U.S. Penal Code has occurred. After obtaining an indictment from a federal grand jury, the U.S. attorney files charges against the accused in the district court in which he or she serves. Criminal activity as defined by Congress covers a wide range of behavior, including interstate theft of an automobile, illegal importation of narcotics, assassination of a president, conspiracy to deprive persons of their civil rights, and even the killing of a migratory bird out of season. For the past decade or so the most numerous types of criminal code violations have been embezzlement and fraud, larceny and theft, drunk driving and other traffic offenses, drug-related offenses, and forgery and counterfeiting. Some federal crimes, such as robbery, are comparatively uniform in occurrence in each of the ninety-four U.S. judicial districts, whereas others are endemic to certain geographic areas. For example, those districts next to the Mexican border get an inordinate number of illegal drug and immigration cases. (In Texas during the 1998 fiscal year, drug and illegal entry cases accounted for a staggering 70 percent of all criminal filings.)[1]

After charges are filed against an accused, and if no plea bargain has been made, a trial is conducted by a U.S. district judge. In court the defendant enjoys all the privileges and immunities granted in the Bill of Rights (such as the right to a speedy and public trial) or by congressional legislation or Supreme Court rulings (for instance, a twelve-person jury must render a unanimous verdict). Defendants may waive the right to a trial by a jury of their peers. A defendant who is found not guilty of the crime is set free and may never be tried again for the same offense (the Fifth Amendment's protection against double jeopardy). If the accused is found guilty, the district judge determines the appropriate sentence within a range set by Congress. The length of a sentence cannot be appealed so long as it is within the range prescribed by Congress. A verdict of not guilty may not be appealed by the government, but convicted defendants may appeal if they believe that the judge or jury made an improper legal determination.

Civil Cases. A majority of the district court caseload is civil in nature; that is, suits between private parties or between the U.S. government, acting in its non-prosecutorial capacity, and a private party. Civil cases that originate in the U.S. district courts may be placed in several categories. The first is litigation concerning the interpretation or application of the Constitution, acts of Congress, or U.S. treaties. Examples of cases in this category include the following: a petitioner claims that one of his or her federally protected civil rights has been violated, a litigant alleges that he or she is being harmed by a congressional statute that is unconstitutional, and a plaintiff argues that he or she is suffering injury from a treaty that is improperly affecting him. The key point is that a federal question must be raised for the U.S. trial courts to have jurisdiction. It is not enough to say that the federal courts should hear a case "because this is an important issue" or "because an awful lot of money is at stake." Unless one is able to invoke the Constitution or a federal law or treaty, the case must be litigated elsewhere (probably in the state courts).

Some minimal dollar amounts traditionally had to be in controversy in some types of cases before the trial courts would hear them, but such amounts have been waived if the case falls into one of several general categories. For example, an alleged violation of a civil rights law, such as the Voting Rights Act of 1965, must be heard by the federal instead of the state judiciary. Other types of cases in this category are patent and copyright claims, passport and naturalization proceedings, admiralty and maritime disputes, and violations of the U.S. postal laws.

Another broad category of cases over which the U.S. trial courts exercise general original jurisdiction includes diversity of citizenship disputes. These disputes involve parties from different states, or the dispute is between an American citizen and a foreign country or citizen. Thus if a citizen of New York were injured in an automobile accident in Chicago by a driver from Illinois, the New Yorker could sue in federal court, because the parties to the suit were of "diverse citizenship." The requirement that at least $75,000 be at stake in diversity cases does not appear to be much of a barrier to the gates of the federal judiciary. Even if physical injuries come to less than $75,000, one can always ask for "psychological damages" to push the amount in controversy above the jurisdictional threshold.

Federal district courts also have jurisdiction over petitions from convicted prisoners who contend that their incarceration (or perhaps their denial of parole) is in violation of their federally protected rights. In the vast majority of these cases prisoners ask for a writ of habeas corpus, an order issued by a judge to determine whether a person has been lawfully imprisoned or detained. The judge would demand that the prison authorities either justify the detention or release the petitioner. Prisoners convicted in a state court must take care to argue that a federally protected right was violated—for example, the right to be represented by counsel at trial. Otherwise the federal courts would have no jurisdiction. Federal prisoners have a somewhat wider range for their appeals, given that all their rights and options are within the penumbra of the U.S. Constitution.

Finally, the district courts have the authority to hear any other cases that Congress may validly prescribe by law. For example, although the Constitution grants to the U.S. Supreme Court original jurisdiction to hear "Cases affecting Ambassadors, other public Ministers and Consuls," Congress has also authorized the district courts to have concurrent original jurisdiction over cases involving such parties.

U.S. Courts of Appeals

The U.S. appellate courts have no original jurisdiction whatsoever; every case or controversy that comes to one of these intermediate-level panels has been first argued in some other forum. These tribunals, like the district courts, are the creations of Congress, and their structure and functions have varied considerably over time. Basically Congress has granted the circuit courts appellate jurisdiction over two general categories of cases. The first of these are ordinary civil and criminal appeals from the federal trial courts, including the U.S. territorial courts, the U.S. Tax Court, and some District of Columbia courts. In criminal cases the appellant is the defendant because the government is not free to appeal a verdict of not guilty. (However, if the question in a criminal case is one of defining the legal right of the defendant, then the government may appeal an adverse trial court ruling.) In civil cases the party that lost in the trial court is usually the appellant, although the winning party can appeal if it is not satisfied with the lower-court judgment.

The second broad category of appellate jurisdiction includes appeals from certain federal administrative agencies and departments and also from the important independent regulatory commissions, such as the Securities and Exchange Commission and the National Labor Relations Board. In recent years about 7 percent of the civil docket has consisted of administrative appeals. Because so many administrative and regulatory bodies have their home base in Washington, D.C., the appeals court for that circuit gets an inordinate number of such cases.

U.S. Supreme Court

The U.S. Supreme Court is the only federal court mentioned by name in the Constitution, which spells out the general contours of the High Court's jurisdiction. Although the Supreme Court is usually thought of as an appellate tribunal, it does have some general original jurisdiction. Probably the most important subject of such jurisdiction is a suit between two or more states. For example, every so often the states of Texas and Louisiana spar in the Supreme Court over the proper boundary between them. By law the Sabine River divides the two states, but with great regularity this effluent changes its snaking course, thus requiring the Supreme Court (with considerable help from the U.S. Army Corps of Engineers) to determine where Louisiana ends and the Lone Star State begins.

In addition the High Court shares original jurisdiction (with the U.S. district courts) in certain cases brought by or against foreign ambassadors or consuls, in cases between the United States and a state, and in cases commenced by a state against citizens of another state or against aliens. In situations such as these, where jurisdiction is shared, the courts are said to have concurrent jurisdiction. Cases over which the Supreme Court has original jurisdiction are often important, but they do not constitute a sizable proportion of the overall caseload. In recent years less than 1 percent of the High Court's docket consisted of cases heard on original jurisdiction.

The U.S. Constitution declares that the Supreme Court "shall have appellate Jurisdiction . . . under such Regulations as the Congress shall make." Over the years Congress has passed much legislation setting forth the "Regulations" determining which cases may appear before the nation's most august judicial body. In essence, appeals may reach the Supreme Court through two main avenues. First, there may be appeals from all lower federal constitutional and territorial courts and also from most, but not all, federal legislative courts. Second, the Supreme Court may hear appeals from the highest court in a state—as long as there is a substantial federal question.

Most of the High Court's docket consists of cases in which it has agreed to issue a writ of certiorari—a discretionary action. Such a writ (which must be supported by at least four justices) is an order from the Supreme Court to a lower court demanding that it send up a complete record of a case so that the Supreme Court can review it. Historically the Supreme Court has agreed to grant the petition for a writ of certiorari in only a tiny proportion of cases—usually less than 10 percent of the time, and in recent years the number has been closer to only 1 percent.

Another method by which the Supreme Court exercises its appellate jurisdiction is certification. This procedure is followed when one of the appeals courts asks the Supreme Court for instructions regarding a question of law. The justices may choose to give the appellate judges binding instructions, or they may ask that the entire record be forwarded to the Supreme Court for review and final judgment.

Jurisdiction and Policy Making of State Courts

The jurisdictions of the fifty separate state court systems in the United States are established in virtually the same manner as those within the national court system. Each state has a constitution that sets forth the authority and decision-making powers of its trial and appellate judges. Likewise, each state legislature passes laws that further detail the specific powers and prerogatives of judges and the rights and obligations of those who bring suit in the state courts. Because no two state constitutions or legislative bodies are alike, it is no surprise that the jurisdictions of individual state courts vary from one state to another. For example, one state constitution may give its supreme court original jurisdiction over all cases in which a state is suing one of its counties while another state constitution may confer such jurisdiction only on the low-level circuit courts. Similarly, one state legislature might define felony theft as the stealing of $2,000 or more, sending the case automatically to a county criminal court, whereas a case involving less than $2,000 would go to a municipal court authorized to handle only minor crimes. In another state, the legislature might draw the line between felony and petty theft at $1,000. Thus, while court jurisdictions vary from one state to another and from the national model, they are all derived in part from a constitution and in part from enactments of legislative bodies.

State courts are substantively important in terms of policy making in the United States. Well over 99 percent of the judicial workload in the United States consists of state, not federal, cases, and 95 percent of all judges in the United States work at the state level.[2] Moreover, the comparison is more than just one of numbers; the decisions of state jurists frequently have a great impact on public policy. For example, during the 1970s a number of suits were brought into federal court challenging the constitutionality of a state's spending vastly unequal sums on the education of its schoolchildren. (This occurred because poorer school districts could not raise the same amount of money as could wealthy school districts.) The litigants claimed that children in the poorer districts were victims of unlawful discrimination in violation of their equal protection rights under the U.S. Constitution. The Supreme Court said they were not, however, in a conservative-dominated five-to-four decision.[3] But the matter did not end there. Litigation was then instituted in many states arguing that unequal educational opportunities were in violation of various clauses in the state constitutions. During the past three decades such suits have been brought twenty-eight times in some twenty-four states. In fourteen of these cases state supreme courts invalidated their state's method of financing education, thus requiring the reallocation of billions of dollars. In some instances these decisions altered the entire structure of the state educational system.[4]

Considerable evidence is available that in recent years many minority groups and supporters of liberal causes, unable to obtain relief in the face of conservative Burger and Rehnquist Court majorities, have turned their litigation efforts toward the state judiciaries. The constitutional guarantees in most states are just as supportive of the rights of minorities as is the U.S. Constitution, and the judiciaries in many states are dominated by liberal and progressive judges who are as much predisposed toward the claims of minorities and civil libertarians as any liberal justice who ever sat on the Warren Court of the 1950s and 1960s.

The cause of gay and lesbian rights is one policy that seems to have fared better in the hands of state judges than in the federal tribunals. For instance in November 1998 the Georgia Supreme Court overturned by a six-to-one vote the state's anti-sodomy law under the privacy provisions of the Georgia constitution even though the same law had been upheld in 1986 by the U.S. Supreme Court (*Bowers v. Hardwick,* 478 U.S. 186). On December 20, 1999, the Vermont Supreme Court ruled that the state must guarantee the same protections and benefits to committed gay and lesbian couples that it does to heterosexuals. (The state legislature soon passed a law implementing the state court's requirement.) In April 2000 the New Jersey Supreme Court determined that "lesbian partners who raise children have the same rights of any parent when deciding custody issues."[5] In other areas, too, state courts have demonstrated a liberal, activist bent. In 1998 the Illinois Supreme Court struck down that state's sweeping tort reform legislation, declaring that limits on damages, discovery, and joint and several liability violated the Illinois constitution.[6] One critical observer bemoaned in an editorial in the *Wall Street Journal,* "In hundreds of other cases across the country, state supreme courts have issued decisions using 'independent state grounds' to impose heightened standards for law enforcement, overturn the death penalty, require public funding of abortions, invalidate public school financing schemes, grant public access to private property, recognize a constitutional right to possess and use drugs and many other policy goals never even dreamed of by the Warren Court."[7] Increasingly then states are finding that their constitutions are more protective of civil liberties than the U.S. Supreme Court's interpretation of the federal constitution.[8]

Although all analysts seem to agree on the importance of state court policy making, not all concur that liberal causes are the sole beneficiaries of these activities. A study of all constitutionally based criminal procedure decisions of the courts of last resort of all fifty states during the 1970s and 1980s "reveals that the *adoption* of Burger-Rehnquist Court doctrines for state law far outpaces their rejection. Indeed, for every state high court decision repudiating U.S. Supreme Court doctrine there are at least two cases endorsing it."[9] This phenomenon has surely existed in the state of California, where a conservative majority on its Supreme Court "has more narrowly construed the rights accorded defendants in criminal prosecutions." Moreover, "because of the California court system's size and influence, the weight of its decision extends far beyond the state's borders." Furthermore, in the economic arena California's conservative court

has taken the lead in a movement to greatly limit the liability of business people for misbehavior of various kinds. The court has eviscerated thousands of lawsuits by employees seeking punitive damages for wrongful discharge. It has disallowed big damage awards obtained by consumers against insurance companies. It has prevented drug companies from being held liable for damages caused consumers by certain products.[10]

The purpose of this discussion is neither to document systematically all the policy-making thrusts of state judges nor to predict the ideological direction of state court decision making. Instead it is to emphasize that what is happening at the state court level is of great importance to all Americans—to their pocketbooks and to their personal rights and liberties. Gone are the days when many public law scholars believed that only federal court activity had any keen impact on people's lives, because the state judicial tribunals only immersed themselves in judicial trivia. The work of state courts is worthy of everyone's full interest and attention.

Jurisdiction and Legislative Politics

One political reality regarding the jurisdiction of the federal and state courts that cannot be overemphasized is that, for all intents and purposes, Congress and the fifty state legislatures determine what sorts of issues and cases the courts in their separate realms will hear. And equally important, what the omnipotent legislative branches give, they may also take away. Some judges and judicial scholars argue that the U.S. Constitution (in Article III) and the respective state documents confer a certain inherent jurisdiction upon the judiciaries in some key areas, independent of the legislative will. Nevertheless, the jurisdictional boundaries of American courts clearly are a product of legislative judgments—determinations often flavored with the bittersweet spice of politics.

Congress may advance a particular cause by giving courts the authority to hear cases in a public policy realm that previously had been forbidden territory for the judiciary. For example, when Congress passed the Civil Rights Act of 1968, it gave judges the authority to penalize individuals who interfere with "any person because of his race, color, religion or national origin and because he is or has been . . . traveling in . . . interstate commerce" (18 U.S.C.A., Sec. 245). Prior to 1968 the courts had no jurisdiction over incidents that stemmed from interference by one person with another's right to travel. Likewise Congress may discourage a particular social movement by passing legislation to make it virtually impossible for its advocates to have any success in the courts. For example, when the Hawaiian Supreme Court approved same-sex marriages in 1993, a conservative and frightened Congress was determined to discourage judges in other states from rendering similar decisions. The result was the Defense of Marriage Act, which President Bill Clinton signed into law on September 20, 1996. In part the law was designed to prevent judges—both state and federal—from reading any meaning into the Fourteenth Amendment to the U.S. Constitution that would condone same-sex marriages. Among other things, the law defined marriage as "only a legal union between one man and one woman," and it permitted state courts to ignore judgments from courts in other states "respecting" marriages between two persons of the same gender. In addition, since the controversial Hawaiian Court ruling in 1993 at least thirty states have passed legislation to specifically ban gay marriages.[11]

Perhaps the most vivid illustration of congressional power over federal court jurisdiction occurred just after the Civil War, and the awesome nature of this legislative prerogative haunts the judiciary to this day. On February 5, 1867, Congress empowered the federal courts to grant habeas corpus to individuals imprisoned in violation of their constitutional rights. The Supreme Court was authorized to hear appeals of such cases. William McCardle was incarcerated by the military government of Mississippi for being in alleged violation of the Reconstruction laws. McCardle was alleged to have published "incendiary and libelous" articles that attacked his "unlawful restraint by military force." He sought relief in the circuit court, but it was denied. He then appealed to the Supreme Court, which agreed to take the case.

After the arguments had been made before the High Court (but prior to a decision), Congress got into the act. Its anti-Southern majority feared that the Court would use the *Ex Parte McCardle* case as a vehicle to strike down all or part of the Reconstruction Acts—something Congress had no intention of permitting. And so, over President Andrew Johnson's veto, the following statute was enacted: "That so much of the act approved February 5, 1867 [as] authorized an appeal from the judgment of the Circuit Court to the Supreme Court of the United States, or the exercise of any such jurisdiction by said Supreme Court, on appeals which have been, or may hereafter be taken, [is] hereby repealed." Thus, while the Court was in the process of deciding the case, Congress removed the subject matter from the federal docket. And was all this strictly legal and constitutional? Yes, indeed. Stunned by Congress's action but obedient to the clear strictures of the Constitution, the Court limply ruled that McCardle's appeal must now "be dismissed for want of jurisdiction."[12]

In other words, while discussing what courts do or may do, do not lose sight of the commanding reality that the jurisdiction of U.S. courts is established by "the United States of America in Congress assembled." Likewise the jurisdictions of the courts in the states are very much governed by—and the political product of—the will of the state legislatures.

Judicial Self-Restraint

The activities that judges are forbidden to engage in, or at least discouraged from engaging in, deal not so much with technical matters of jurisdiction as with justiciability—the question of whether judges in the system ought to hear or refrain from hearing certain types of disputes. It is only by exploring both sides of the demarcation line between prescribed and proscribed activity that insight can be gained into the role and function of the federal and state courts. In the following sections ten separate aspects of judicial self-restraint, ten principles that serve to check and contain the power of American judges, will be examined.[13] These maxims originate from a variety of sources—the U.S. Constitution and state constitutions, acts of Congress and of state legislatures, the common law tradition—and whenever possible their roots and the nature of their evolution will be noted. Some apply more to appellate courts than to trial courts, as will be indicated. Although the primary examples provided will be illustrative of the federal judiciary, most apply to state judicial systems as well.

A Definite Controversy Must Exist

The U.S. Constitution states that "the judicial Power shall extend to all Cases, in Law and Equity, arising under this Constitution, the Laws of the United States, and Treaties made . . . under their Authority" (Article III, Section 2). The key word here is *cases*. Since 1789 the federal courts have chosen to interpret the term in its most literal sense; there must be a controversy between legitimate adversaries who have met all the technical legal standards to institute a suit. The dispute must concern the protection of a meaningful, nontrivial right or the prevention or redress of a wrong that directly affects the parties to the suit. Three corollaries to this general principle breathe a little life into its rather abstract-sounding admonitions.

The first is that the federal courts do not render advisory opinions, rulings about situations that are hypothetical or that have not caused an authentic clash between adversaries. A dispute must be real and current before a court will agree to accept it for adjudication. For example, in 1902 Congress passed a law allocating certain pieces of land to the Cherokee Indians. Because such disbursements often stimulate a good deal of question about property rights, Congress sought to head off any possible disputes by authorizing certain land recipients to bring suits against the U.S. government in the court of claims, with appeal to the Supreme Court. They were permitted to do so "on their own behalf and on behalf of all other Cherokee citizens" who received land "to determine the validity of any acts of Congress passed since the said act." Stripped of the legalese, the law thus said: "If you have any hypothetical questions about how the law might affect anyone, just sue the United States, and the courts will answer these questions for you." The Supreme Court politely but pointedly said, "We don't do that sort of thing; we settle only real, actual cases or controversies." The act of Congress was found to be nothing more

than an attempt to provide for judicial determination, final in this court, of the constitutional validity of an act of Congress. [It] is true the United States is made a defendant to this action, but *it has no interest adverse to the claimants.* The object is not to assert a property right as against the government, or to demand compensation for alleged wrongs because of action on its part. . . . In a legal sense the judgment [amounts] to no more than an expression of opinion upon the validity of the [1902 act]. If such actions as are here attempted [are] sustained, the result will be that this court, instead of keeping within the limits of judicial power, and deciding cases or controversies arising between opposing parties, [will] be required to give opinions in the nature of advice concerning legislative action—a function never conferred upon it by the Constitution. [Emphasis added.][14]

A second corollary of the general principle is that the parties to the suit must have proper standing. This notion deals with the matter of who may bring litigation to court. Although there are many aspects of the term *standing*, the most prominent component is that the person bringing suit must have suffered (or be immediately about to suffer) a direct and significant injury. As a general rule, a litigant cannot bring a claim on behalf of others (except for parents of minor children or in special types of suits called class actions). In addition, the alleged injury must be personalized and immediate—not part of some generalized complaint.

On January 1, 1997, a new law took effect granting the president a line-item veto. A line-item veto permits the chief executive to cancel individual spending and tax items contained in appropriations bills that he has already signed into law. Immediately after the law was passed, six members of Congress who opposed the line-item veto filed suit in federal court to challenge its validity. They claimed that the statute violated the constitutional separation of powers doctrine, which requires that the powers of the chief executive be kept distinct from the powers of Congress. On April 10 a federal district court judge agreed, ruling that the Line Item Veto Act gave the president the unprecedented and "revolutionary" power to repeal a part of a statute, a legislative function that no president can exercise and that Congress may not delegate.

When the case reached the Supreme Court, the justices, by a seven-to-two vote, overruled the lower-court judge.[15] Refusing to go into the merits of the case at all, the majority noted that as of the date of the Court's decision, President Clinton had not yet used his line-item veto power; therefore, no one could claim any immediate, direct, or personal injury from the statute. Chief Justice William H. Rehnquist, speaking for the majority, said that "we have consistently stressed that a plaintiff's complaint must establish that he has a 'personal stake' in the alleged dispute. . . . The institutional injury [the plaintiffs] . . . allege is wholly abstract and widely dispersed, and their attempt to litigate this dispute at this time and in this form is contrary to historical experience."[16] That temporarily put an end to the matter. The nation had to wait until Clinton first used the veto, and then someone had to come forward who claimed an injury from the president's action and who wished to challenge the law in court.

The wait was a short one. Within months President Clinton began energetically using the line-item veto, canceling more than eighty items in taxing and spending bills passed by Congress. One of these was a provision of the Balanced Budget Act of 1997 that provided funds for hospitals in New York City and another gave tax breaks to potato growers in Idaho. A federal district court determined that this time at least one party in each suit potentially suffered real and significant financial injury from the vetoes: New York stood to lose hundreds of millions of dollars for its Medicaid programs, and the potato growers were about to lose a lucrative tax break that helped to keep them economically competitive. After the suits were consolidated, the court then ruled that the Line Item Veto law violated the presentiment clause (Article I, Section 7, Clause 2) of the Constitution. The U.S. Supreme Court later affirmed the district court in its now famous six-to-three ruling.[17] The key point again is that no judicial rulings are made on the substantive merits of a case unless and until someone is able to convince the court that he or she will suffer or has suffered real injury from the objectionable law.

The third corollary of this general principle is that courts ordinarily will not hear a case that has become moot—when the basic facts or the status of the parties have significantly changed in the interim between when the suit was filed and when it comes before the judge(s). The death of a litigant or the fact that the litigants have ceased to be warring parties would render a case moot in most tribunals.

For example, in 1974 the U.S. Supreme Court agreed to hear a petition from Marco DeFunis, who challenged the constitutionality of the admissions policy of the University of Washington Law School. The law school gave preferential treatment to certain minority racial groups, even though such applicants did not rate as high as other, nonminority applicants according to the school's evaluation procedures based on objective tests and grades. DeFunis, a nonminority applicant, charged reverse discrimination in violation of his Fourteenth Amendment rights. During the initial trial of this case at the state court level, DeFunis had been admitted to the law school (on a sort of conditional basis), and when the case eventually reached the Supreme Court, he was in his final quarter of law school. (The law school conceded at oral argument before the Supreme Court that it would permit DeFunis to graduate if he continued to fulfill all requirements.) When the Supreme Court learned of this, a majority determined that the case had become moot. "The controversy between the parties has thus ceased to be 'definite and concrete' and no longer 'touches the legal relations of parties having adverse legal interests,' " said the Court.[18]

However, sometimes judges for their own reasons may decide that a case is still ripe for adjudication, even though the status of the facts and parties would seem to have radically altered. Examples include cases where someone has challenged a state's refusal to permit an abortion or to permit the life-support system of a terminally ill person to be switched off. (In such cases, by the time the suit reaches an appellate court, the woman may already have given birth or the moribund person may have died.) In these cases the judges believed that the issues were so important that they needed to be addressed by the court. To declare such cases moot would, practically speaking, prevent them from ever being heard in time by an appellate body.

A great deal of flexibility and common sense is built into the U.S. legal system—factors that allow for discretion in judges' decision making. The principle of judicial self-restraint offers a counterpoint, guiding judges to what they may not do. They may not decide an issue unless there is an actual case or controversy. From this it follows that they do not consider abstract, hypothetical questions; they do not take a case unless the would-be litigants can demonstrate direct and substantial personal injury; and they (usually) do not take cases that have become moot. This principle is an important one because it means that judges are not free to wander about the countryside like medieval knights slaying all the evil dragons they encounter. They may rule only on concrete issues brought by truly injured parties directly affected by the facts of a case.

Although federal judges do not rule on abstract, hypothetical issues, many state courts are permitted to do so in some form or other (such as those in Colorado, Massachusetts, and South Dakota).[19] Federal legislative courts may give advisory opinions as well. Also, American judges are empowered to render declaratory judgments, which define the rights of various parties under a statute, a will, or a contract. The judgments do not entail any type of coercive relief. As Justice Rehnquist once put it, "A declaratory judgment is simply a statement of rights, not a binding order."[20] The federal courts were given the authority to act in this capacity in the Federal Declaratory Judgment Act of 1934, and about three-fourths of the states grant their courts this power. Although a difference exists between an abstract dispute that the federal courts (at least) must avoid and a situation where a declaratory judgment is in order, in the real world the line between the two is often a difficult one for jurists to draw.

Even though U.S. courts may not rule on abstract questions or on matters for which no significant injury is to be found, this is by no means the pattern throughout the rest of the world. In Norway, for example, its Parliament may ask its Constitutional Court for advice about the constitutionality of a law before it is ever passed. In Ireland the president is permitted to ask the courts for an opinion about a bill's constitutionality before he signs it into law. Likewise in Canada members of its executive cabinet may ask the country's Supreme Court for advisory opinions on almost any topic, including bills pending in or enacted by the provincial legislative bodies. And in Germany its Land (state) governments may petition the Constitutional Court for abstract opinions about legal matters. Still, even in these countries obtaining advisory opinions from the courts is mainly a prerogative of government official and agencies—not private citizens.

A Plea Must Be Specific

Another constraint upon the judiciary is that judges will hear no case on the merits unless the petitioner is first able to cite a specific part of the Constitution as the basis of the plea. For example, the First Amendment forbids government from making a law "respecting an establishment of religion." In 1989 the state of New York created a special school district in Orange County solely for the benefit of the Satmar Hasids, a group of Hasidic Jews with East European roots that strongly resists assimilation into modern society. Most of the children attended parochial schools in the Village of Kiryas Joel, but these private schools were unable to handle retarded and disabled students, and the Satmars claimed that such children within their community would be traumatized if forced to attend a public school. Responding to this situation the state legislature created a special district encompassing a single school that served only handicapped children from the Hasidic Jewish community. This arrangement was challenged by the association representing New York state's school boards. In June 1994 the U.S. Supreme Court ruled that the creation of the one-school district effectively delegated political power to the orthodox Jewish group and therefore violated the First Amendment's ban on governmental "establishment of religion." [21] Whether or not everyone agrees that the New York law was constitutional, few, if any, doubt that the school board association met the specific criteria for securing judicial review: The Constitution clearly forbids the government from delegating political power to a specific religious entity. The government here readily acknowledged that it had passed a law for the unique benefit of a singular religious community.

However, if one went into court and contended that a particular law or official action "violated the spirit of the Bill of Rights" or "offended the values of the founders," a judge would dismiss the proceeding on the spot. For if judges were free to give concrete, substantive meaning to vague generalities such as these, there would be little check on what they could do. Who is to say what is the "spirit of the Bill of Rights" or the collective motivation of those who hammered out the Constitution? Judges who were free to roam too far from the specific clauses and strictures of the constitutional document itself would soon become judicial despots.

Despite what has just been said, in the real world this principle is not as simple and clear-cut as it sounds, because the Constitution contains many clauses that are open to a wide variety of interpretations. For example, the Constitution forbids Congress from passing any law abridging "freedom of speech," but such a term has been virtually impossible for jurists to define with any degree of precision. The Eighth Amendment prohibits "excessive bail" for criminal defendants, but what is excessive? The states are forbidden, in the Fourteenth Amendment, Section 1, from abridging "the privileges and immunities of citizens of the United States," but who is to say what these privileges and immunities are? The Constitution gives hardly a clue. Although petitioners must cite a particular constitutional clause as the basis for their plea—as opposed to some ambiguous concept—there are nevertheless enough vague clauses in the Constitution to give federal judges plenty of room to maneuver and make policy.

The United States is not the only country with a constitution that contains ambiguous words and potentially conflicting clauses to which judges have felt free to give new and imaginative meanings. For instance, Article 40 of the Irish Constitution "guarantees liberty for the exercise" of the rights of citizens "to express freely their convictions and opinions" and "to assemble peaceable without arms." But this same Article also stipulates that all of these rights are "subject to public order and morality." And it specifically hedges these guarantees by excluding from the protected realm speech that is "blasphemous, seditious, or indecent" and assemblies that serve "to cause a breach of the peace or to be a danger or nuisance to the general public." Or, for example, Section 92 of the Australian Constitution provides that "trade, commerce and intercourse among the States . . . shall be *absolutely free*" [emphasis added]. But Section 51 empowers Parliament "to make laws for the peace, order, and good government of the Commonwealth with respect to (1) Trade and Commerce with other countries, and among the States."

Beneficiaries May Not Sue

A third aspect of judicial self-restraint is that a case will be rejected out of hand if the petitioner has apparently been the beneficiary of a law or an official action that he or she has subsequently chosen to challenge. Suppose that Farmer Brown has long been a member of the Soil Bank Program (designed to cut back on grain surpluses). Under the program, he agreed to take part of his land out of production and periodically was paid a subsidy by the federal government. After years as a participant he learns that his lazy, ne'er-do-well neighbors, the Joneses, are also drawing regular payments for letting their farmland lie fallow. The idea that his neighbors are getting something for nothing starts to offend Farmer Brown, and he begins to harbor grave doubts about the constitutionality of the whole program. Armed with a host of reasons that Congress had acted illegally, Brown challenges the legality of the Soil Bank Act in the local federal district court. As soon as it is brought to the judge's attention that Farmer Brown had himself been a member of the program and had gained financially from it, the suit is dismissed: One may not benefit from a particular governmental endeavor or official action and subsequently attack it in court.

Appellate Courts Rule on Legal—Not Factual—Questions

In the real world appellate court justices often find it difficult to tell whether a particular legal dispute is a question of who did what to whom (the facts of the case) or of how to weigh and assess a series of events (the legal interpretation of the facts). A working proposition of state and federal appellate court practice is that these courts will generally not hear cases if the grounds for appeal are that the trial judge or jury wrongly amassed and identified the basic factual elements of the case. It is not that trial judges and juries always do a perfect job of making factual determinations. Rather, there is the belief that they are closer, sensorially and temporally, to the parties and physical evidence of the case. The odds are, so the theory goes, that they will do a much better job of making factual assessments than would an appellate body reading only a stale transcript of the case some months or years after the trial.[22] However, legal matters—which laws to apply to the facts of a case or how to assess the facts in light of the prevailing law—are appropriate for appellate review. On such issues collegial, or multijudge, appellate bodies presumably have a legitimate and better capacity "to say what the law is," as Chief Justice John Marshall put it.

Nevertheless, some qualification must be offered. In most jurisdictions, appellate courts will hear appeals under "the clearly erroneous rule"; that is, when the petitioner contends that the trial court's determination of the facts was obviously and utterly wrong. The issue would not be a minor quibble about what the facts were but a belief that the trial court had made a finding that totally flew in the face of common sense. Likewise appellate courts may be willing to review an administrative agency's factual determinations that were allegedly made "without substantial evidence." Despite these qualifications, however, it is still fair to say that trial courts are the primary determiners of the facts or evidence in cases even though such determinations are not always absolutely conclusive.

For example, if X were convicted of a crime and the sole grounds for her appeal were that the judge and jury had mistakenly found her guilty (that is, incorrectly sifted and identified the facts), the appeals court would probably dismiss the case out of hand. However, assume that X provided evidence that she had asked for and been refused counsel during her FBI interrogation and that her confession was therefore illegal. At trial the district judge ruled that the Fifth Amendment's right against self-incrimination did not apply to X's interrogation by the FBI. The defendant argued to the contrary. Such a contention could be appealed because the issue is one of legal, not factual, interpretation.

The fact that U.S. appellate courts are generally restricted to interpreting the law and not to identifying and assembling facts is one additional check on the scope of their decision making.

The Supreme Court Is Not Bound (Technically) by Precedents

If the High Court is free to overturn or circumvent past and supposedly controlling precedents when it decides a case, this might appear to be an argument for judicial activism—not restraint. However, this practice must be placed in the restraint column. If the Supreme Court were inescapably bound by the dictates of its prior rulings, it would have very little flexibility. It would not be free to back off when discretion advised a cautious approach to a problem; it would not have liberty to withdraw from a confrontation in which it might not be in the nation's or the Court's interest to engage. By occasionally allowing itself the freedom to overrule a past decision or to ignore a precedent that would seem to be controlling, the Supreme Court establishes a corner of safety to which it can retreat if need be. When wisdom dictates that the Court change direction or at least keep an open mind, this principle of self-restraint is readily plucked from the judicial kit bag.

Other Remedies Must Be Exhausted

Another principle of self-restraint often frustrates the anxious litigant but is essential to the orderly administration of justice: Courts in the United States will not accept a case until all other remedies, legal and administrative, have been exhausted. Although this caveat is often associated with the U.S. Supreme Court, it is a working principle for virtually all American judicial tribunals. In its simplest form this doctrine means that one must work up the ladder with one's legal petitions. Federal cases must first be heard by the U.S. trial courts, then reviewed by one of the appellate tribunals, and finally heard by the U.S. Supreme Court. This orderly procedure of events must and will occur despite the importance of the case or of the petitioners who filed it. For instance, in 1952 President Harry S. Truman seized the American steel mills to prevent a pending strike that he believed would imperil the war effort in the Korean conflict. Both labor and management were suddenly told they were now working for Uncle Sam. The mill owners were furious and immediately brought suit, charging that the president had abused the powers of his office. A national legal-political crisis erupted. One might think that the Supreme Court would immediately take a case of this magnitude. Not so. In the traditional and orderly fashion of American federal justice, the controversy first went to the local district court in Washington, D.C., just as if it were the most ordinary dispute. Not until after the district court had ruled did the nation's highest tribunal have the opportunity to sink its teeth into this hearty piece of judicial meat. (The Supreme Court did, however, concede the need for expeditious behavior by granting certiorari before the court of appeals could rule on the merits of the case—thereby shortening the normal appellate process.)

Exhaustion of remedies refers to possible administrative relief as well as to adherence to the principle of a three-tiered judicial hierarchy. Such relief might be in the form of an appeal to an administrative officer, a hearing before a board or committee, or formal consideration of a matter by a legislative body. Consider a hypothetical illustration. Professor Ben Wheatley is denied tenure at a staunchly conservative institution. He is told that tenure was not granted because of his poor teaching record and lack of scholarly publications. He contends that denial of tenure is in retaliation for his having founded the nearby Sunshine Socialist Society, a nudist colony for gay atheists. He has the option of a hearing before the university's Grievance Committee, but he declines it, saying, "It would do no good; it would just be a waste of time." Instead, he takes his case immediately to the local federal district court, claiming that his Fourteenth Amendment rights have been violated. When the case is brought before the trial court, the judge says to Professor Wheatley: "Before I will even look at this matter, you must first take your case before the official, duly established Grievance Committee at your university. It doesn't matter whether you believe that you will win or lose your petition before the committee. You must establish your record there and avail yourself of all the administrative appeals and remedies that your institution has provided. If you are then still dissatisfied with the outcome, you may at that time invoke the power of the federal district courts."

Thus, judicial restraint means that judges do not jump immediately into every controversy that appears to be important or that strikes their fancy. The restrained and orderly administration of justice requires that before any court may hear a case, all administrative and inferior legal remedies must first be exhausted.

Courts Do Not Decide "Political Questions"

U.S. judges are often called upon to determine the winner of a contested election, to rule on the legality of a newly drawn electoral district, or to involve themselves in voting rights cases. How then can the argument be made that political questions are out of bounds for the American judiciary? The answer lies in the narrow, singular use of the word *political*. To U.S. judges, the executive and the legislative branches of government are political in that they are elected by the people for the purpose of making public policy. The judiciary, in contrast, was not designed by the founders to be an instrument manifesting the popular will and is therefore not political. According to this line of reasoning, then, a political question is one that ought properly to be resolved by one of the other two branches of government (even though it may appear before the courts wrapped in judicial clothing). When judges determine that something is a political question and therefore not appropriate for judicial review, what they are saying in effect is this: "You litigants may have couched your plea in judicial terminology, but under our form of government, issues such as this ought properly to be decided at the ballot box, in the legislative halls, or in the chambers of the executive."

For example, when the state of Oregon gave its citizens the right to vote on popular statewide referendums and initiatives around the end of the nineteenth century, the Pacific States Telephone and Telegraph Company objected.[23] (The company feared that voters would bypass the more business-oriented legislature and pass laws restricting its rates and profits.) The company claimed that by permitting citizens directly to enact legislation, the state has "been reduced to a democracy," whereas Article IV, Section 4, of the Constitution guarantees to each state "a Republican Form of Government"—a term that supposedly means that laws are to be made only by the elected representatives of the people, not by the citizens directly. Pacific States Telephone demanded that the Supreme Court take action. Opting for discretion rather than valor, the High Court refused to rule on the merits of the case, declaring the issue to be a political question. The Court reasoned that because Article IV primarily prescribes the duties of Congress, it follows that the founders wanted Congress—not the courts—to oversee the forms of government in the several states. In other words, the Court was being asked to invade the decision-making domain of one of the other (political) branches of government. And this it refused to do.

In recent decades an important political versus nonpolitical dispute has concerned the matter of reapportionment of legislative districts. Prior to 1962 a majority on the Supreme Court refused to rule on the constitutionality of legislative districts with unequal populations, saying that such matters were "nonjusticiable" and that the Court dared not enter what Justice Felix Frankfurter called "the political thicket." According to traditional Supreme Court thinking, the founders wanted legislatures to redistrict themselves—perhaps with some gentle prodding from the electorate. However, with the Supreme Court's decision in *Baker v. Carr*, the majority made an about-face.[24] Since 1962 the Court has held in scores of cases that the equal protection clause of the Fourteenth Amendment requires legislative districts to be of equal population size and, furthermore, that the courts should see to it that this mandate is carried out.

The refusal of the Supreme Court in recent decades to involve itself in foreign relations has likewise exemplified its desire to ignore the siren call of the political realm. For example, during the Vietnam War the Court repeatedly declined many ardent pleas to rule on the constitutionality of U.S. involvement.[25] Also, when President Jimmy Carter acted on his own initiative to end the Mutual Defense Treaty between the United States and Taiwan, this action was challenged in the courts by a number of senators and representatives. The High Court, consistent with tradition, refused to involve itself in this political question.[26]

Whether judges should take it on themselves to do what the founders probably wanted only political leaders to do is a question not confined to the United States. In India, for example, the national judiciary has been criticized by many for taking on issues that the writers of the Indian constitution wished to be addressed by Parliament alone, such as matters of air and water pollution. Article 21 of the Indian Constitution provides its people with "a right to life." In 1991 its Supreme Court ruled that this Article meant that the people had a right to pollution-free air and water, and later on it ordered the government to take on a series of measures to educate the public on matter of environmental pollution.[27]

The Burden of Proof Is on the Petitioner

Another weighty principle of self-restraint is the general agreement among the nation's jurists that an individual who would challenge the constitutionality of a statute bears the burden of proof. This is just a different way of saying that laws and official deeds are all presumed to be legal unless and until proven otherwise by a preponderance of evidence. The question of who has the burden of proof is of keen interest to lawyers because, in effect, it means: Which side has the bigger job to perform in the courtroom? And which party must assume the lion's share of the burden of convincing the court—or lose the case entirely? Thus, if one were attacking a particular statute, one would have to do more than demonstrate that it was "questionable" or "of doubtful constitutionality"; one must persuade the court that the evidence against the law was clear-cut and overwhelming—not often an easy task. In giving the benefit of the doubt to a statute or an executive act, judges have yet another area in which to exercise restraint.

The only exception to this burden of proof principle is in the realm of civil rights and liberties. Some jurists who are strong civil libertarians have long contended that when government attempts to restrict basic human freedoms, the burden of proof should shift to the government. And in several specific areas of civil rights jurisprudence that philosophy now prevails. For example, the U.S. Supreme Court has ruled in a variety of cases that laws that treat persons differently according to their race or gender are automatically subject to "special scrutiny." This means that the burden of proof shifts to the government to demonstrate a compelling or overriding need to differentiate persons according to their ethnic origins or sex. For instance, the government has long argued (successfully) that some major restrictions can be placed on women in the armed forces that prevent them from being assigned to full combat duty.

Laws Are Overturned on the Narrowest Grounds Only

Sometimes during a trial a judge clearly sees that the strictures of the Constitution have been offended by a legislative or executive act. Even here, however, ample opportunity is available to proceed with caution. Judges have two common ways to act in a restrained manner even when they must reach for the blue pencil.

First, a judge may have the option of invalidating an official action on statutory, instead of constitutional, grounds. Statutory invalidation means that a judge overturns an official's action because the official acted beyond the authority delegated to him or her by the law. Such a ruling has the function of saving the law itself while still nullifying the official's misdeed.

Suppose that Congress continues to authorize postal officials to seize all obscene nude photographs that are shipped through the mail. A photographer attempts to mail pictures taken at his art studio, but the pictures are seized by postal officials. The photographer protests that the statute violates his First Amendment rights and the case is eventually taken to the federal courts. Assuming that the judges are generally sympathetic to the position of the photographer, they have two basic options. They may declare the statute to be in violation of the Constitution and thus null and void, or they may select another stance that permits them to have it both ways. They may decide that the law itself passed constitutional muster, but that the postal official in question mistakenly decided that the nude photos were obscene. Thus the statute is preserved and a direct confrontation between the courts and Congress is averted, but the courts are able to give the petitioner virtually all of what he wants. This is an example of deciding a case on statutory grounds.

Second, judges may, if possible, invalidate only that portion of a law they find constitutionally defective instead of overturning the entire statute. For instance, in 1963 Congress passed the Higher Education Facilities Act, which provided construction grants for college buildings. Part of the law declared that for a twenty-year period, no part of the newly built structures could be used for "sectarian instruction, religious worship, or the programs of a divinity school." Because church-related universities as well as public institutions benefited from the act, the entire law was challenged in court as being in violation of the establishment of religion clause of the First Amendment. The Supreme Court determined that the basic thrust of the law did not violate the Constitution, but it did find the "twenty-year clause" to be objectionable. After all, the Court reasoned, most buildings last a good deal longer than two decades, and a building constructed at public expense could thus house religious activities during most of its lifetime. Instead of striking down the entire act, however, the Court majority merely substituted the word *never* for the phrase *twenty years*.[28] Thus the baby was not thrown out with the bath water and judicial restraint was maintained.

No Rulings Are Made on the "Wisdom" of Legislation

This final aspect of judicial self-restraint is probably the least understood by the public, the most often violated by the courts, and yet potentially the greatest harness on judicial activism in existence. What this admonition means, if followed strictly, is that the only basis for declaring a law or an official action unconstitutional is that it violates the Constitution on its face. Statutes do not offend the Constitution merely because they are unfair, are fiscally wasteful, or constitute bad public policy. Official actions can be struck down only if they step across the boundaries clearly set forth by the founders. If taken truly to heart, this means that judges and justices are not free to invoke their own personal notions of right and wrong or of good and bad public policy when they examine the constitutionality of legislation.

A keen expression of this phenomenon of judicial self-restraint is found in Justice Potter Stewart's dissenting opinion in the case of *Griswold v. Connecticut*. The Court majority had struck down the state's law that forbade the use of contraceptive devices or the dissemination of birth control information. Stewart said, in effect, that the law was bad, but that its weaknesses did not make it unconstitutional.

Since 1897 Connecticut has had on its books a law which forbids the use of contraceptives by anyone. I think this is an uncommonly silly law. As a practical matter, the law is obviously unenforceable, except in the oblique context of the present case. . . . But we are not asked in this case to say whether we think this law is unwise, or even asinine. We are asked to hold that it violates the United States Constitution. And that I cannot do.[29]

Another spinoff of this principle is that a law may be passed that all agree is good and wise but that is nevertheless unconstitutional; conversely, a statute may legalize the commission of an official deed that all know to be bad and dangerous but that still does not offend the Constitution. Permitting the police to dispose of known criminals without benefit of trial would probably save taxpayers a good deal of money and also reduce the crime rate, but it would be a clear, prima facie violation of the Constitution. However, a congressional tax on every sex act might be constitutionally permissible but would be a very unwise piece of legislation—not to mention difficult to enforce. Thus when the issue is laws or official acts, the adjectives *goodness* and *constitutionality* are no more synonymous than are *badness* and *unconstitutionality*.

Although few legal scholars would disagree with what has just been said, virtually all would point out that the principle of not ruling on the "wisdom" of a law is difficult to follow in the real world and is often honored in the breach. This is so because the Constitution, a rather brief document, is silent on many areas of public life and contains a number of phrases and admonitions that are open to a variety of interpretations. For instance, the Constitution says that Congress may regulate interstate commerce. But what exactly is commerce, and how extensive does it have to be before it is of an "interstate" character? As human beings, judges have differed in the way they have responded to this question. The Constitution guarantees a person accused of a crime the right to a defense attorney. But does this right continue if one appeals a guilty verdict and, if so, for how many appeals? Strict constructionists and loose constructionists have responded differently to these queries.

In all, despite the inevitable intrusion of judges' personal values into their interpretation of many portions of the Constitution, virtually every jurist subscribes to the general principle that laws can be invalidated only if they offend the Constitution—not the personal preferences of the judges.

Summary

In this chapter we have focused on what federal and state courts are supposed to do and on what they must refrain from doing. They adjudicate cases that come within their lawful original or appellate jurisdiction. Federal district courts hear criminal cases and civil suits that deal with federal questions, diversity of citizenship matters, prisoners' petitions, and any other issues authorized by Congress. The appellate courts, having no original jurisdiction whatever, take appeals from the district courts and from numerous administrative and regulatory agencies. The U.S. Supreme Court has original jurisdiction over suits between two or more states and in cases where ambassadors or public ministers are parties to a suit. Its appellate jurisdiction, regulated entirely by Congress, permits it to hear appeals from the circuit courts and from state courts of last resort. Since 1988 Congress has delegated to the High Court the right to control its own appellate caseload. As for state courts, the previous chapter summarized the primary contours of their jurisdictions, but in this chapter we emphasized the great importance of the issues that are adjudicated at the state level.

Under the U.S. legal system, federal courts are not to adjudicate questions unless a real case or controversy is at stake, although many state courts may render advisory opinions. All pleas to the courts must be based on a specific portion of the Constitution. Judges are also to dismiss suits in which a petitioner is challenging a law from which he or she has benefited. Federal and state appellate courts may rule only on matters of law—not on factual questions. Not being bound entirely by its precedents, the Supreme Court is free to exercise flexibility and restraint if it wishes to do so. All courts insist that litigants exhaust every legal and administrative remedy before a case will be decided. Courts in the United States are to eschew political questions and insist that the burden of proof rests on those who contend that a law or official action is unconstitutional. If judges must nullify an act of the legislature or the executive, they are to do so on the narrowest grounds possible. Finally, courts ought not rule on the wisdom or desirability of a law but are to strike down legislation only if it clearly violates the letter of the Constitution.

NOTES

1. Deborah Tedford, "Focus of Federal Docket Shifts: Immigration, Drugs Now 70 Percent of Texas Cases," *Houston Chronicle*, August 29, 1999, A1.

2. Richard A. Posner, *The Federal Courts: Challenge and Reform* (Cambridge, Mass.: Harvard University Press, 1996), 37.

3. *San Antonio Independent School District v. Rodriguez*, 411 U.S. 1 (1973).

4. William Kinney Swinford, "Resolving the Dispute over Methods of Financing Elementary and Secondary Education," Ph.D. dissertation, Ohio State University, 1993, 3–4.

5. "Court Deems Gay Ex 'Psychological Patent,' " *Houston Chronicle*, April 7, 2000, A2.

6. Mark S. Pulliam, "State Courts Take Brennan's Revenge," *Wall Street Journal*, January 4, 1999, A11.

7. Ibid.

8. For an excellent empirical analysis of the nature of state supreme court policy making, see Craig F. Emmert and Carol Ann Traut, "State Supreme Courts, State Constitutions, and Judicial Policymaking," *Justice System Journal* 16 (1992): 37–48. See also Charles S. Lopeman, *The Activist Advocate: Policy Making in State Supreme Courts* (Westport, Conn.: Praeger Publishers, 1999).

9. Barry Latzer, "The Hidden Conservatism of the State Court 'Revolution,' " *Judicature* 74 (1991): 190.

10. Richard B. Schmitt, "Right Turn: California High Court Makes Mark on Law by Limiting Damages," *Wall Street Journal*, July 11, 1989, A1.

11. "State High Court Strikes Down Effort to Legalize Gay Marriages," *Houston Chronicle*, December 11, 1999, A12.

12. *Ex Parte McCardle*, 74 U.S. (7 Wall.) 506 (1869).

13. For our discussion of the many aspects of judicial self-restraint we acknowledge our debt to Henry J. Abraham, on whose classic analysis of the subject we largely relied. See Henry J. Abraham, *The Judicial Process*, 7th ed. (New York: Oxford University Press, 1998), chap. 9.

14. *Muskrat v. United States*, 219 U.S. 346 (1911).

15. *Raines v. Byrd*, 521 U.S. 811 (1997).

16. Edward Felsenthal, "Justices Clear Way for Line-Item Veto, Ruling Challengers Lack Legal Standing," *Wall Street Journal*, June 27, 1997, A16.

17. *Clinton v. New York*, 524 U.S. 417 (1998).

18. *DeFunis v. Odegaard*, 416 U.S. 317 (1974).

19. Seven state constitutions expressly impose on their state supreme courts a duty to render advisory opinions (Colorado, Florida, Maine, Massachusetts, New Hampshire, Rhode Island, and South Dakota). In Alabama and Delaware, state courts have upheld laws authorizing advisory opinions even in the absence of a constitutional mandate. In North Carolina, the power to issue advisory opinions comes from a series of judicial decisions. For a general discussion of this topic, see "The State Advisory Opinion in Perspective," *Fordham Law Review* 44 (1975): 81–113.

20. *Steffel v. Thompson*, 415 U.S. 452 (1974) at 482.

21. *Board of Education of Kiryas Joel Village School District v. Grumet*, 512 U.S. 687 (1994).

22. One innovation in this realm is worth noting. At the present time in five federal courtrooms and in parts of six states, appeals judges are able to view videotapes of trials whose judgments are appealed to them. For an interesting discussion of this practice and conjecture about its future implications, see Junda Woo, "Videotapes Give Appeals Cases New Dimension," *Wall Street Journal*, April 14, 1992, B1.

23. *Pacific States Telephone & Telegraph v. Oregon*, 223 U.S. 118 (1912).

24. *Baker v. Carr*, 369 U.S. 186 (1962).

25. *Massachusetts v. Laird*, 400 U.S. 886 (1970).

26. *Goldwater v. Carter*, 444 U.S. 996 (1979).

27. For an excellent discussion of this particular case and also of the degree to which the Indian Supreme Court engages in judicial activism, see Robert Moog, "Activism on the Indian Supreme Court," *Judicature* 82 (1998): 124–132.

28. *Tilton v. Richardson*, 403 U.S. 672 (1971).

29. *Griswold v. Connecticut*, 381 U.S. 479 (1965).

SUGGESTED READINGS

Abraham, Henry J. *The Judicial Process,* 7th ed. New York: Oxford University Press, 1998. A traditional but classic discussion of the judicial process—especially Chapter 9, which focuses on judicial self-restraint.

Halpern, Stephen C., and Charles M. Lamb, eds. *Supreme Court Activism and Restraint.* Lexington, Mass.: Lexington Books, 1982. An excellent series of individual essays about the history and the pros and cons of judicial activism and restraint.

Judicature 81 (1998). The entire issue is dedicated to courts and justice abroad, with a special emphasis on matters of jurisdiction and policy-making boundaries.

Stumpf, Harry P., *American Judicial Politics,* 2d ed. Upper Saddle River, N.J.: Prentice Hall, 1998. A concise, up-to-date textbook on the judicial process at both the state and federal levels.

Tate, C. Neal, and Torbjorn Vallinder, eds. *The Global Expansion of Judicial Power.* New York: New York University Press, 1995. This is a series of up-to-date accounts of how the power and jurisdiction of courts has been expanding throughout much of the modern world.

The Third Branch: Newsletter of the Federal Courts. Published by the Administrative Office of the U.S. Courts. Washington, D.C.: Government Printing Office. A monthly report on activities, problems, and events related to day-to-day operations of the federal judiciary.

CHAPTER 3

Federal Judges

President Clinton's appointments of women and minorities to the federal bench far surpassed his three predecessors. Judge Vanessa Gilmore of Houston smiles during a round of applause after her swearing in.

✎ At least half of President Bill Clinton's judicial appointees were women or minorities—a marked contrast with his predecessors who appointed largely white males. Were Clinton's actions important for symbolic or political reasons only, or do women and minorities think and behave somewhat differently as judges?

✎ In virtually all foreign countries no one could become a federal judge unless he or she first had attended a formal judges college, passed a rigid set of exams, or had many years of specialized training. The United States, however, imposes no formal requirements whatsoever on a prospective federal judge; the presidential appointee need only be approved by the Senate. Would the United States benefit from emulating the model of other nations, or has its system served the citizenry well?

✎ When senators are deciding whether or not to support a president's judicial nominations, should they consider only the nominees' qualifications or should they also consider how the nominees might vote in cases that are of interest to the senators?

THE MAIN ACTORS in the federal system are the men and women who serve as judges and justices.

As the black-robed decision makers to whom most Americans still look with such reverence become the focus of analysis, keep several questions in mind: What characteristics do these people have that distinguish them from the rest of the citizenry? What are the qualifications—both formal and informal—for appointment to the bench? How are the judges selected and who are the participants in the process? Is there a policy link between the citizenry, the appointment process, and the subsequent decisions of the jurists? How are they socialized into their judicial roles; that is, how do judges learn to be judges? And how are judges disciplined and when are they removed from the bench?

Background Characteristics of Federal Judges

Americans cling eagerly to the log cabin-to-White House myth of attaining high public office—the notion that someone born in the humblest of circumstances (such as Abraham Lincoln) may one day grow up to be the president of the United States, or at least a U.S. judge. As with most myths, it has a kernel of truth. In principle virtually anyone can become a prominent public official, and a few well-known examples can be cited of people who came from poor backgrounds and climbed to the pinnacle of power. One example is Thurgood Marshall, the great-grandson of a slave and the son of a Pullman car steward who became a Supreme Court justice. Another is Warren E. Burger, who served as chief justice; his father earned his daily bread as a traveling salesman and as a railroad car inspector. More typical, however, is the most recent Supreme Court appointee, Stephen G. Breyer, a multimillionaire whose wife is from a family of British nobility. The main criticism leveled against Breyer prior to his appointment was that he was overinvested in the wealthy insurance firm of Lloyds of London. For a long time uncontested data have clearly shown that America's federal judges, like other public officials and the captains of commerce and industry, come from a narrow stratum of American society. Although potential judges are not necessarily the sons and daughters of millionaires, it is at least helpful if they come from a special segment of the nation's middle and upper-middle classes.

District Judges

Background data for all federal district judges for the past 210 years have never been collected, but a good deal is known about judges who have served in recent decades. Table 8-1 profiles some key characteristics of trial jurists appointed by Presidents Jimmy Carter, Ronald Reagan, George Bush, and Bill Clinton.

In terms of their primary occupation before assuming the federal bench, a plurality had been judges at the state or local level. About 37 percent of Reagan's judges had had extensive judicial experience, and almost 45 percent of Carter's judicial team had previously worn the black robe. The next largest blocs were employed either in the political or governmental realms or in moderate- to large-sized law firms. Those working in small law firms or as professors of law made up the smallest bloc.

Their educational background reveals something of their elite nature. All graduated from college; about half attended either the costly Ivy League schools or other private universities to receive their undergraduate and law degrees. Most adult Americans have never gone to college, and of those who have, only a tiny portion could meet the admission requirements—not to mention the expense—of most private or Ivy League schools.

About half of the district judges had had some experience on the bench, and about four out of ten had served at one time as a public prosecutor. This recent phenomenon has caused some court observers to conclude that "we may be evolving toward the European system of a career judiciary."[1]

Judges differ in yet another way from the population as a whole. Among trial judges—and all U.S. judges for that matter—a strong tendency toward "occupational heredity" exists. That is, judges tend to come from families with a tradition of judicial and public service.[2] One of former president Reagan's trial court appointees, Howell Cobb of Beaumont, Texas, is typical of this phenomenon. The nominee's hometown paper said of him:

The appointee is the fourth generation of a family of lawyers and judges. His great-grandfather, a Confederate officer, served as secretary of the Treasury under President James Buchanan and was governor of Georgia and speaker of the U.S. House of Representatives. Cobb's grandfather was a justice on the Georgia Supreme Court, and his father was a circuit judge in Georgia. Cobb's son, a lawyer in El Paso, also follows tradition. "Most trial lawyers aspire to a seat on the bench," Cobb said.[3]

Traditionally being a woman or a racial minority or both has not been an asset if one coveted a judicial robe. Although the United States is about 51 percent female, judging has been almost exclusively a man's business. Until the Carter presidency less than 2 percent of the lower judiciary was female, and even with conscious effort to change this phenomenon, only 14.4 percent of Carter's district judges were women. The same holds for racial minorities, whose numbers on the trial bench

TABLE 3-1 Background Characteristics of Presidents' District Court Appointees, 1977–1999

Characteristic	Bill Clinton	George Bush	Ronald Reagan	Jimmy Carter
Occupation				
Politics/government	10.9%	10.8%	13.4%	5.0%
Judiciary	46.8	41.9	36.9	44.6
Large law firm				
100+ members	6.9	10.8	6.2	2.0
50–99	5.2	7.4	4.8	5.9
25–49	3.6	7.4	6.9	5.9
Moderate-size firm				
10–24 members	8.3	8.8	10.0	9.4
5–9	7.3	6.1	9.0	10.4
Small firm				
2–4	5.2	3.4	7.2	10.9
solo	3.2	1.4	2.8	2.5
Professor of law	1.6	0.7	2.1	3.0
Other	1.2	1.4	0.7	0.5
Experience				
Judicial	51.2	46.6	46.2	54.0
Prosecutorial	40.7	39.2	44.1	38.1
Neither	29.8	31.8	28.6	30.7
Undergraduate education				
Public	43.6	44.6	36.6	56.4
Private	42.3	41.2	49.7	33.7
Ivy League	14.1	14.2	13.8	9.9
Law school education				
Public	41.1	52.7	42.4	50.5
Private	39.5	33.1	45.9	32.7
Ivy League	19.4	14.2	11.7	16.8
Gender				
Male	71.8	80.4	91.7	85.6
Female	28.2	19.6	8.3	14.4
Ethnicity/race				
White	73.8	89.2	92.4	78.7
African American	19.0	6.8	2.1	13.9
Hispanic	5.2	4.0	4.8	6.9
Asian	1.6	—	0.7	0.5
Native American	0.4	—	—	—
Percentage white male	51.2	73.0	84.8	68.3
American Bar Association rating				
Exceptionally well qualified/well qualified	58.1	57.4	53.5	51.0
Qualified	40.7	42.6	46.6	47.5
Not qualified	1.2	—	—	1.5

Table continues on next page

TABLE 3-1   Background Characteristics of Presidents' District Court Appointees, 1977–1999 *(continued)*

Characteristic	Bill Clinton	George Bush	Ronald Reagan	Jimmy Carter
Political identification				
Democrat	89.1	5.4	4.8	90.6
Republican	4.8	88.5	91.7	4.5
Other	0.4	—	—	—
None	5.7	6.1	3.4	5.0
Past party activism	52.4	60.8	59.0	60.9
Net worth				
Less than $200,000	15.3	10.1	17.6	35.8[a]
$200,000–499,999	23.0	31.1	37.6	41.2
$500,000–999,999	27.4	26.4	21.7	18.9
$1+ million	34.5	32.4	23.1	4.0
Average age at nomination	49.1	48.1	48.7	49.6
Total number of appointees	248	148	290	202

SOURCE: Sheldon Goldman and Elliot Slotnick, "Clinton's Second Term Judiciary: Picking Judges Under Fire," *Judicature* 82 (1999): 264–286.

[a] These figures are for appointees confirmed by the 96th Congress for all but six Carter district court appointees (for whom no data were available).

have always been small, not only in absolute numbers but also in comparison with figures for the overall population. Until the present time only Jimmy Carter, who made affirmative action a cornerstone of his presidency, had appointed a significant number of non-Anglos to the federal bench—over 21 percent. Under the Clinton administration, however, a complete about-face took place. At the end of his first six years in office the official count reveals that a whopping 49 percent of his judicial appointees have been either women or minorities. This figure (which represents both district and appeals court judges) is compared with percentages of only 28, 14, and 34 for Presidents Bush, Reagan, and Carter, respectively. The impact of Clinton's revolutionary appointment strategy on the policy output of the federal courts is currently under study by judicial scholars.

The American Bar Association (ABA) ratings reveal that few make it to the federal bench who are not rated as "qualified" by this self-appointed evaluator of judicial fitness. The difference in quality between the Republican and Democratic appointees is trivial; both Bush's and Clinton's appointees have received comparatively strong ratings.

About nine out of ten district judges have been of the same political party as the appointing president, and until the Clinton administration about 60 percent had had a record of active partisanship. The Clinton cohort contained fewer active partisans—about 52 percent.

That district judge nominees constitute an elite group is clearly revealed in the statistics for their net worth at the time of their appointment to the bench. Although these figures do not prove that all potential jurists were wealthy, they do suggest that few candidates for the bench had to ponder the source of their next meal. The Carter cohort seems to have been the least wealthy when they assumed the bench, whereas a third of Bush and Clinton's judicial nominees were millionaires at the time they took the judicial oath.

As for age, the typical judge has been about forty-nine at the time of appointment. Age variations from one presidency to another have been small, with no discernable trend over the years from one administration to another.

Appeals Court Judges

Because the statistics and percentages of the appellate court appointees of the four presidents from Carter through Clinton are similar to those for the trial judges, we shall offer some commentary only on those figures that suggest a difference between the two sets of judges (see Table 8-2).

Appeals judges are much more likely to have previous judicial experience than their counterparts on the trial court bench. Also, Presidents Carter, Reagan, and Clinton were more apt to look to the ranks of law school professors for their appeals court appointments than was President Bush.

If the trend toward seeking out private school and Ivy League graduates was strong for trial judge appointments, it is even more pronounced for those selected for seats on the appeals courts. The only exception is for the Clinton appellate cohort. Only 54 percent of the Clinton jurists gained admittance to such schools, while 70 percent of Bush judges attended elite undergraduate institutions. Still, compared with the population at large or even U.S. district judges, appellate court jurists appear to be solid members of America's social and economic elite.

In terms of opposite-party selections, little difference is seen between trial and appellate court appointments. However, appeals judges have a slight tendency to be more active in their respective parties than their colleagues on the trial bench.

The Clinton initiative to make the bench more accurately reflect U.S. gender and racial demographics is evident in the ranks of the appellate judges as well. A third of his jurists are women. This is compared with just 19, 5, and 20 percent of the

TABLE 3-2   Background Characteristics of Presidents' Appeals Court Appointees, 1977–1999

Characteristic	Bill Clinton	George Bush	Ronald Reagan	Jimmy Carter
Occupation				
Politics/government	4.2%	10.8%	6.4%	5.4%
Judiciary	56.3	59.5	55.1	46.4
Large law firm				
100+ members	12.5	8.1	5.1	1.8
50–99	2.1	8.1	2.6	5.4
25–49	4.2	—	6.4	3.6
Moderate-size firm				
10–24 members	8.3	8.1	3.9	14.3
5–9	4.2	2.7	5.1	1.8
Small firm				
2–4	—	—	1.3	3.6
solo	—	—	—	1.8
Professor	8.3	2.7	12.8	14.3
Other	—	—	1.3	1.8
Experience				
Judicial	62.5	62.2	60.3	53.6
Prosecutorial	35.4	29.7	28.2	32.1
Neither	27.1	32.4	34.6	39.3
Undergraduate education				
Public	45.8	29.7	24.4	30.4
Private	33.3	59.5	51.3	51.8
Ivy League	20.8	10.8	24.4	17.9
Law school education				
Public	39.6	29.7	41.0	39.3
Private	25.0	40.5	35.9	19.6
Ivy League	35.4	29.7	23.1	41.1
Gender				
Male	66.7	81.1	94.9	80.4
Female	33.3	18.9	5.1	19.6
Ethnicity/race				
White	77.1	89.2	97.4	78.6
African American	10.4	5.4	1.3	16.1
Hispanic	10.4	5.4	1.3	3.6
Asian	2.1	—	—	1.8
Percentage white male	50.0	70.3	92.3	60.7
American Bar Association rating				
Exceptionally well qualified/ well qualified	77.1	64.9	59.0	75.0
Qualified	22.9	35.1	41.0	25.0

TABLE 3-2　Background Characteristics of Presidents' Appeals Court Appointees, 1977–1999 *(continued)*

Characteristic	Bill Clinton	George Bush	Ronald Reagan	Jimmy Carter
Political identification				
Democrat	85.4	5.4	—	82.1
Republican	6.3	89.2	96.2	7.1
Other	—	—	1.3	—
None	8.3	5.4	2.6	10.7
Past party activism	56.3	70.3	65.4	73.2
Net worth				
Less than $200,000	6.3	5.4	15.6[a]	33.3[b]
$200,000–499,999	12.5	29.7	32.5	38.5
$500,000–999,999	31.3	21.6	33.8	17.9
$1+ million	50.0	43.2	18.2	10.3
Average age at nomination	51.2	48.7	50.0	51.8
Total number of appointees	48	37	78	56

SOURCE: Sheldon Goldman and Elliot Slotnick, "Clinton's Second Term Judiciary: Picking Judges Under Fire," *Judicature* 82 (1999): 264–286.

[a]Net worth was unavailable for one appointee.

[b]Net worth only for Carter appointees confirmed by the 96th Congress with the exception of five appointees for whom net worth was unavailable.

Bush, Reagan, and Carter judges, respectively. And the Clinton team is composed of more African Americans, Hispanics, and Asians than the cohorts of any other president. When the gender and race variables are combined, the contrast between the Clinton team and other presidential cohorts is even more vivid. Only 50 percent of Clinton's appellate judges are white males. White males constituted 70, 92, and 61 percent of the judges appointed by Bush, Reagan, and Carter, respectively. Clinton's efforts to increase the representation of women and minorities on the bench have not gone unnoticed in other countries, at least by those whose judicial systems bear some semblance to the United States'. For example, international judicial scholar Henry Abraham noted that in recent years "there has been mounting criticism [in Britain] of the [judicial] selection process, because of the scarcity of women and minorities among the high judges. . . . Tony Scrivener, QC, Chairman of the Bar, promised to endeavor to alleviate that condition and also to advance the candidacies of more liberal members of the profession to judgeships."[4]

Finally, candidates for the appeals courts seem to be as blessed with financial resources as their brothers and sisters selected to preside over the trial courts. For example, about 43 percent of Bush's nominees to the appellate court bench and 50 percent of Clinton's nominees had a net worth of over $1 million at the time of their appointment.

Supreme Court Justices

Since 1789, 106 men and 2 women have sat on the bench of America's highest judicial tribunal. If judges of the trial and appeals courts have been culled primarily from America's cultural elite, then members of the U.S. Supreme Court are the crème de la crème.

Although perhaps 10 percent of the justices were of essentially humble origin, the remainder "were not only from families in comfortable economic circumstances, but were chosen overwhelmingly from the socially prestigious and politically influential gentry class in the late 18th and early 19th century, or the professionalized upper class thereafter." [5] A majority of the justices came from politically active families, and about a third were related to jurists and closely connected with families with a tradition of judicial service. Thus the justices were reared in far from commonplace American families.

Until the 1960s the High Court had been all white and all male, but in 1967 President Lyndon B. Johnson appointed Thurgood Marshall as the first black member of the Court. When Marshall retired in 1991, President Bush nominated Clarence Thomas, a man who shared Marshall's ethnic heritage, though not his liberal views. In 1981 the gender barrier was broken when President Reagan named Sandra Day O'Connor to the Court, and thirteen years later she was joined by Ruth Bader Ginsburg. In terms of religious background, the membership of the Court has been overwhelmingly Protestant, and most of these have been affiliated with the more prestigious denominations (such as the Episcopal, Presbyterian, and Unitarian churches). Thus in terms of ethnicity, gender, and religious preference, the Court is by no means a cross-section of American society.

As for the nonpolitical occupations of the justices, all 108 had legal training and all had practiced law at some stage in their careers. An inordinate number had served as corporation attorneys before their appointments. Only 22 percent had state or federal judicial experience immediately prior to their appointments, although more than half had served on the bench at some time before their nomination to the Supreme Court. As with their colleagues in the lower federal judiciary, the justices were much more likely to have been politically active than the average American, and virtually all shared many of the ideological and political orientations of their appointing president.

An Appraisal of the Statistics

Several conclusions are readily apparent from the summary data just presented. First, federal judges in the United States are an elite within an elite. They come from upper- or upper-middle-class families that are politically active and that have a tradition of public and, often, judicial service. Is the narrow judicial selection process the result of pure chance? Has there been a sinister conspiracy for the past two centuries to keep women, blacks, Roman Catholics, the poor, and so on out of the U.S. judiciary, or are the causes more subtle and complex? The evidence points to the latter explanation.

Legislation has never been passed that forbade non-Anglos to wear the black robe. But laws, traditions, and unwritten codes have kept them from entering the better law schools, from working in the more prestigious law firms and corporations, and from making the kind of social and political connections that may lead to nomination to judicial office. Likewise, no statutes have excluded the children of the poor from consideration for a seat on the bench. But few youngsters from impoverished homes can afford expensive, high-quality colleges and law schools that would give them the training and the contacts they would need. Traditionally, too, many more young men than young women were encouraged to apply to law school. For instance, Supreme Court Justice Ginsburg remembers that while she was at Harvard Law School during the 1950s, the dean held a reception for the nine women in her class of more than five hundred. "After dinner," she recalled, "the dean asked each of us to explain what we were doing at the law school occupying a seat that could have been filled by a man. When my turn came, I wished I could have pushed a button and vanished through a trapdoor."[6] The process of exclusion, then, has not been part of a conscious, organized conspiracy; instead, it has been the inevitable consequence of more subtle social and economic forces in society.

Another observation about the background profile of federal judges is worthy of mention. Because they tend to come from the same kinds of families, to go to the same universities and law schools, and to belong to churches, clubs, and societies that uphold similar values, federal judges generally are much more alike than they are different. There may be Democrats and Republicans, former defense attorneys and former prosecutors on the bench, but to a significant degree virtually all play the game by the same rules. What one scholar has said about the recruitment process for the appeals courts is true for federal judgeships in general:

Broadly speaking [the recruitment process] tends to reward supporters of the presidential party; weed out incompetents, mavericks, and ideological extremists; and ensure substantial professional and political experience among those who wield federal appellate power. Forged thereby are continuous links between judges and their political and professional surroundings. Restricted thereby are the types of persons inducted into Courts of Appeals. The multiple filters through which recruits must pass put a premium on moderate, middle-class, and political lawyers, successful people advantaged in life.[7]

The fact that the recruitment process produces a corps of jurists who agree on how the judicial game is to be played is the primary reason that the loosely organized judicial hierarchy does not come flying apart. It is a key explanation for the predictability of most judicial decisions. The judicial machinery runs as smoothly and consistently as it does not because of outside watchdogs or elaborate enforcement mechanisms but because the principal participants largely share the same values and orientations and are working to further similar goals.

Formal and Informal Qualifications of Federal Judges

Despite the absence of formal qualifications for a federal judgeship, there are well-defined informal requirements.

Formal Qualifications

Students often torture one another with horror stories of the hurdles to be overcome to achieve success in a particular profession. Would-be medical students are awed by the high grade point averages and aptitude scores required for admission to medical schools; potential university professors shrink at the thought of the many years of work necessary to obtain a Ph.D., only to face the publish-or-perish requirements for a tenured position. It would be logical, then, to assume that the formal requirements for becoming a federal judge—and surely a Supreme Court justice—must be formidable indeed. Not so. No constitutional or statutory qualifications are stipulated for serving on the Supreme Court or the lower federal courts. The Constitution merely indicates that "the judicial Power of the United States, shall be vested in one supreme Court" as well as in any lower federal courts that Congress may establish (Article III, Section 1) and that the president "by and with the Advice and Consent of the Senate, shall appoint . . . Judges of the supreme Court" (Article II, Section 2). Congress has applied the same selection procedure to the appeals and the trial courts. There are no exams to pass, no minimum age requirement, no stipulation that judges be native-born citizens or legal residents, and no requirement that judges even have a law degree.

Informal Requirements

At least four vital although informal factors determine who sits on the federal bench in America: professional competence, political qualifications, self-selection, and the element of pure luck.

Professional Competence. Although candidates for U.S. judicial posts do not have to be attorneys—let alone prominent ones—it has been the custom to appoint lawyers who have distinguished themselves professionally (or at least not to appoint those without merit). Merit may mean no more than an association with a prestigious law firm, publication of a few law review articles, or respect among fellow attorneys. A potential judge need not necessarily be an outstanding legal scholar. Nevertheless, one of the unwritten codes is that a judicial appointment is different from run-of-the-mill patronage. Thus although the political rules may allow a president to reward an old ally with a seat on the bench, even here tradition has created an expectation that the would-be judge have some reputation for professional competence, the more so as the judgeship in question goes from the trial court to the appeals court to the Supreme Court level.

A modern-day example of the unwritten rule that potential judges be more than just warm bodies with a law degree is found in President Richard M. Nixon's nomination of G. Harrold Carswell to the Supreme Court in 1970. After investigations by the press and the Senate Judiciary Committee revealed that Carswell's record was unimpressive at best, his nomination began to stall on the floor of the Senate. To his aid came the well-meaning senator Roman Hruska of Nebraska, who stated in part: "Even if Carswell were mediocre, there are a lot of mediocre judges and people and lawyers. They are entitled to a little representation, aren't they, and a little chance? We can't have all Brandeises, and Frankfurters, and Cardozos and stuff like that there."[8] With such support Carswell must have wondered why he needed any detractors. In any case the acknowledgment by a friendly senator that the Supreme Court nominee was "mediocre" probably did more than anything else to prompt the Senate to reject Carswell. Although tradition may allow judgeships to be political payoffs and may not require eminence in the nominee, candidates for federal judicial posts are expected to meet a reasonable level of professional competence.

Political Qualifications. When at least 90 percent of all federal judicial nominees are of the same political party as the appointing president, even the most casual observer must notice that certain political requirements are likely being fulfilled for a seat on the bench. The fact that well over half of all federal judges were politically active before their appointments—in comparison with a 10 percent figure for the total population—is further evidence of this phenomenon. In this respect the American practice is not unique in the world. Even countries that pride themselves on keeping politics out of the judicial selection, for example, Canada, still often see it manifested at some level. As one keen observer of the Canadian political scene noted: "Most judges appointed by both federal and provincial Liberal governments are Liberal, judges appointed by Conservative governments are Conservative."[9] What are the political criteria used for American judicial appointments? In some cases a judgeship may be a reward for major service to the party in power or to the president or a senator. For example, when federal judge Peirson Hall (of the Central District of California) was asked how important politics was to his appointment, he gave this candid reply:

I worked hard for Franklin Roosevelt in the days when California had no Democratic Party to speak of. In 1939 I began running for the Senate, and the party convinced me it would be best if there wasn't a contest for the Democratic nomination. So I withdrew and campaigned for Martin Downey. They gave me this judgeship as sort of a consolation prize—and one, I might add, that I have enjoyed.[10]

Although examples like this are not uncommon, it would be a mistake to think of federal judgeships merely as political plums handed out to the party faithful. As often as not, a seat on the bench goes to a reasonably active or visible member of the party in power but not necessarily to someone who has made party service the central focus of a lifetime.

Political activity that might lead to a judgeship includes service as chair of a state or local party organization, an unsuccessful race for public office, or financial backing for partisan causes.

The reason most nominees for judicial office must have some record of political activity is twofold. First, to some degree judgeships are still considered part of the political patronage system; those who have served the party are more likely to be rewarded with a federal post than those who have not paid their dues. Second, even if a judgeship is not given as a direct political payoff, some political activity on the part of a would-be judge is often necessary. Otherwise, the candidate would simply not be visible to the president or senator(s) or local party leaders who send forth the names of candidates. If the judicial power brokers have never heard of a particular lawyer because that attorney has no political profile, his or her name will not come to mind when a vacancy occurs on the bench.

Self-Selection. For those seeking the presidency or running for Congress, shyness does not pay. One needs to declare one's candidacy, meet a formal filing deadline, and spend considerable time and money to advertise one's qualifications. Although Americans profess to admire modesty and humility in their leaders, successful candidates for elected office do well not to overindulge these virtues. With the judiciary, however, the informal rules of the game are different. Many would consider it undignified and lacking in judicial temperament for someone to announce publicly a desire for a federal judgeship—much less to campaign openly for such an appointment.

However, some would-be jurists orchestrate discreet campaigns on their own behalf or at least pass the word that they are available for judicial service. Few will admit to seeking an appointment actively, but credible anecdotes suggest that attorneys often position themselves in such a way that their names will come up when the powers-that-be have a vacant seat to fill. In 1993, for instance, the *Wall Street Journal* carried a story about a vacancy on the U.S. Court of Appeals for the Federal Circuit, a court that deals with an inordinate number of patent appeals and one that is followed closely by business interests. The article noted that "a lively battle" had broken out among business groups over who should occupy the vacant seat and that

even major corporations have taken the highly unusual step of weighing in for their favored candidates, while some other candidates have taken to fairly aggressive self-promotion. . . . Among those pushing for such a judge [one committed to science and technology] is John B. Pegram. His preferred choice: himself. In the past few months, Mr. Pegram . . . has written to the White House, offering himself up as a candidate, and made contact with a number of members of Congress, trumpeting his credentials.[11]

At judicial swearing-in ceremonies it is often said that "the judgeship sought the man (or woman) rather than vice versa," and surely this does happen. But sometimes the judgeship does its seeking with a little nudge from the would-be jurist.

The Element of Luck. If all that were involved in the picking of a Supreme Court justice or a lower-court judge were professional and political criteria, the appointment process would be much easier to explain and predict. If, for instance, one wanted to know who was going to be appointed to a vacancy on the Sixth Circuit bench, one would need only to identify the person in the Sixth Circuit to whom the party was most indebted and who had a reputation for legal competence. The problem is that the prevailing party owes much to hundreds of capable attorneys in the Sixth Circuit. Why should one of them be selected and several hundred not? Until judicial scholarship becomes more of a science and less of an art, accurate predictions cannot be made about who will wear the black robe; there are just too many variables and too many participants in the selection process. Consider, for example,

President Harry S. Truman's appointment of Carroll O. Switzer to fill a vacant judgeship in 1949.

The story begins in 1948 when Truman was seeking a full term as president. The campaign had not gone well from the start. Even the party faithful could barely muster a faint cheer when Truman proclaimed to sparse crowds, "We're gonna win this election and we're gonna make those Republicans like it. Just you wait 'n' see." Almost everyone predicted Truman would lose, and lose badly. Then one morning his campaign train stopped in the little town of Dexter, Iowa. An unexpectedly large number of farmers had put aside their milking chores and the fall corn harvest to see the feisty little man from Missouri "give those Republicans hell." Truman picked up a real sense of enthusiasm among the cheering crowd, and for the first time in the campaign he smelled victory.

On the campaign platform with Truman that morning was Carroll Switzer, a bright young Des Moines attorney who was the (unsuccessful) Democratic candidate for Iowa governor that year. No evidence exists that Truman met Switzer before or after that one propitious day. But when a vacancy occurred on the U.S. bench a year later, Truman's mind jumped like a spring to the name of his lucky horseshoe, Carroll Switzer. A longtime administrative assistant to an Iowa senator related the story as follows:

> I am sure that this day at Dexter was the first time President Truman and his staff were sure he could win—later proved right. I am sure that he recalled that day favorably when an appointment . . . came up in the Iowa judgeship. . . . Every time the Iowa judgeship came up, Truman would hear of no one but Switzer. Truman would say "That guy Switzer backed me when everyone else was running away, and, by God, I'm going to see that he gets a judgeship."[12]

That morning in Dexter was Switzer's lucky day. Although he had the professional and political credentials for a judicial post, no one could have foreseen that he would happen to appear with Truman the day the national winds of political fortune began to blow in the president's favor. Had it been any other day, Switzer might never have been more than just a bright attorney from Des Moines.

This account illustrates the point that a good measure of happenstance exists in virtually all judicial appointments. Being a member of the right party at the right time or being visible to the power brokers at a lucky moment often has as much to do with becoming a judge as the length and sparkle of one's professional résumé.

The Federal Selection Process and Its Participants

The skeletal framework of judicial selection is the same for all federal judges, although the roles of the participants vary depending upon the level of the U.S. judiciary. All nominations are made by the president after due consultation with the White House staff, the attorney general's office, certain senators, and other politicos. Furthermore, the FBI customarily performs a routine security check. After the nomination is announced to the public, various interest groups that believe they have a stake in the appointment may lobby for or against the candidate. Also, the candidate's qualifications will be evaluated by a committee of the American Bar Association. The candidate's name is then sent to the Senate Judiciary Committee, which conducts an investigation of the nominee's fitness for the post. If the committee's vote is favorable, the nomination is sent to the floor of the Senate, where it is either approved or rejected by a simple majority vote.

The President

Technically, the chief executive nominates all judicial candidates, but history has shown that the president manifests greater personal involvement in appointments to the Supreme Court than to the lower courts. This is so for two major reasons. First, Supreme Court appointments are seen by the president—and by the public at large—as generally more important and politically significant than openings on the lesser tribunals. Presidents often use their few opportunities for High Court appointments to make a political statement or to set the tone of their administration. For example, during the period of national stress prior to U.S. entry into World War II, Democratic president Franklin D. Roosevelt (FDR) elevated Republican Harlan Stone to chief justice as a gesture of national unity. In 1969 President Nixon used his appointment of the conservative Warren Burger to make good on his campaign pledge to restore "law and order." And President Reagan in 1981 hoped to dispel his reputation for being unsympathetic toward the women's movement by being the first to name a woman to the High Court. Likewise, President Clinton's appointment to the Court of two political moderates, Ruth Bader Ginsburg and Stephen Breyer, was viewed by many as an attempt to demonstrate to the public that he was a "new Democrat" and not a left-wing radical. Because appointments to the lower judiciary are less newsworthy, they are less likely to command the personal involvement of the president, who will probably rely much more heavily on the judgment of the White House staff or the Justice Department in selecting and screening candidates for appeals and trial court benches.

Second, presidents are less likely to devote much attention to lower-court appointments because tradition has allowed for individual senators and local party bosses to influence and often dominate such activity. The practice known as senatorial courtesy is a major restriction on the president's capacity to make district judge appointments. The conditions of this unwritten rule of the game are these: Senators of the president's political party who object to a candidate that the president wishes to appoint to a district judgeship in their home state have a virtual veto over the nomination. They exercise this veto through use of the blue slip—the printed form that a senator from the nominee's state is supposed to return to the Senate Judiciary Committee to express his or her views about the particular candidate.[13] So significant a restriction is this on the chief executive's appointing prerogatives that it caused one former assistant attorney general to quip: "The Constitution is backwards. Article II, Section 2 should read: 'The senators shall nominate, and by and with the consent of the President, shall appoint.'"[14] Many senators regard their prerogatives in this realm to be ordained by the founders. For example, under the Reagan administration when Texas senator Phil Gramm was asked to defend his key role in the appointment of district judges in his state, he said, "I'm given the power to make the appointment. . . . The people elected me to do that."[15] Senatorial courtesy does not apply to appellate court appointments, although presidents customarily defer to senators of their party from states that make up the appellate court circuit. Thus in lower-court appointments presidents have less incentive to devote effort to a game in which they are not the star player.

The president also has authority "to fill up all Vacancies that may happen during the recess of the Senate, by granting Commissions which shall expire at the End of their next Session" (Article II, Section 2). One reason a chief executive may wish to make a recess appointment is to fill a judicial vacancy on a court that has a large backlog of business. The other reason is more political. A president may find it easier to secure confirmation for a sitting judge than for a candidate named while the Senate is in session. That is, the Senate might be less likely to reject a fait accompli. So for example, when the Senate in the fall of 1999 rejected the appointment of the African American nominee Ronnie White for a federal judgeship for what many believed were racially biased reasons, the Congressional Black Caucus called on President Clinton to bypass the Senate and use recess appointments for six pending nominations of African American nominees. The caucus was aware that of the 309 recess appointments made in the nation's history, the Senate ultimately confirmed 85 percent of them.[16]

The Department of Justice

Assisting the president and the White House staff in the judicial selection process are the two key presidential appointees in the Justice Department—the attorney general of the United States and the deputy attorney general. Their primary job is to seek out candidates for federal judicial posts who conform to general criteria set by the president. For example, if a vacancy were to occur on the Seventh Circuit appellate bench, the attorney general (or a staff member) might phone the U.S. attorneys in the states of Illinois, Indiana, and Wisconsin and ask, "Are there some attorneys in your district who would make good judges and who are members of our political party or who at least share the president's basic philosophy?" Once several names are obtained, the staff of the Justice Department will subject each candidate to further scrutiny. They may order an FBI investigation of the candidate's character and background; they will usually read copies of all articles or speeches the candidate has written or evaluate a sitting judge's written opinions; they might check with local party leaders to determine that the candidate is a party faithful and is in tune with the president's major public policy positions.

In the case of district judge appointments, where names are often submitted by home-state senators, the Justice Department's function is more that of screener than of initiator. Regardless of who comes up with a basic list of names, the Justice Department's primary duty is to evaluate the candidates' personal, professional, and political qualifications. In performing this role the department may work closely with the White House staff, with the senators involved in the nomination, and with party leaders who may wish to have some input in the choice of the potential nominee.

Under the Clinton administration jurists were selected jointly by the White House Counsel's Office and the Justice Department's Office of Policy Development. At the Justice Department each potential judge was assigned to a particular attorney who examined the candidate's professional credentials, including any relevant judicial decision making. At the Office of White House Counsel candidates were screened for their political credentials. For example, the office makes sure that the Republican chair of the Senate Judiciary Committee would have no objection to the nominee.[17]

State and Local Party Leaders

Regional party politicos have little to say in the appointment of Supreme Court justices, where presidential prerogative is dominant, and their role in the choice of appeals court judges is minimal. However, in the selection of U.S. trial judges their impact is formidable, especially when appointments occur in states in which neither senator is of the president's political party. In such cases the president need not fear that senatorial courtesy will be invoked against a district court nominee and thus will be more likely to consult with state party leaders rather than with the state's senators. For example, during the Kennedy and Johnson administrations the Democratic mayor of Chicago, Richard J. Daley, personally approved every federal judge appointed in the Northern District of Illinois.

Interest Groups

A number of pressure groups in the United States, representing the whole political spectrum from left to right, often lobby either for or against judicial nominations. Leaders of these groups—civil liberties, business, organized labor, civil rights—have little hesitation about urging the president to withdraw the nomination of someone whose political and social values are different from their own or about lobbying the Senate to support the nomination of someone who is favorably perceived. As one recent study concluded, "Organized interests, at least in the 1980s and early 1990s, mobilized often, on a variety of nominations, mustered an impressive array of capabilities and resources, and employed a wide range of activities on each."[18]

When President Bush nominated Clarence Thomas for a Supreme Court position in 1991, a variety of interest groups clamored to make their views known. For example, Dr. William F. Gibson, speaking for the liberal National Association for the Advancement of Colored People (NAACP), said, "Thomas' judicial philosophy is simply inconsistent with the historical positions taken by the NAACP." Coordinating his action with the NAACP announcement, the voice of organized labor, President Lane Kirkland of the AFL-CIO, declared that the "president's apparent resolve to make the court the preserve of the far right wing leaves us no other choice [but to oppose the nomination]."[19] However, conservative interest groups rallied to Thomas's support. John Motley, the top lobbyist for the nation's largest association of small businesses, the National Federation of Independent Business, said of Thomas:

Some of the individual-freedom views he holds would call into question some labor-management decisions past courts have reached and affect the minimum-wage issue. If that's true, it provides one of the strongest arguments I've seen in a long time for the small business community to get involved in a high court nomination.[20]

Interest groups lobby for and against nominees at all levels of the federal judiciary. As two well-known students of the subject recently concluded, "The participation of organized interests in judicial nominations in recent years extends well beyond the highly visible cases of [Robert H.] Bork, [David H.] Souter, and [Clarence] Thomas. Although these cases have obvious significance for cases reaching the Supreme Court, nominations for federal district judgeships, circuit judgeships, and other appointed positions in the executive branch that are subject to senatorial confirmation also have important implications for organized interests."[21]

The American Bar Association

For more than four decades, the Committee on the Federal Judiciary of the ABA has played a key role in evaluating the credentials of potential nominees for positions on the federal bench. The committee, whose fifteen members represent all the U.S. circuits, evaluates candidates on the basis of numerous criteria, including judicial temperament, age, trial experience, character, and intelligence. A candidate approved by the committee is rated either "qualified" or "well qualified," whereas an unacceptable candidate is stamped with a "not qualified" label. (Traditionally the committee rated the very best candidates as "exceptionally well qualified," but this category was dropped in 1991.)

The traditional composition of the committee has made it the subject of some controversy. Because it has been made up largely of older, well-to-do, Republican, business-oriented corporation attorneys, some observers have argued that their evaluation of potential judicial candidates has been biased in favor of their peers. A strong suspicion exists that the committee has seen being wealthy and conservative as positive traits and being liberal and outspoken as uncharacteristic of "a sound judicial temperament." It should come as no surprise, then, that the ABA's committee has generally worked more closely with Republican presidents than with Democratic administrations.

Bucking the recommendations of the committee is a risky business, and presidents are likely to think long and hard before nominating a candidate tagged with the "not qualified" label.[22] President John F. Kennedy in 1962 successfully pushed for the appointment of Sarah T. Hughes (of the Northern District of Texas) despite opposition from the ABA, which argued that she was too old. Lobbying from none other than the vice president (Lyndon Johnson) and the Speaker of the House (Sam Rayburn) was required to ease the nomination through.[23]

Some presidents have gone back and forth in terms of their willingness to be bound by the pronouncements of the ABA committee. For example, when he first took office, President Nixon indicated that he would appoint no one who did not have the blessing of the ABA. However, after Senate defeat of two of Nixon's Supreme Court nominees, Clement Haynsworth and G. Harrold Carswell, the ABA began to cast a more critical eye on Nixon's choices. (The ABA had approved the Haynsworth and Carswell nominations and felt somewhat humiliated when investigations by the press and the Senate turned up a variety of negative factors overlooked by the committee.) Late in 1971, when he was trying to fill two vacancies on the Supreme Court, Nixon brought up the possibility of nominating Sen. Robert C. Byrd of West Virginia. Attorney General John Mitchell told Nixon that securing ABA approval would be a problem because Byrd had attended a "night law school" and had little experience as a practicing attorney. Nixon's reported reply to Mitchell indicates that the president's total confidence in the judgment of the ABA had waned. "Fuck the ABA," said Nixon. And from that time on, the president refused to submit names to the ABA committee until after he had already selected and publicized them.

Since President Nixon and Watergate, two changes seem to have occurred in the ABA. First, it appears to have severed some of its close ties to the conservative establishment and taken stands on public policy issues that offend traditional dogma. For instance, it has come out for federal support of legal aid for the poor. Second, its impact on the judicial selection process may be less now than in past decades. President Carter's setting up of the U.S. Circuit Judge Nominating Commission was seen in part as a successful end run around the bar association, and when President Reagan appointed Sandra Day O'Connor to the Supreme Court, the ABA was not even consulted.

The relationship between the Bush administration and the ABA was generally a comfortable one, despite some minor initial conflict over whether or not the association should consider the nominees' political philosophy and ideology. (Bush's advisers called for less emphasis on such matters.) Under President Clinton a similar climate of quiet harmony prevailed. For example, during his first six years in office 58 percent of his district court nominees and 77 percent of his appellate court nominees received the ABA's "well-qualified" label—percentages higher than Carter's, Reagan's first-term, or Bush's nominees received.

The Senate Judiciary Committee

The rules of the Senate require its Judiciary Committee to pass on all nominations to the federal bench and to make recommendations to the Senate as a whole. Its role is thus to screen individuals who have already been nominated, not to suggest names of possible candidates. The committee by custom holds hearings on all nominations, at which time witnesses are heard and deliberations take place behind closed doors. The hearings for district court appointments are largely perfunctory because the norm of senatorial courtesy has, for all intents and purposes, already determined whether the candidate will pass senatorial muster. However, for appeals court nominees—and surely for an appointment to the Supreme Court— the committee hearing is a serious proceeding.

Acting as a sort of watchdog of the Senate, the committee can affect the selection process in several ways. "First, it can delay Senate action on confirmation in the hope of embarrassing the president or to test his determination to make a particular appointment." As a general rule, the longer the delay, the poorer the nominee's chances are of securing approval. The failure of two of Reagan's Supreme Court nominees, Robert H. Bork and Douglas H. Ginsburg, to receive Senate approval was the result, in part, of the elongated committee hearings, which permitted the opposition forces to gather negative data and flex their lobbying muscles. Second, the committee can simply recommend against Senate confirmation. Finally, committee opponents of the nomination might engage in an extensive Senate floor debate, which "affords still another opportunity for senators to seek to embarrass the administration by questioning the wisdom of a particular appointment."[24]

Historically the Judiciary Committee has had a distinctly Southern and conservative flavor. As a result, it often did not look kindly upon appointees to the appeals courts and the Supreme Court who were thought to be too liberal—particularly on civil rights matters. Sen. James O. Eastland of Mississippi, the powerful committee chair for many years, often exacted a terrible toll from presidents who sought to put integrationists on the upper federal courts. For example, when President Kennedy tried to secure the appointment of the black and liberal Thurgood Marshall for a seat on the appellate court bench, Senator Eastland refused to support the nomination unless he could get his old college chum, William Harold Cox, a seat on the federal district court in Mississippi. Cox, who on the bench referred to blacks as "niggers" and "chimpanzees," is regarded as the worst of several racist judges Kennedy was "forced" to appoint in the South. As one black civil rights leader put it: "The brothers had to pay a lot of dues" to get Thurgood Marshall appointed to the bench.[25]

Perhaps the most vivid reminder of the power of the Senate Judiciary Committee came in the fall of 1991, in its much-publicized (and perhaps overly thorough) hearings on the nomination of Clarence Thomas to the Supreme Court. Even before public hearings began, the committee had requested some thirty thousand pages of documentation from Thomas. During weeks of intense questioning, the committee investigated almost every conceivable aspect of the nominee's background, philosophy, and credentials. The committee concluded its work with a dramatic weekend-long, televised hearing concerning sexual harassment charges brought by a former employee of Thomas, Anita F. Hill. Although the conduct of the committee during these proceedings is still being debated, few Americans came away from the spectacle unacquainted with the Judiciary Committee of the United States Senate.

After the Republican takeover of Congress as a result of the 1994 elections, control of the Judiciary Committee passed into the hands of conservative GOP senator Orrin G. Hatch of Utah. Between 1994 and 1996 the relationship between the Clinton administration and Hatch was relatively good, although Clinton's success rate in getting his nominees approved by the Republican Senate did decline markedly.[26] The unwritten rule said that if Clinton did not send up for consideration the names of any potential jurists who were too overtly liberal, then Hatch would grease the skids for easy committee approval. This arrangement seemed to work well for Clinton, whose main objective was to put more women and minorities on the bench rather than to fill the judiciary with left-of-center judges.

All this changed abruptly during the 1996 presidential election campaign when Republican candidate Robert Dole began charging that Clinton was filling the judiciary with highly activist, liberal judges. Although as a senator Dole had voted to confirm both of Clinton's Supreme Court appointees (Ginsburg and Breyer) and virtually all of Clinton's lower-court appointees, and although the empirical evidence suggested that the Clinton judges were not all that liberal, Dole as a candidate continued to charge that Clinton's judicial appointments were an "all-star team of liberal leniency" that had set off a "crisis" in the courts.[27]

The acrimony between Clinton and the GOP over judicial appointments continued after the 1996 election. By the summer of 1997 the Judiciary Committee had entered a state of virtual paralysis on the matter of confirming Clinton's judicial nominations. In May 1997 about one hundred judicial vacancies were unfilled, and the wait from nomination to confirmation reached a record 183 days.[28] Wrangling between Republicans and Democrats increased, while in the House of Representatives right-wing legislators (such as House Majority Whip Tom DeLay) mounted a drive to impeach activist-liberal judges.[29] By 1998, however, the situation began to improve somewhat, and the administration began to have a little more success in getting its nominations approved. The reasons for this were noted by a leading expert in this area, Professor Sheldon Goldman: "These include improvements in the administration's own handling of judicial selection matters, the role of Chief Justice

[William H.] Rehnquist in drawing attention to the untenable state of affairs in appointment processes, and in the final analysis, widespread and hostile reaction to the hubris displayed by the conservative right—in particular, a number of conservative senators who had been largely responsible for the gridlock of 1996–97."[30]

The Senate

The final step in the judicial appointment process for federal judges is a majority vote by the Senate. The Constitution states that the Senate must give its "advice and consent" to judicial nominations made by the president. Historically two general views have prevailed of the Senate's prescribed role. Presidents, from the time of George Washington, and a few scholars have taken the position that the Senate ought quietly to go along with the presidential choices unless overwhelmingly strong reasons exist to the contrary. Other scholars and, not unexpectedly, most senators have held to the views of Sen. Birch Bayh of Indiana and Sen. Robert Griffin of Michigan that the Senate "has the right and the obligation to decide in its own wisdom whether it wishes to confirm or not to confirm a Supreme Court nominee."[31] In practice the role of the Senate in the judicial confirmation process has varied, depending on the level of the federal judgeship being considered.

For district judges the norm of senatorial courtesy prevails. That is, if the president's nominee is acceptable to the senator(s) of the president's party in the state in which the judge is to sit, the Senate is usually happy to give its advice and consent with a quiet nod. For appointments to the appeals courts, senatorial courtesy does not apply, because the vacancy to be filled covers more than just the state of one or possibly two senators. But senators from each state in the circuit in which the vacancy has occurred customarily submit names of possible candidates to the president. An unwritten rule is that each state in the circuit should have at least one judge on that circuit's appellate bench, a practice often followed when the vacancy is that of a state's only representative on the circuit bench. As long as the norms are adhered to and the president's nominee has reasonably good qualifications, the Senate as a whole usually goes along with the recommendations of the chief executive.

The Senate has been inclined traditionally to go toe-to-toe with the president if disagreement arises over a nominee's fitness for the High Court. Since 1789, presidents have sent the names of 144 persons to the Senate for its advice and consent. Of this number, 30 were either rejected or "indefinitely postponed" by the Senate, or the names were withdrawn by the president. Thus presidents have been successful about 79 percent of the time, and their batting average seems to be improving, given that as many as one-third of the nominations were rejected by the Senate in the nineteenth century. The record shows that presidents have met with the most success in getting their High Court nominations approved when (1) the nominee comes from a noncontroversial background and has middle-of-the-road political leanings, and (2) the president's party also controls the Senate, or at least a majority shares the president's basic attitudes and values. As one study of 2,054 Senate roll-call votes on Supreme Court nominations from Earl Warren to Anthony M. Kennedy concluded: "When a strong president nominates a highly qualified, ideologically moderate candidate, the nominee passes the Senate in a lopsided, consensual vote. Presidents have often nominated this type of candidate and consequently consensual votes have been fairly common. When presidents nominate a less well qualified, ideologically extreme candidate, especially when the president is in a weak position, then a conflictual vote is likely."[32]

Policy Links among the Citizenry, the President, and the Federal Judiciary

Because this book is about policy making, it is appropriate to examine the links between the policy values of the elected chief executive and the decisional propensities of federal judges. If in electing one presidential candidate over another, the citizenry expresses its policy choices, do such choices spill over into the kind of judges presidents appoint and the way those judges decide policy-relevant cases? For instance, if the people decide in an election that they want a president who will reduce the size and powers of the federal bureaucracy, does that president subsequently appoint judges who share that philosophy? And, equally important, when those judges hear cases that give them the opportunity either to expand or to reduce the extent of a bureaucrat's power, do they opt for the reduction of authority? Recent evidence, while incomplete, suggests the existence of some policy links.

This phenomenon will be examined through two questions. First, what critical factors must exist for presidents to be able to obtain a judiciary that reflects their own political philosophy? Second, what empirical evidence is there to suggest that judges' decisions to some degree carry the imprint of the presidents who selected them?

The President and the Composition of the Judiciary

Four general factors determine whether chief executives can obtain a federal judiciary that is sympathetic to their political values and attitudes.

Presidential Support for Ideologically Based Appointments. One key aspect of the success of chief executives in appointing a federal judiciary that mirrors their own political beliefs is the depth of their commitment to do so. Some presidents may be content merely to fill the federal bench with party loyalists and pay little attention to their nominees' specific ideologies. Some may consider ideological factors when appointing Supreme Court justices but may not regard them as important for trial and appellate judges. Other presidents may discount ideologically grounded appointments because they themselves tend to be nonideological. Still others may place factors such as past political loyalty ahead of ideology in selecting judges.

Bill Clinton was a chief executive in the first category; that is, he was a president without a clearly defined set of ideological positions. More than once he acknowledged that he would probably go down in history as the most conservative Democrat who has occupied the White House during the twentieth century. Frequently referring to himself as a "new Democrat," Clinton tried to distance himself from the more liberal image that characterized the Democratic Party during most of the twentieth century. Throughout his administration Clinton sought to establish a judicial cohort that "looks like America"; that is, a team reflective of the nation's diverse ethnicity and gender instead of a cohort characterized by any singular ideological perspective.

As a president, Harry Truman had strong political views, but when selecting judges he placed loyalty to himself ahead of the candidate's overall political orientation. Truman's premium on personal loyalty rather than ideology is generally reflected in the group of men he put on the bench. For example, scant linkage existed between Truman's personal liberal stance on civil rights and equal opportunity and his judicial selections: He appointed no blacks and no women at all, and at least three of his key Southern district court appointees have been identified as having been very unfriendly to the cause of civil rights.[33]

If Clinton and Truman exemplify presidents who eschewed ideological criteria, Ronald Reagan provides a good example of a chief executive who selected his judicial nominees with a clear eye toward their compatibility with his own conservative philosophy. During his two terms, Reagan appointed 368 judges to the district and appeals courts. Of these, 94 percent were Republicans, 93 percent were white, and 92 percent were males; the majority were well-off (46 percent had net worths of over $500,000 and more than one in five were millionaires); virtually all had established records as political conservatives and as apostles of judicial self-restraint. As the Reagan administration's conservative programs began to bog down in the more liberal-minded Congress, the Reagan team looked more and more toward implementing their values through their judicial appointment strategy. As White House communications director Patrick J. Buchanan put it, "[Our conservative appointment strategy] . . . could do more to advance the social agenda—school prayer, anti-pornography, anti-busing, right-to-life and quotas in employment—than anything Congress can accomplish in 20 years."[34] President Reagan was not the only modern president to pack the bench with those who shared his political and legal philosophies. Presidents Johnson and Carter both successfully appointed activist liberal judges.

The Number of Vacancies to Be Filled. A second element affecting the capacity of chief executives to establish a policy link between themselves and the judiciary is the number of appointments available to them. The more judges a president can select, the greater the potential of the White House to put its stamp on the judicial branch. For example, George Washington's influence on the Supreme Court was significant because he was able to nominate ten individuals to the High Court. Jimmy Carter's was nil, because no vacancies occurred during his term as president.

The number of appointment opportunities depends on several factors: how many judicial vacancies are inherited from the previous administration (Clinton, for example, was left with a whopping one hundred district and trial court vacancies—14 percent of the total—by former president Bush), how many judges and justices die or resign during the president's term, how long the president serves, and whether Congress passes legislation that significantly increases the number of judgeships. Historically, the last factor seems to have been the most important in influencing the number of judgeships available, and politics in its most basic form permeates this process. A study of proposals for new-judges bills in thirteen Congresses tested the following two hypotheses: (1) "proposals to add new federal judges are more likely to pass if the party controls the Presidency and Congress than if different parties are in power," and (2) "proposals to add new federal judges are more likely to pass during the first two years of the President's term than during the second two years." The author concluded that his "data support both hypotheses—proposals to add new judges are about 5 times more likely to pass if the same party controls the Presidency and Congress than if different parties control, and about 4 times more likely to pass during the first two years of the President's term than during the second two years." He then noted that these findings serve "to remind us that not only is judicial selection a political process, but so is the creation of judicial posts."[35] Thus the number of vacancies that a president can fill—a function of politics, fate, and the size of the judicial workloads—is another variable that helps determine the impact a chief executive has on the composition of the federal judiciary.

The President's Political Clout. Another factor is the scope and proficiency of presidential skill in overcoming any political obstacles. One such stumbling block is the U.S. Senate. If the Senate is controlled by the president's political party, the White House will find it much easier to secure confirmation than if opposition forces control the Senate. Sometimes when the opposition is in power in the Senate, presidents are forced into a sort of political horse-trading to get their nominees approved. For example, in the summer of 1999 President Clinton was obliged to make a deal with the conservative chairman of the Senate Judiciary Committee, Orrin Hatch. To obtain smooth sailing for at least ten of Clinton's judicial nominations that had gotten blockaded in the Senate, the president agreed to nominate for a federal judgeship a conservative Utah Republican, Ted Stewart, who was vigorously opposed by liberals and environmental groups. "Administration officials defended the deal, saying they would get more than an acceptable amount in return for nominating Stewart, whom they acknowledged would not be chosen for the Federal bench by a Democratic President under ordinary circumstances."[36]

The Senate Judiciary Committee is another roadblock preventing presidents who have the requisite will from placing their chosen men and women on the federal bench. Some presidents have been more adept than others at easing their candidates through the jagged rocks of the Judiciary Committee rapids. Both Presidents Kennedy and Johnson, for example, had to deal with the formidable committee chairman James Eastland of Mississippi, but only Johnson seems to have had the political adroitness to get most of his liberal nominees approved. Kennedy lacked this skill. Under the Clinton administration, despite the president's considerable political acumen, he was never able to parlay those skills into much clout with the conservative and often hostile Senate Judiciary Committee.

The president's personal popularity is another element in the political power formula. Chief executives who are well liked by the public and command the respect of opinion makers in the news media, the rank-and-file of their political party, and the leaders of the nation's major interest groups are much more likely to prevail over any forces that seek to thwart their judicial nominees. Personal popularity is not a stable factor and is sometimes hard to gauge, but presidents' standing with the electorate clearly helps determine the success of their efforts to influence the composition of the American judiciary. For example, in 1930, President Herbert Hoover's choice for a seat on the Supreme Court, John J. Parker, was defeated in the Senate by a two-vote margin. If the nomination had been made a year or so earlier, before the onset of the Great Depression took Hoover's popularity by the throat, Parker might have gotten on the Supreme Court. Likewise, in 1968 President Johnson's low esteem among voters and the powers-that-be may have been partially responsible for Senate rejection of his candidate for chief justice, Abe Fortas, and also for the Senate's refusal to replace Fortas with Johnson's old pal Homer Thornberry. As one observer commented, "Johnson failed largely because most members of the Senate 'had had it' with the lame-duck President's nominations."[37] Conversely, President Dwight D. "Ike" Eisenhower's success in getting approval for an inordinately large number of nominees dubbed "not qualified" by the ABA (13.2 percent) may be attributed, in part at least, to his great popularity and prestige.

The Judicial Climate the New Judges Enter. A final matter affects the capacity of chief executives to secure a federal judiciary that reflects their own political values: the current philosophical orientations of the sitting district and appellate court judges with whom the new appointees would interact. Because federal judges serve lifetime appointments during good behavior, presidents must accept the composition and value structure of the judiciary as it exists when they first take office. If the existing judiciary already reflects the president's political and legal orientation, the impact of new judicial appointees will be immediate and substantial. However, if new chief executives face a trial and appellate judiciary whose values are radically different from their own, the impact of their subsequent judicial appointments will be weaker and slower to materialize. New judges must respect the controlling legal precedents and the constitutional interpretations that prevail in the judiciary at the time they enter it, or they risk being overturned by a higher court. Such a reality may limit the capacity of a new set of judges to get in there and do their own thing—at least in the short run.

When Franklin Roosevelt became president in 1933, he was confronted with a Supreme Court and a lower federal judiciary that had been solidly packed with conservative Republican jurists by his three GOP predecessors in the White House. A majority of the High Court and most lower-court judges viewed most of Roosevelt's New Deal legislation as unconstitutional, and it was not until 1937 that the Supreme Court began to stop overturning virtually all of FDR's major legislative programs.

To make matters worse, his first opportunity to fill a Supreme Court vacancy did not come until the fall of 1937. Thus, despite the ideological screening that went into the selection of FDR's judges, it seems fair to assume that, at least between 1933 and 1938, Roosevelt's trial and appellate judges had to restrain their liberal propensities in the myriad of cases that came before them. This may explain in part why the voting record of the Roosevelt court appointees is not much more liberal than that of the conservative judges selected by Roosevelt's three Republican predecessors; the Roosevelt team just did not have much room to maneuver in a judiciary dominated by staunch conservatives.

The decisional patterns of the Eisenhower judges further serve to illustrate this phenomenon. Although the Eisenhower appointees were more conservative than those selected by Presidents Truman and Roosevelt, the differences in their rulings were small. One major reason was that the Eisenhower jurists entered a realm that was dominated from top to bottom by Roosevelt and Truman appointees, who were for the most part liberals. Ike's generally conservative judges were only marginally less constrained than were Roosevelt's liberal jurists in the face of a conservative-dominated judiciary.

President Reagan's impact on the judicial branch continues to be substantial. By the end of his second term, he had appointed an unprecedented 368 federal judges, 50 percent of those on the bench. When he entered the White House, the Supreme Court was already teetering to the right because of Nixon's and Gerald R. Ford's conservative appointments. Although Carter's liberal appointees still had places on the trial and appellate court benches, Reagan found a good many conservative Nixon and Ford judges on the bench when he took office. Thus he has had a major role in shaping the entire federal judiciary in his own conservative image for some time to come. The Bush judges had a much easier time making their impact felt, because they entered a judicial realm wherein well over half the judges already professed conservative, Republican values. However, President Clinton's impact on the judiciary has been slower to manifest itself because his judicial nominees entered an arena in which over 75 percent of the trial and appellate court seats were held by judges appointed by prior GOP presidents with very conservative orientations. Still, bit by bit the more ideologically moderate thrust of the Clinton cohort is making itself felt. At the end of his presidency almost half of all federal judgeships bore the Clinton stamp.

Presidents' Values and Their Appointees' Decisions

What evidence is there that presidents have been able to secure a judiciary in tune with their own policy values and goals? Or, when the people elect a particular president, is there reason to believe that their choice will be expressed in the kinds of judges that are appointed and the kinds of decisions that those judges render?

To answer these questions we examined the liberal-conservative voting patterns of the teams of district court judges appointed by fifteen presidents during the twentieth century. This comprehensive study is the only one that covers enough presidents, judges, and cases to allow for some meaningful generalizations. In essence the focus is on whether liberal presidents appointed trial judges who decided cases in a more liberal manner and whether conservative chief executives were able to obtain district court jurists who followed their policy views.

In the realm of civil rights and civil liberties, liberal judges would generally take a broadening position; that is, they would seek in their rulings to extend these freedoms. Conservative jurists, by contrast, would prefer to limit such rights. For example, in a case in which a government agency wanted to prevent a controversial person from speaking in a public park or at a state university, a liberal judge would be more inclined than a conservative to uphold the right of the would-be speech giver. Or in a case concerning school integration, a liberal judge would be more likely to take the side of the minority petitioners. In the area of government regulation of the economy, liberal judges would probably uphold legislation that benefited working people or the economic underdog. Thus, if the secretary of labor sought an injunction against an employer for paying less than the minimum wage, a liberal judge would be more disposed to endorse the labor secretary's arguments whereas a conservative judge would tend to side with business, especially big business. Another broad category of cases often studied by judicial scholars is criminal justice. Liberal judges are, in general, more sympathetic to the motions made by criminal defendants. For instance, in a case in which the accused claimed to have been coerced by the government to make an illegal confession, liberal judges would be more likely than their conservative counterparts to agree that the government had acted improperly.

Figure 8-1 indicates the percentage of liberal decisions rendered by the district court appointees of Presidents Woodrow Wilson through Clinton. Fifty-one percent of the decisions of the Wilson judges are liberal, which puts these jurists almost on a par with those of Lyndon Johnson and Jimmy Carter for having the most liberal voting record. The liberal pattern of the Wilson judges is not surprising. Wilson was one of the staunchest liberal presidents of the twentieth century—particularly on economic issues. Moreover, he chose his judges on a highly partisan, ideological basis: 98.6 percent of his appointments to the lower courts were Democrats—the record for any president in the twentieth century.

Succeeding Wilson in the White House were the three Republican chief executives of the 1920s: Warren G. Harding and his "return to normalcy" in 1921, followed by the equally conservative Calvin Coolidge and Hoover. The right-of-center policy values of these three presidents (and the undisputed Republican domination

FIGURE 3-1 Percentage of Liberal Decisions Rendered by District Court Appointees of Presidents Wilson through Clinton

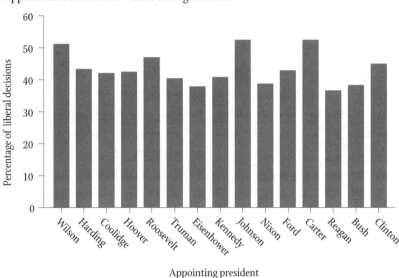

Appointing president

SOURCE: Unpublished data collected by Robert A. Carp, Ronald Stidham, and Kenneth Manning.

of the Senate during their incumbencies) are mirrored in the decisional patterns of the trial judges they selected. The liberalism score drops by 8 percentage points from Wilson to Harding, 51 to 43, and stays around that same level for the Coolidge and Hoover judicial teams.

With Franklin Roosevelt's judges a shift was made back to left-of-center. At 47 percent liberal, the Roosevelt jurists are 5 percentage points more liberal than those of his immediate predecessor, Herbert Hoover. FDR used ideological criteria to pick his judges, and he put the full weight of his political skills behind that endeavor. He once instructed his dispenser of political patronage, James A. Farley, in effect to use the judicial appointment power as a weapon against senators and representatives who were balking at New Deal legislation: "First off, we must hold up judicial appointments in States where the [congressional] delegation is not going along [with our liberal economic proposals]. We must make appointments promptly where the delegation is with us. Second, this must apply to other appointments. I'll keep in close contact with the leaders."[38]

At first the comparatively conservative voting record of the Truman judges seems a bit strange in view of Truman's personal commitment to liberal economic and social policy goals. Only 40 percent of the Truman judges' decisions were liberal, a full 7 percentage points less than Roosevelt's jurists—and even 2 percentage points below the Hoover nominees. However, Truman counted personal loyalty much more heavily than ideological standards when selecting his judges, and as a result many conservatives found their way into the ranks of the Truman judges.

Because of Truman's lack of interest in making policy-based appointments, coupled with strong opposition in the Senate and lack of popular support throughout much of his administration, his personal liberalism was generally not reflected in the policy values of his judges. Eisenhower's judges were more conservative than Truman's, as expected, but the difference is not great. This resulted in part because Eisenhower paid little attention to purely ideological appointment criteria and also because his judges had to work in the company of an overwhelming Democratic majority throughout the federal judiciary. These factors must have curbed many of the conservative inclinations of the Eisenhower jurists.

The 41 percent liberalism score of the judges appointed by John F. Kennedy represents a swing to the left. This is to be expected, and at first blush it may appear strange that Kennedy's team on the bench was not more left-of-center. However, Kennedy had problems in dealing with the conservative, Southern-dominated Senate Judiciary Committee; he lacked political clout in the Senate, which often made him a pawn of senatorial courtesy; and he was unable to overcome the stranglehold of local Democratic bosses, who often prized partisan loyalty over ideological purity—or even competence—when it came to appointing judges.

Lyndon Johnson's judges moved impressively toward the left, and his judges were more liberal than Wilson's and much more so than Kennedy's. This can be accounted for on the basis of the four criteria that predict a correspondence between the values of chief executives and the orientation of their judges. Johnson knew how to bargain with individual senators and was second to none in his ability to manipulate and cajole those who were initially indifferent or hostile to issues (or candidates) he supported. His impressive victories in Congress—for example, the antipoverty legislation and the civil rights acts—are monuments to his skill. Undoubtedly, too, he used his political prowess to secure a judicial team that reflected his liberal policy values. In addition, Johnson was able to fill a large number of vacancies on the bench, and his liberal appointees must have felt at home ideologically in a judiciary headed by the liberal Warren Court.

If the leftward swing of the Johnson team is dramatic, it is no less so than the shift to the right made by the Nixon judges. Only 39 percent of the decisions of Nixon's jurists were liberal. Nixon placed enormous emphasis on getting conservatives nominated to judgeships at all levels. He possessed the political clout to secure

Senate confirmation for most lower-court appointees—at least until Watergate, when the Nixon wine turned to vinegar—and the rightist policy values of the Nixon judges must have been prodded by a Supreme Court that was growing more and more conservative.

The 43 percent liberalism score of the Ford judges puts them right between the Johnson and Nixon jurists in terms of ideology. That Ford's jurists were less conservative than Nixon's is not hard to explain. First, Ford himself was much less of a political ideologue than his predecessor, as reflected in the way in which he screened his nominees and in the type of individuals he chose. (Ford's appointment of the moderate John Paul Stevens to the Supreme Court versus Nixon's selection of the highly conservative William H. Rehnquist illustrates the point.) Also, because Ford's circuitous route to the presidency did not enhance his political effectiveness with the Senate, he would not have had the clout to force highly conservative Republican nominees through a liberal, Democratic Senate, even if he had wished to.

With a score of 52 percent, Jimmy Carter shares with Lyndon Johnson the record for having appointed judges with the most liberal voting records of the fifteen presidents under consideration. Despite Carter's call for an "independent" federal judiciary based on "merit selection," his judges were selected with a keen eye toward their potential liberal voting tendencies.[39] That a correspondence exists between the values of President Carter and the liberal decisional patterns of his judges should come as no surprise. Carter was clearly identified with liberal social and political values, and although his economic policies were perhaps more conservative than those of other recent Democratic presidents, Carter's commitment to liberal values in the areas of civil rights and liberties and of criminal justice was not in doubt. Carter, too, had ample opportunity to pack the bench. The Omnibus Judgeship Act of 1978 passed by a friendly Democratic Congress created a record 152 new federal judicial openings for Carter to fill. Carter also possessed a fair degree of political clout with a Judiciary Committee and Senate controlled by Democrats. Finally, the Carter judicial team found many friendly liberals (appointed by Presidents Johnson and Kennedy) already sitting on the bench.

Reagan's judicial team has the distinction of having the most conservative voting record of all the judicial cohorts in our study. Only 37 percent of their decisions bear the liberal stamp. President Reagan's conservative values and his commitment to reshaping the federal judiciary were well known. Early in his first presidential campaign Reagan had inveighed against left-leaning activist judges, and he promised a dramatic change. As did his predecessor, Reagan had the opportunity, through attrition and newly created judgeships, to fill the judiciary with persons of his own inclinations. (At the end of his second term about half the federal judiciary bore the Reagan label.) This phenomenon was aided by Reagan's great personal popularity throughout most of his administration and a Senate that his party controlled during six of his eight years in office. Finally, the Reagan cohort entered the judicial realm with conservative greetings from the sitting right-of-center Nixon and Ford judges.

The judicial cohort appointed by President Bush continues in the conservative vein established by the Reagan administration, although at 38 percent the Bush cohort reflects the more moderate center of the Republican Party that characterized the appointees of Presidents Eisenhower and Nixon. The fact that the Bush team is more liberal than the Reagan cohort may be explained in two ways. First, on the policy issues of the day Bush was generally more moderate than Reagan; his critics in the Republican Party were those on the far right who claimed he was too liberal, that he had often abandoned the "conservative revolution" that Reagan had set in motion. Second, as the Bush judges have increasingly interacted with the more moderate and diverse Clinton jurists, their voting behavior has been nudged to the left.

President Clinton and the Federal Judiciary

What kind of men and women did President Clinton select for service on the federal bench and what has been the ideological direction of their decision making? The behavior of Clinton's judges has resulted in 45 percent liberal decision making. While this is certainly more progressive than the 37 and 38 percent figures for Presidents Reagan and Bush, respectively, it is decidedly more conservative than the 52 percent liberal landmarks of Presidents Johnson and Carter. In a word, the Clinton judges are moderate. This comes as no surprise, given the explanatory model that we have set forth.

First, Clinton did not manifest any desire to make ideologically based judicial appointments. Instead, his goal was to put more women and minorities on the federal bench. As for ideology, one key member of the president's judicial selection team who worked in both the Justice Department and the White House put it this way: "Neither side is running an ideology shop. Neither of us consider ourselves to be the guardians of some kind of flame. . . . [T]his is not a do or die fight for American Culture. This is an attempt to get . . . highly competent lawyers on the federal bench so they can resolve disputes."[40]

While Clinton did inherit a large number of unfilled judicial slots from the Bush administration, his Republican Congresses were loath to enact any type of omnibus judgeship bill that would have enhanced his capacity to pack the judiciary. Clinton also evinced little desire to expend political muscle in pushing through controversial candidates over Judiciary Committee and Senate objections. The woman primarily in charge of Clinton's judicial selections, Eleanor Dean Acheson, confirmed the administration's unwillingness to do major battle over judicial appointments: "There are a couple of cases in which we decided that even if we thought we had a shot at winning a fight. . . that it was not worth the time and resources . . . because these fights go for months and months, and during that period it is very difficult to concentrate."[41]

Finally, the climate into which the Clinton judges entered was not conducive to liberal decision making. When the Clinton cohort took their seats on the federal bench, about three-quarters of sitting judges—including the supervisory appellate panels—were conservative Republicans appointed primarily by Presidents Reagan and Bush. Thus even if the Clinton judges had been closet liberals, they would have little opportunity to vent these values in a judiciary so dominated by those of a more conservative persuasion.

Given the moderate nature of the Clinton judges' decision making, it seems a bit strange that his jurists came under such great criticism from Republican senators and representatives, some of whom even called for the impeachment of Clinton's so-called liberal-activist judges. To explore this topic in greater depth, we broke down the totality of decision making for the six most recent presidencies into three categories of cases (see Table 8-3): criminal justice (such as motions made by criminal defendants), civil rights and liberties (such as freedom of speech, abortion, and racial discrimination), and labor and economic regulation (such as disputes between labor and management and governmental efforts to regulate the economy). If the Clinton judges are inordinately liberal, some evidence should emerge as we turn our analytic microscope up this additional notch.

In the realm of criminal justice 33 percent of the Clinton judges' decisions are liberal, which is greater than the 31 percent figure for the Bush judges, but less than the 39 percent for Carter's judicial team. In the area of civil rights and liberties 41 percent of Clinton's judges voted on the liberal side—only 2 percentage points above the scores for Presidents Nixon and Ford. Again, this number is more liberal than the 33 percent figure for the Bush and Reagan jurists, but more conservative than the 52 percent number for Jimmy Carter's judges. Finally, in the realm of labor and economic regulation decisions, Clinton's team, at 58 percent, does manifest something of a liberal tendency, just 3 percentage points under Carter's score of 61. This is somewhat ironic because the Republicans spent most of their energies at-

TABLE 3-3   Percentage of Liberal District Court Decisions for Three Categories of Cases, Presidents Nixon through Clinton

Appointing President	Criminal Justice	Civil Rights and Liberties	Labor and Economic Regulation
Nixon	27	39	48
Ford	33	39	53
Carter	39	52	61
Reagan	26	33	49
Bush	31	33	50
Clinton	33	41	58

SOURCE: Unpublished data collected by Robert A. Carp, Ronald Stidham, and Kenneth Manning.

tacking the criminal justice and civil liberties decisions of the Clinton judges—not that his jurists are more inclined to support employees in their disputes with management and the government in its efforts to regulate the environment. In sum, the data suggest that the Clinton judges are on the whole not particularly liberal in their decision making. Clinton judges are ideologically moderate.

President George W. Bush and the Federal Judiciary

What can be expected for the federal judiciary now that George W. Bush has been elected president? To respond, we will refer to our four-part model, which addresses whether a chief executive can obtain a federal judiciary that is sympathetic to his political values and attitudes. First, is the new president personally committed to making ideologically based appointments? The evidence suggests a qualified affirmation that President Bush will use ideology as a basis for his judicial nominations. While the president thus far has not indicated that he will select judges on as strict a conservative litmus test as, say, President Reagan, he has publicly expressed admiration for Justice Antonin Scalia, who usually interprets the Constitution as restraining congressional power to regulate commerce and seeks to limit the expansion of many Bill of Rights freedoms (generally conservative positions). Bush also denounced as a judicial "overreach" into the authority of the states the Supreme Court's 1973 decision in *Roe v. Wade* that granted women a right to choose abortion, and he went on record during the presidential campaign to say that he would "fight for a ban on partial birth abortion."[42] Likewise he stated during the presidential campaign that he would "appoint justices who would solidify the court's inclination to narrowly define constitutional rights, limit federal authority and give more power to state legislatures." He told CNN in January 2000, "I am going to name judges who will strictly interpret the Constitution and not use the bench from which to legislate. I am going to name strict constructionists to the Supreme Court."[43] But on a moderating note, Bush shares to some degree former president Clinton's desire to increase the number of women and minorities on the bench (and elsewhere in government). Between 1995 and the summer of 2000, Bush, as governor of Texas, appointed 3,017 individuals to state boards, commissions, and vacant judgeships. Of these, 1,109 were female, 258 were black, and 397 were Hispanic.[44] While none of these women and minority appointees likely was a staunch liberal, Bush, like Clinton, may be as interested in bringing a broader range of individual to the bench as he is in appointing persons solely on the basis of pure conservative ideology.

Second, what about the number of vacancies to be filled? At the Supreme Court level President Bush will find several justices whose age and health have given rise to speculation about potential vacancies. When Bush took office, Justice John Paul Stevens was eighty, Chief Justice William Rehnquist was seventy-six, and Justice Sandra Day O'Connor was seventy. And in recent years health problems have dogged both Justices O'Connor and Ginsburg. Thus President Bush might be able to make several new High Court appointments in just his first several years in office. At the lower court levels, with the help of a Congress dominated by Republicans and conservative Democrats, Bush has a much better chance than did Clinton of having Congress pass an omnibus judges bill that would enable him to fill an increased number of judicial positions. And one can add to this equation the fact that as the Clinton term ended, the Senate was more and more reluctant to fill judicial vacancies, hoping that soon they might be filled by a new Republican president. As of early summer of 2000 there were forty-six vacancies in the district courts and twenty such openings in the courts of appeal.[45] Thus President Bush can expect a distinctly better than average opportunity to affect the composition of the Supreme Court and a fairly positive opportunity to fill the ranks of the lower courts with Republican jurists.

Third, what is the president's political clout vis-à-vis the Senate and its Judiciary Committee as well as the president's overall popularity with the electorate? Given that the Senate is now evenly divided between Republicans and Democrats, this will surely hinder President Bush from having a *carte blanche* in securing approval of his judicial nominees. This will probably cause him to appoint judges who are more moderate in their ideology rather than individuals who are too right of center. The level of the president's popularity over time remains to be seen, however.

Fourth, what is the judicial climate into which the new judges will enter as Bush appointees? Recall that President Franklin Roosevelt's liberal appointees made little headway at first in a judiciary dominated almost completely by conservative Republican judges appointed by Roosevelt's predecessors. However, President George W. Bush's father, when he took office in 1989, inherited a judiciary that was slowly tilting in a conservative direction (because of President Reagan's many prior appointments). Therefore after just a few judicial appointments on his part he was able to strongly augment the ideological turn in a conservative vein.

On the Supreme Court level, President George W. Bush is finding a Supreme Court very closely divided between conservative and moderate justices.[46] [We prefer the word *moderate* to *liberal* because in our opinion there are no longer any liberals on the court—at least as that term has been traditionally used.] For example, in the past two years a very large number of very important, high-profile cases were decided by five-to-four decisions. For example, the Court decided to permit the Boy Scouts of America to exclude homosexual scoutmasters, ruled that states may not criminalize "partial birth abortions," decided that Congress does not have authority to provide federal civil remedies for victims of gender-motivated violence, and said that Congress cannot strip the states of their immunity from lawsuit except under narrow circumstances.[47] If just one justice had changed his or her mind in these cases, the decision would have gone in the other direction. So if President Bush is able to replace the eighty-year-old moderate, Justice Stevens, with a conservative jurist, conservatives likely will have a solid, working majority on the Court. And if the new president is able to make several new appointments to the Court, he will give the conservatives a secure hold on the Court for years to come. As for the lower courts, roughly half of the judges are moderates or liberals appointed by Clinton and Carter; the remainder are conservatives appointed primarily by Presidents Bush and Reagan. Thus the new chief executive will be in a position to tilt the balance in his own ideological direction, given the likelihood that he will be able to replace about one quarter of the lower-court judges during his first term through normal attrition.

In sum, our model suggests that President Bush should be able to move the federal judiciary in a decidedly more conservative direction. He has indicated a clear desire to appoint more conservative jurists (albeit this commitment is perhaps tempered by a desire to appoint more women and minorities to the courts). He should have at least an average number of new vacancies to fill; but his clout in getting his nominees through the evenly divided Senate should be more problematic. Finally, given the narrow division of the federal judiciary between conservatives and moderates, President Bush is in a critical position to tilt the ideological balance in a somewhat more conservative vein.

The Judicial Socialization Process

When scholars use the term *socialization,* they are referring to the process whereby individuals acquire the values, attitudes, and behavior patterns of the existing social system. Factors that aid the process include family, friends, education, coworkers, religious training, political party affiliation, and the communications media. Social scientists also apply the term *socialization* to the process by which a person is formally trained to perform the specific tasks of a particular profession. It is the second meaning of the term, then, that will be of concern here.

Much significant socialization occurs before the judges first mount the bench. From their parents, teachers, exposure to the news media, and so on, future judges learn the rules of the American political game. That is, by the time they are teenagers they have absorbed key values and attitudes that will circumscribe subsequent judicial behavior: "the majority should rule on general matters of public policy, but minorities have their rights, too"; "judges ought to be fair and impartial"; or "the Constitution is an important document and all political leaders should be bound by it." In college and law school, future judges acquire important analytic and communications skills, in addition to the basic substance of the law. After a couple of decades of legal practice, the preparation for a judgeship is in its final stage. The future judge has learned a good deal about how the courts and the law work and has specialized in several areas of the law. Despite all this preparation, sometimes called "anticipatory socialization," most new judges in America still have much to learn even after donning the black robe.[48]

In many other countries, preparing to be a judge is like preparing to be a physician, an engineer, or a pharmacist—one goes to a particular professional school in which one receives many years of in-depth training and perhaps an on-the-job internship. Since 1959 in France, for example, all would-be judges are intensively trained for a minimum of twenty-eight months in the prestigious École Nationale de la Magistrature. They enter judicial service only after passing rigorous, competitive examinations. Not only does the United States lack formalized training procedures for the judicial profession, but there is also the naive assumption that being a lawyer for a decade or so is all the experience one needs to be a judge. After all, don't most lawyers, like judges, work in the courtroom? Isn't it enough for the lawyer-turned-judge just to mount the bench and put on a new hat? To the contrary, becoming a judge in America requires a good deal of freshman socialization (short-term learning and adjustment to the new role) and occupational socialization (on-the-job training over a period of years).

Typical new trial court appointees may be first-rate lawyers and experts in a few areas of the law in which they have specialized. As judges, however, they are suddenly expected to be experts on all legal subjects, are required to engage in judicial duties usually unrelated to any tasks they performed as lawyers (for example, sentencing), and are given a host of administrative assignments for which they have had no prior experience (for example, learning how to docket efficiently several hundred diverse cases).[49] The following statements by U.S. trial judges reveal what it was like for them as the new kid on the judicial block. (Virtually all the judges who were interviewed for this book were promised anonymity, and thus no references will appear.)

Before I became a federal judge I had been a trial lawyer dealing mainly with personal injury cases and later on with some divorce cases. Needless to say, I knew almost nothing about criminal law. With labor law I had had only one case in my life on this subject, and that was a case going back to the early days of World War II. In other words when I became a federal judge I really had an awful lot to learn about many important areas of the law.

My legal background and experience really didn't prepare me very well for the kind of major judicial problems I face. For instance, most lawyers don't deal with constitutional issues related to the Bill of Rights and the Fourteenth Amendment; rather they deal with much more routine questions, such as wills and contracts. Civil liberties questions were really new to me as a judge, and I think this is true for most new judges.

A report about a George Bush (senior) appointee to the trial bench confirms the persistence of this phenomenon. Before becoming a U.S. district judge, Melinda F. Harmon

was a Houston [Texas] attorney for Exxon for 12 years. She had no experience in criminal litigation or in constitutional law, fields that will make up a significant portion of her case load as a federal judge. Harmon acknowledged at her confirmation hearing that she would have to rely on "on-the-job training" to become prepared for the federal bench. She said she used part of her trip to Washington to stop by the federal judicial training center and check out seven videotapes to help her prepare.[50]

At the appeals court level there is also a period of freshman socialization—despite the circuit judge's possible prior judicial experience—and former trial judges appear to make the transition with fewer scars. As a couple of appeals judges in effect said of their first days on the circuit bench: "I was no blushing violet in fields I knew something about. How effective I was is another question." Even an experienced former trial judge recalled his surprise that "it takes a while to learn the job—and I'm not addressing myself to personal relationships. . . . That's a very different job." Another appeals judge, regarded by his peers as a leader from the beginning, said, "I don't know how I got through my first year."[51] During the transition time (the period of learning the appellate court ropes), circuit judges tend to speak less for the court than their more experienced colleagues. They often take longer to write opinions, defer more often to senior colleagues, or just wallow about in indecision.

The learning process for new Supreme Court justices is even harder—if the personal testimonies of justices as diverse as Benjamin Cardozo, Frank Murphy, Harlan F. Stone, Earl Warren, William Brennan, and Arthur Goldberg are to be believed. As one scholar has noted, "Once on the Court, the freshman Justice, even if he has been a state or lower federal court judge, moves into a strange and shadowy world."[52] Perhaps this is the metaphor that Chief Justice William Howard Taft had in mind when he confided that in joining the Court he felt that he had come "to live in a monastery." As with new appeals court judges, novice Supreme Court justices tend to defer to senior associates, to write fewer majority and dissenting opinions, and to manifest a good deal of uncertainty. New High Court appointees may have more judicial experience than their lower-court colleagues, but the fact that the Supreme Court is involved in broad judicial policy making—as opposed to the error correction of the appeals courts and the norm enforcement of the trial courts— may account for their initial indecisiveness. Still, not all new justices experience what scholars have come to call "the freshman effect," and of those who do, not all manifest it in the same way.[53]

Supreme Court appointee David Souter's first year on the Court provides a good example of "the freshman effect phenomenon." Near the end of his first term on the Court, one observer noted that "Souter has gotten off to a notably slow start and written only one opinion of the 64 released this term, a unanimous ruling on a procedural point about jury selection" (hardly a bombshell case).[54] It was pointed out in *Newsweek* that

He may be a New Englander, but Justice David Souter hasn't shown much Yankee independence in his first term. . . . So far Souter has voted with the majority in all 40 of the decisions in which he has participated. Each of the other eight justices has written at least one dissenting opinion and joined the dissenting side several other times. Souter also lags behind in writing majority decisions—producing only one while the other justices have averaged six each. In the next few weeks, Souter may catch up; but some blame his anemic output for the court's end-of-term gridlock. "There's just one reason and that's the total breakdown in one chamber," says a former court clerk.[55]

Given the need on the part of all new federal jurists for both freshman and occupational socialization, where do they go for instruction? Although there are many agents of socialization for novice judges, the evidence is strong that the older, more experienced judges have the primary responsibility for this task: The system trains and nurtures its own. As one trial judge said, "My prime sources of help were the two judges here in [this city]. They sent me various things even before I was appointed, and I was glad to get them." Another recalled, "I had the help I needed right down here in the corner of this building on this floor," pointing in the direction of another judge's chambers. One district judge gave a more graphic description of his "schooling":

They [the other trial judges] let me sit next to them in actual courtroom situations, and they explained to me what they were doing at every minute. We both wore our robes and we sat next to each other on the bench. I would frequently ask them questions and they would explain things to me as the trial went along. Other times I would have a few free minutes and I would drop into another judge's courtroom and just sit and watch. I learned a lot that way.

For both the rotating appeals court judges and their trial court peers, then, the lion's share of training comes from their more senior, experienced colleagues on the bench—particularly the chief judge of the circuit or district.[56] For example, when Houston's senior federal trial judge Norman Black passed away in July 1997, one of his junior colleagues, Judge David Hittner, said of him: "Norman taught a lot of us younger federal judges how to do this job."[57] One scholar has noted that "the impact of chief judges was most noticeable on freshmen. . . . ('If all the judges are new, he'll pack a wallop out of proportion to one vote.')"[58] Likewise on the Supreme Court, older associates, often the chief justice, play a primary part in passing on to novice justices the essential rules and values on which their very serious game is based.[59]

The training seminars provided by the Federal Judicial Center for newly appointed judges should also be mentioned again in this regard because over the years the center has played an ever-increasing role in the training and socialization of new jurists. Although some of these seminars are conducted by outsider specialists—subject matter experts in the law schools—the key instructors still tend to be seasoned judges whose real-life experience on the bench commands the respect of the new members of the federal judiciary.

The fact that judges in America still require socialization even after their appointments is interesting in and of itself, but the question arises: What is the significance of all this for the operation of the judicial-legal system? First, the agents of socialization that are readily available to the novice jurists allow the system to operate more smoothly, with a minimum of down time. If new judges were isolated from their more experienced associates, geographically or otherwise, they would require much more time to learn the fine points of their trade and presumably a greater number of errors would be foisted upon hapless litigants.

Second, the judicial system is a loose hierarchy that is constantly subjected to centrifugal and centripetal forces from within and without. The fact that the system is able to provide its own socialization—that the older, experienced jurists train the novices—serves as a sort of glue that helps bond the fragmented system together. It allows the judicial values, practices, and orientations of one generation of judges to be passed on to another. It gives continuity and a sense of permanence to a system that operates in a world where chaos and random behavior appear to be the order of the day.

The Retirement and Removal of Judges

In their final stage, judges cease performing their judicial duties, by choice, because of ill health or death, or because of the disciplinary actions of others.

Disciplinary Action against Federal Judges

All federal judges appointed under the provisions of Article III of the Constitution hold office "during good Behavior," which means in effect for life or until they choose to step down. The only way they can be removed from the bench is by impeachment (indictment by the House of Representatives) and conviction by the Senate. In accordance with constitutional requirements (for Supreme Court justices) and legislative standards (for appeals and trial court judges), impeachment may occur for "Treason, Bribery, or other high Crimes and Misdemeanors." An impeached jurist would face trial in the Senate, which could convict by a vote of two-thirds of the members present.[60]

The impeachment of a federal judge is a rare event, although recently it has become a more familiar topic. In October 1989, the Senate voted to convict Judge Alcee L. Hastings on eight of the seventeen charges brought in impeachment proceedings against him. The case against the judge was filed less than two years after this black Carter appointee assumed the bench. The matter began when a convicted felon with long-standing associations with organized crime walked into the U.S. Attorney's Office in Miami and asked for a plea bargain. If drug charges would be reduced or dropped against him, he would be willing to provide information about a bribery scheme in Judge Hastings's court. An investigation followed, and criminal charges were brought against the judge, who was accused of soliciting and accepting a bribe and of "corruptly influencing and impeding the administration of justice." Ironically the judge was found not guilty of the charges, but during the course of the trial he had inadvertently revealed information that suggested that he ran his courtroom in an unethical, though not criminal, manner. Less than one month after the trial an investigation was commenced into Hastings's behavior by the chief judge of the Eleventh Circuit, John Godbold. A circuit judicial council called more than 110 witnesses and examined more than twenty-eight hundred exhibits. The committee found against Hastings and then officially informed the House of Representatives that Hastings had engaged in conduct that "might constitute one or more grounds for impeachment." The House of Representatives conducted an inquiry through the use of a subcommittee and on its recommendation voted 413 to 3 to impeach the judge. A trial was then held in the Senate. While some of the charges were thrown out, Judge Hastings was convicted on several counts and was promptly stripped of his judgeship.[61] Two weeks later the same fate befell Judge Walter L. Nixon, who was convicted on two of three impeachment charges. However, since 1789 the House has initiated such proceedings against only thirteen jurists—although about an equal number of judges resigned just before formal action was taken against them. Of these thirteen cases, only seven resulted in a conviction, which removed them from office. Considering all the men and women who have sat on the federal bench during the past two centuries, that is not a bad record. (In the past decade, four members of Congress were convicted of felonies in a single session.)

Although outright acts of criminality by those on the bench are few, a gray area of misconduct may put offending judges somewhere in the twilight zone between acceptable and impeachable behavior. What to do with the federal jurist who hears a case despite an obvious conflict of interest, who consistently demonstrates biased behavior in the courtroom, who too often totters into court after a triple-martini lunch? A case in point is Judge Willis Ritter, who used to sit on the federal bench in Salt Lake City. One observer described Ritter as

ecumenically mean, which is to say he seems to dislike most persons who come into his court, be they defendant, government lawyer, private trial attorney, or ordinary citizen. Ritter is also selective about his fellow judges. He was once so estranged from another Utah federal judge that they wouldn't ride on the elevator together, much less speak; for a while the court clerk divided cases so that they didn't have to appear in the courthouse on the same day. . . . Ritter is one of the few federal judges in the nation who becomes so emotionally involved in his hearings that appeals courts often order him not to retry cases when they are reversed.[62]

One lawyer who had managed to fall from Judge Ritter's graces recalled an incident. As the lawyer was starting to present his case in open court, from out of the blue the judge began to hiss at him and continued to do so throughout the attorney's presentation. "Like a snake, he was going 'ssssss' all the time I was speaking," the astounded lawyer recounted later. "I never ever have been before a judge of this kind."[63]

Had Ritter committed impeachable offenses? He had not been guilty of "Treason, Bribery, or other high Crimes and Misdemeanors," although one could question whether he was serving "during good Behavior." Historically, little has been done in such cases other than issuance of a mild reprimand by colleagues (a useless gesture for a Judge Ritter) or impeachment (a recourse considered too drastic in most cases). In recent decades, however, actions have been taken to fill in the discipline gap. In 1966, for example, the Supreme Court upheld an action taken by the Tenth Circuit Judicial Council against U.S. District Judge Stephen S. Chandler of Oklahoma. The council had stripped him of his duties and authority (while permitting him to retain his salary and title) for a series of antics both on and off the bench that made Judge Ritter seem venerable by comparison.

In addition, on October 1, 1980, a new statute took effect, on which Congress had labored for several years. Titled the Judicial Councils Reform and Judicial Conduct and Disability Act, the law has two distinct parts.[64] The first part authorizes the Judicial Council in each circuit, composed of both appeals and trial court judges and presided over by the chief judge of the circuit, to "make all necessary and appropriate orders for the effective and expeditious administration of justice within its circuit." The second part of the act establishes a statutory complaint procedure against judges. Basically, it permits an aggrieved party to file a written complaint with the clerk of the appellate court. The chief judge then reviews the charge and may dismiss it if it appears frivolous, or for a variety of other reasons. If the complaint seems valid, the chief judge must appoint an investigating committee consisting of himself or herself and an equal number of trial and circuit court judges. After an inquiry the committee reports to the council, which has several options: (1) the judge may be exonerated; (2) if the offender is a bankruptcy judge or magistrate, he or she may be removed; and (3) an Article III judge may be subject to private or public reprimand or censure, certification of disability, request for voluntary resignation, or prohibition against further case assignments. However, removal of an Article III judge is not permitted; impeachment is still the only recourse. If the council determines that the conduct "might constitute" grounds for impeachment, it will notify the Judicial Conference, which in turn may transmit the case to the U.S. House of Representatives for consideration.

Since the act went into effect there has been no shortage of complaints. Between 1983 and 1990, 1,586 were filed, an average of more than 200 each year. Of these, the chief judges dismissed 1,224, and the circuit councils dismissed another 290. While some cases are still pending, some type of action was taken against fifty-four judges. (For example, the councils publicly censured one judge, privately censured another, issued a private warning to two more, and recommended that two be impeached by the House of Representatives.) Because of the confidential nature of this process, it is difficult to keep a hard count of all the disciplinary actions. But at least eleven judges chose to retire after judicial conduct complaints were filed and a number of others took senior status or reduced workloads because of deteriorating physical or mental health.[65] Thus, there is reason to believe that the Judicial Conduct Act is having some meaningful impact, although its effects cannot be measured with total precision.

Disability of Federal Judges

Perhaps the biggest problem has not been the removal of criminals and crackpots from the federal bench. Instead, it has been the question of what to do with jurists who have become too old and infirm to carry out their judicial responsibilities effectively. As the former chief judge of the Fifth Circuit Court of Appeals John Brown tersely put it, "Get rid of the aged judges, and you get rid of most of the problems of the federal judiciary: drunkenness, incompetence, senility, cantankerous behavior on the bench."[66] For example, Justice William O. Douglas suffered a stroke while on the Supreme Court but refused afterward to resign, even when it was clear to all that he should do so. In 1974 Chief Justice Burger "believed Douglas was developing the paranoid qualities of many stroke victims. Douglas complained that there were plots to kill him and to remove him from the bench. Once he was wheeled into the Chief's chambers and maintained it was his. Rumors circulated among the staff that Douglas thought he was the Chief Justice." But he stayed on. A year later he was still interpreting the Constitution for more than 200 million Americans although he "was in constant pain and barely had the energy to make his voice audible. He was wheeled in and out of conference, never staying the entire session, leaving his votes with [William J.] Brennan [Jr.] to cast. [Louis F.] Powell [Jr.] counted the number of times Douglas fell asleep. Brennan woke him gently when it came time to vote." Eventually Douglas resigned, but he remained on the bench longer than he should have. On the Court at the same time as Douglas were Justices John Harlan and Hugo Black. The latter, at eighty-five, was in such poor health that Douglas was counseling him to resign. "But Black would not accept the advice."[67]

In contrast to Black, Harlan continued to run his chambers from his hospital bed. Nearly blind, he could not even see the ash from his own cigarette, but he doggedly prepared for the coming term. One day a clerk brought in an emergency petition. Harlan remained in bed as he discussed the case with the clerk. They agreed that the petition should be denied. Harlan bent down, his eyes virtually to the paper, wrote his name, and handed the paper to his clerk. The clerk saw no signature. He looked over at Harlan. "Justice Harlan, you just denied your sheet," the clerk said, gently pointing to the scrawl on the linen. Harlan smiled and tried again, signing the paper this time.[68]

Although the federal judiciary as a whole is not proportionally in the same state of ill health and advanced age as was the Supreme Court during the early 1970s, the problem of what to do with the aged or mentally disabled judge has not disappeared. Congress has tried with some success to tempt the more senior judges into retirement by making it financially more palatable to do so. Since 1984 federal judges have been permitted to retire with full pay and benefits under what is called the rule of eighty; that is, when the sum of a judge's age and number of years on the bench is eighty. Congress has also permitted judges to go on senior status instead of accepting full retirement. In exchange for a reduced caseload they are permitted to retain their office and staff and—equally important—the prestige and self-respect of being an active judge. Despite the congressional inducements to retire, "more vacancies occur as a result of death in harness, particularly at the higher levels, than in any other way."[69]

Some credible evidence suggests that judges often time their resignations to occur when their party controls the presidency so that they will be replaced by a jurist of similar political and judicial orientation. As one researcher concluded, "Among the Appeals and District judges there is a substantial contingent who bring to the bench political loyalties that encourage them, more often than not, to maneuver their departure in such a way that will maximize the chance for the appointment of a replacement by a president of their party."[70] This observation has been given even greater weight by a 1990 study that correlated federal trial judges' retirement patterns with a wide variety of variables. The study found, among other things, that especially since 1954, "judicial retirement/resignation rates have been strongly influenced by political/ideological considerations, and infused with partisanship."[71] Predicting electoral outcomes can sometimes be problematic, however, as indicated by this account of an Iowa district judge's decision about retirement:

By 1948 Iowa Southern District Federal Judge Charles A. Dewey had decided that the time had come for him to retire. The seventy-one-year-old jurist had served on the federal bench for two full decades, and he felt that he had earned the right to his government pension. As a good Republican, however, he felt that it would be best to withhold his resignation until after the November election when "President Thomas E. Dewey" would be in a position to fill the vacancy with another "right-minded" individual like himself. Much to Judge Dewey's chagrin, his namesake did not receive the popular mandate in the presidential election, and Judge Dewey did not believe that he could carry on for another four years until the American people finally "came to their senses" and put a Republican in the White House. Therefore, shortly after the November election, Judge Dewey tendered his resignation.[72]

A similar note is sounded by former chief justice William Howard Taft, who clung to his High Court position lest he be replaced with someone whose policy values were more progressive than his own: "As long as things continue as they are, and I am able to answer in their place, I must stay in the Court in order to prevent the Bolsheviki [that is, American Communists] from gaining control."[73] And more recently the liberal black Supreme Court justice Thurgood Marshall vowed not to "retire from the Court as long as Reagan remains in the White House."[74] (He kept his pledge throughout the Reagan years, but finally, in June 1991, a rather bitter and decrepit Thurgood Marshall yielded to Father Time and announced his resignation, saying, "I'm old and I'm coming apart." Republican George Bush was president.)

These illustrations provide further evidence that many jurists view themselves as part of a policy link among the people, the judicial appointment process, and the subsequent decisions of the judges and justices.

Summary

This chapter began with a collective portrait of the men and women who have served in the federal judiciary. We noted that despite the occasional maverick, the jurists have come from a narrow stratum within America's social and economic elite. The result is a core of judges who share similar values and who therefore strive, with minimal coercion, to keep the judicial system functioning in a relatively harmonious manner. Though formal qualifications for a seat on the bench are few, tradition has established several informal criteria, including a reasonable degree of professional competence, the right political affiliation and contacts, at least some desire for the job itself, and a bit of luck thrown in for good measure.

At the national level the judicial selection process includes a variety of participants, despite the constitutional mandate that the president shall do the appointing with the advice and consent of the Senate. If presidents are to dominate this process and name individuals having similar policy values to the bench, several conditions must be met: Chief executives must want to make ideologically based appointments, they must have an ample number of vacancies to fill, they must be adroit leaders with political clout, and the existing judiciary must be attuned to their policy goals. If most of these conditions are met, presidents tend to get the kind of judges they want. In other words, an identifiable policy link exists among the popular election of the president, the appointment of judges, and the substantive content of the judges' decisions.

Although much judicial socialization occurs before the judges don their black robes, a good deal of learning takes place after they assume the bench. Because both freshman socialization and occupational socialization are furthered by senior colleagues, the values and practices of one generation of judges are smoothly passed on to the next. Thus continuity in the system is maintained.

The disciplining and removal of corrupt or mentally unfit judges is still a problem, although at the national level it may be eased as the Judicial Conduct Act of 1980 seems to be having some effect. The fact that so many judges time their resignations to allow a president (or a governor) of similar party identification and values to appoint a replacement is further evidence that the jurists themselves see a substantive link between the appointment process and the content of many of their decisions.

NOTES

1. Richard A. Posner, *The Federal Courts: Challenge and Reform* (Cambridge, Mass.: Harvard University Press, 1996), 20.

2. For a more extensive study of this subject, particularly as it pertains to the U.S. appeals courts and the Supreme Court, see John R. Schmidhauser, *Judges and Justices: The Federal Appellate Judiciary* (Boston: Little, Brown, 1979), 55–58.

3. Debra Sharpe and Peggy Roberson, "Tower Backs Cobb for Federal Judge," *Beaumont Enterprise*, May 4, 1984, A1.

4. Henry J. Abraham, *The Judicial Process*, 7th ed. (New York: Oxford University Press, 1998), 34.

5. Schmidhauser, *Judges and Justices*, 49.

6. Jill Abramson, "Ruth Bader Ginsburg Has Spent Her Career Overcoming the Odds," *Wall Street Journal*, June 15, 1993, A6.

7. J. Woodford Howard Jr., *Courts of Appeals in the Federal Judicial System* (Princeton, N.J.: Princeton University Press, 1981), 121.

8. Howard Ball, *Courts and Politics: The Federal Judicial System* (Englewood Cliffs, N.J.: Prentice-Hall, 1980), 201–202.

9. Peter McCormick, *Canada's Courts*, (Toronto: James Lorimer, 1994), 109.

10. As quoted in Joseph C. Goulden, *The Benchwarmers: The Private World of the Powerful Federal Judges* (New York: Weybright and Talley, 1974), 33.

11. Richard F. Schmitt, "Battle Erupts Over Federal Circuit Seat," *Wall Street Journal*, October 21, 1993, B8.

12. As quoted in Robert A. Carp and C. K. Rowland, *Policymaking and Politics in the Federal District Courts* (Knoxville: University of Tennessee Press, 1983), 55.

13. As a standard procedure, the Senate Judiciary Committee sends to the senator(s) of the state in which a district court vacancy exists a request, printed on a blue form, to approve or disapprove the nomination being considered by the committee. If approval is not forthcoming, the senator retains the slip; if there is no objection, the blue form is returned to the committee.

14. As quoted in Ball, *Courts and Politics*, 176.

15. Cragg Hines, "Dispensing Legal Plums," *Houston Chronicle*, April 21, 1985, A1.

16. David Goldsmith, "Black Lawmakers Ask Clinton to Bypass Senate, Appoint 6," *Houston Chronicle*, November 13, 1999, A14.

17. For an excellent recent discussion of this general matter under the Clinton administration, see Sheldon Goldman and Elliot Slotnick, "Picking Judges under Fire," *Judicature* 82 (1999): 264–284.

18. Gregory A. Caldeira, Marie Hojnacki, and John R. Wright, "The Lobbying Activities of Organized Interests in Federal Judicial Nominations," *Journal of Politics* 62 (2000): 68.

19. Judy Wiessler, "NAACP, AFL-CIO Join Anti-Thomas Fray," *Houston Chronicle*, August 1, 1991, A1.

20. Jeanne Saddler, "Support for High-Court Nominee," *Wall Street Journal*, July 17, 1991, B2.

21. Gregory A. Caldeira and John R. Wright, "Lobbying for Justice: Organized Interests, Supreme Court Nominations, and the United States Senate," *American Journal of Political Science* 42 (1998): 521.

22. The classic study of the role of the American Bar Association (ABA) is Joel B. Grossman, *Lawyers and Judges: The ABA and the Politics of Judicial Selection* (New York: Wiley, 1965).

23. For the humorous and interesting details of this controversy, see Goulden, *The Benchwarmers*, 61–62.

24. Harold W. Chase, *Federal Judges: The Appointing Process* (Minneapolis: University of Minnesota Press, 1972), 21, 23.

25. As quoted in Donald Dale Jackson, *Judges* (New York: Atheneum, 1974), 122.

26. Goldman and Slotnick, "Clinton's First Term Judiciary," *Judicature*, 80 (1997): 254–273.

27. Ronald Stidham, Robert A. Carp, and Donald R. Songer, "The Voting Behavior of President Clinton's Judicial Appointees," *Judicature* 80 (1996): 16–21; and Richard L. Berke, "A Missing Issue in the Big Race," *New York Times*, October 13, 1996, Sec. 4, 1.

28. Viveca Novak, "Empty-Bench Syndrome," *Time*, May 26, 1997, 37.

29. Greg McDonald, "Conservative Lawmakers Propose Impeachment of Activist Judges," *Houston Chronicle*, March 13, 1997, A6.

30. Goldman and Slotnick, "Picking Judges under Fire," 267–268.

31. As quoted in Ball, *Courts and Politics*, 167.

32. Charles M. Cameron, Albert D. Cover, and Jeffrey A. Segal, "Senate Voting on Supreme Court Nominees: A Neoinstitutional Model," *American Political Science Review* 84 (1990): 532. For a more recent and equally sophisticated study of this phenomenon, see Jeffrey A. Segal, Charles M. Cameron, and Al-

bert D. Cover, "A Spatial Model of Roll Call Voting: Senators, Constituents, Presidents, and Interest Groups in Supreme Court Confirmations," *American Journal of Political Science* 36 (1992): 96–121.

33. "Judicial Performance in the Fifth Circuit," *Yale Law Review* 73 (1963): 90–133.

34. Jack Nelson, "Courts Main Hope for Reagan Social Stand," *Houston Chronicle,* March 18, 1986, A6.

35. Jon R. Bond, "The Politics of Court Structure: The Addition of New Federal Judges," *Law and Policy Quarterly* 2 (1980): 182, 183, 187.

36. Neil A. Lewis, "Clinton Critic Is Key to Deal to End Tie-up on Judgeships," *New York Times* Web site http://www.NYTIMES.com/, July 3, 1999.

37. Henry J. Abraham, *The Judicial Process,* 3d ed. (New York: Oxford University Press, 1975), 77.

38. James A. Farley, "Why I Broke with Roosevelt," *Collier's,* June 21, 1947, 13.

39. See Jon Gottschall, "Carter's Judicial Appointments: The Influence of Affirmative Action and Merit Selection on Voting on the U.S. Courts of Appeals," *Judicature* 67 (1983): 165–173.

40. Goldman and Slotnick, "Clinton's First Term Judiciary," 256.

41. Ibid., 257.

42. Stuart Taylor Jr., "The Supreme Question," *Newsweek,* July 10, 2000, 20.

43. Steve Lash, "High Court to be Given New Course?" *Houston Chronicle,* May 26, 2000, A1.

44. "Clinton Extols VP, Hits GOP on Judgeships," *Houston Chronicle,* July 14, 2000, A10.

45. "Judicial Boxscore," *The Third Branch,* 32 (2000): 8.

46. The nine justices are often said to be split into two ideological camps: five conservatives (Justices Antonin Scalia, Clarence Thomas, William H. Rehnquist, Sandra Day O'Connor, and Anthony M. Kennedy) and four moderates (Justices Stephen G. Breyer, Ruth Bader Ginsburg, David H. Souter, and John Paul Stevens). But this is misleading and simplistic because two of the so-called conservatives—Justices O'Connor and Kennedy—often voting in sync, sometimes vote with the moderates on given issues. Be that as it may, five-to-four decisions have been handed down on many important, high-profile cases.

47. *Boy Scouts of America et al. v. Dale* (99-699), decided June 28, 2000; *Stenberg, Attorney General of Nebraska, et al. v. Carhart* (99-830), decided June 28, 2000; *United States v. Morrison et al.* (99-5), decided May 15, 2000; and *Alden v. Maine,* 527 U.S. 706 (1999).

48. This phenomenon also appears to occur among U.S. appeals court judges. See, for example, Stephen L. Wasby, " 'Into the Soup?': The Acclimation of Ninth Circuit Appellate Judges," *Judicature* 73 (1989): 13. This article is a good discussion of the socialization process of appeals court judges in general.

49. New federal district judges with prior state court experience have a somewhat easier time of it, particularly in terms of the psychological adjustment to the judgeship and dealing with some of the administrative problems. However, prior state court experience seems to be of little help in the jurist's efforts to become expert in federal law. See Robert A. Carp and Russell R. Wheeler, "Sink or Swim: The Socialization of a Federal District Judge," *Journal of Public Law* 21 (1972): 367–374.

50. "Easy OK Seen for Houston Judge," *Houston Chronicle,* April 6, 1989, A6.

51. All quoted in Howard, *Courts of Appeals in the Federal Judicial System,* 224.

52. Walter F. Murphy, *Elements of Judicial Strategy* (Chicago: University of Chicago Press, 1964), 50.

53. For a recent and sophisticated study of this subject, see Timothy M. Hagle, " 'Freshman Effects' for Supreme Court Justices," *American Journal of Political Science* 37 (1993): 1142–1157. See also Terry Bowen, "Consensual Norms and the Freshman Effect on the United States Supreme Court," *Social Science Quarterly* 76 (1995): 222–231; and Sandra L. Wood, Linda Camp Keith, Drew Noble Lanier, and Ayo Ogundele, " 'Acclimation Effects' for Supreme Court Justices: A Cross-Validation, 1888–1940," *American Journal of Political Science* 42 (1998): 690–697.

54. Ruth Marcus, "Souter Draws Clear Bench Marks," *Houston Chronicle,* May 28, 1991, A4. Note, however, that not all Supreme Court appointees appear to manifest "the freshman effect." See, for exam-

ple, Albert P. Melone, "Revisiting the Freshman Effect Hypothesis: The First Two Terms of Justice Anthony Kennedy," *Judicature* 74 (1990): 6–13.

55. "Souter: Slow Off the Mark," *Newsweek,* May 27, 1991, 4.

56. For the best discussion of this training, see Howard, *Courts of Appeals in the Federal Judicial System,* chap. 8.

57. Ty Clevenger, "Final Tribute Paid to Black," *Houston Chronicle,* July 28, 1997, A13.

58. Ibid., 229.

59. For examples of this, see Murphy, *Elements of Judicial Strategy,* 49–51.

60. For a good discussion of the impeachment process, including information on what the founders had in mind regarding the terms "High Crimes and Misdemeanors," see "Impeaching Federal Judges: Where Are We and Where Are We Going?" *Judicature* 72 (1989): 359–365. (The article is an edited version of a panel discussion.) See also Mary L. Volcansek, *Judicial Impeachment* (Urbana: University of Illinois Press, 1993).

61. Information about the Hastings impeachment was taken from Volcansek, *Judicial Impeachment,* chaps. 4 and 5.

62. Goulden, *The Benchwarmers,* 298.

63. Philip Hager, "Legal Leaders Seek Way to Unseat Unfit Federal Judges," *Houston Chronicle,* October 2, 1977, A6.

64. For a good discussion of this subject, see Collins T. Fitzpatrick, "Misconduct and Disability of Federal Judges: The Unreported Informal Responses," *Judicature* 71 (1988): 282–283.

65. All data in this paragraph derive from Volcansek, *Judicial Impeachment,* 13–14.

66. As quoted in Goulden, *The Benchwarmers,* 292.

67. Bob Woodward and Scott Armstrong, *The Brethren* (New York: Simon and Schuster, 1979), 361, 392, 156.

68. Ibid., 157.

69. Henry J. Abraham, *The Judicial Process,* 7th ed. (New York: Oxford University Press, 1998), 44.

70. R. Lee Rainey, "The Decision to Remain a Judge: Deductive Models of Judicial Retirement," paper delivered at the annual meeting of the Southern Political Science Association, Atlanta, 1976, 16.

71. Deborah J. Barrow and Gary Zuk, "An Institutional Analysis of Turnover in the Lower Federal Courts, 1900–1987," *Journal of Politics* 52 (1990): 457.

72. Robert A. Carp, "The Function, Impact, and Political Relevance of the Federal District Courts: A Case Study," Ph.D. dissertation, University of Iowa, 1969, 76.

73. As quoted in C. Herman Pritchett, *The Roosevelt Court: A Study of Judicial Votes and Values, 1937–1947* (New York: Macmillan, 1948), 18.

74. "Grading the Presidents," *Newsweek,* September 21, 1987, 33.

SUGGESTED READINGS

Abraham, Henry J. *Justices and Presidents: A Political History of Appointments to the Supreme Court,* 3d ed. New York: Oxford University Press, 1992. Offers an in-depth political history of appointments to the U.S. Supreme Court.

Goldman, Sheldon, and Elliot Slotnick. "Clinton's First Term Judiciary: Many Bridges to Cross." *Judicature* 80 (1997): 254–278. Provides a background profile of the socioeconomic characteristics of the district and appeals court judges appointed by Presidents Carter through Clinton.

Goldman, Sheldon. *Picking Federal Judges: Lower Court Selection from Roosevelt through Reagan.* New Haven: Yale University Press, 1997. Based on thorough, careful scholarship, Goldman writes in easy-to-follow prose about the judicial selection process between 1933 and 1989.

Judicature 77 (1994). The entire issue is dedicated to discussion of electing, selecting, and retaining judges.

Posner, Richard A. *The Federal Courts: Challenge and Reform.* Cambridge, Mass.: Harvard University Press, 1996. A perceptive account of how the federal courts function and the problems they face, written by a judge who is also a judicial scholar.

Ryan, John Paul, et al. *American Trial Judges: Their Work Styles and Performance.* New York: Free Press, 1980. A classic analysis of the role of American trial judges and the ways that their performance might be evaluated.

Stidham, Ronald, et al. "The Voting Behavior of President Clinton's Judicial Appointees," *Judicature* 80 (1996): 16–20. Discusses the impact of the appointing president on the judicial voting behavior of his federal trial and appellate judges.

Twentieth Century Fund Task Force on Judicial Selection. *Judicial Roulette.* New York: Priority Press Publications, 1988. A concise, sophisticated review of the politics of federal judicial selection in recent decades.

Volcansek, Mary L. *Judicial Impeachment: None Called It Justice.* Urbana: University of Illinois Press, 1993. A comprehensive discussion of the removal of federal judges from office for misconduct.

CHAPTER 4

Decision Making by Trial Court Judges

Charles T. Wells, chief justice of the Florida Supreme Court, listens during an appeal of an election contest ruling in Tallahassee on December 7, 2000. The state high court heard arguments from attorneys representing both presidential candidates concerning the state's November 7 presidential election.

⚖ Should a judge's political party affiliation affect the way he or she makes decisions on the bench? Most Americans would say "no" to that question. And yet they prefer to elect their judges and on a party basis. Is there an inherent inconsistency in these preferences?

⚖ Should judges' decisions reflect public opinion? Most Americans would find that offensive. However, no less than Chief Justice of the United States William H. Rehnquist says that it is inevitable and unavoidable that judges reflect public opinion. Sometimes, for example, trial judges are encouraged by the appellate courts to reflect the public mood in their decision making.

⚖ Judges are much more likely to hand down decisions that reflect their own personal values in some situations than in others. What are the circumstances that allow one to predict whether a judge will render a decision "in accordance with the law" or in accordance with his or her own personal attitudes?

ON WHAT BASIS and for what reasons do judges in the United States rule the way they do on the motions, petitions, and judicial policy questions with which they must deal? We shall respond to this query by summarizing the theories and research findings of a large number of judicial scholars who have tried to find out what makes judges tick. (Chapter 11 will examine the special case of decision making on the collegial appellate courts at the state and federal levels.) In this chapter we will examine federal and state jurists as a group because, to a large extent, the variables that influence judicial decision making are the same for judges at both levels of the judiciary. For instance, both types of judges tend to be strongly governed by court precedents and virtually all judges reflect to some degree their political party affiliation. Where differences between federal and state judges can be anticipated, we will take note of it. For example, one would expect public opinion to have less effect on federal judges who are appointed for life than on those state judges who must regularly stand for reelection.

It is useful to begin with a brief discussion of the decision-making environment in which trial judges and their appellate colleagues operate. Because of the differing purposes and organizational frameworks of trial and appellate courts, judges of each type face particular kinds of pressures and expectations. However, all jurists are subject to two major kinds of influences, as described by Richard J. Richardson and Kenneth N. Vines: the legal subculture and the democratic subculture.[1] In any given case, determining the relative weight that any specific influence has on a judge is often difficult. Studies have suggested, though, that when judges, especially trial judges, find no significant precedent to guide them—that is, when the legal subculture cupboard is bare—they tend to turn to the democratic subculture, an amalgam of determinants that includes their own political inclinations.

At the base of the federal and state judicial hierarchies are the trial court judges who preside over the judicial process and who corporately make hundreds of millions of decisions each year. Some decisions pertain to legal points and procedures raised by litigants even before a trial begins, such as a motion by a criminal defendant's lawyer to exclude from trial a piece of illegally obtained evidence. During the trial a judge must rule on scores of motions made by the attorneys in the case—for example, an objection to a particular question asked of a witness or a request to strike from the record contested testimony. Even after a verdict has been rendered, a trial judge may be beset with demands for decisions—for instance, the request by a litigant to reduce a monetary award made by a civil jury.

Trial judges can and occasionally do take ample time to reflect on their more important decisions and may consult with their staff or other judges about how to handle a particular legal problem. Nevertheless, a significant portion of their deci-sion making must be done on the spur of the moment, without the luxury of lengthy reflection or discussion with staff or colleagues. As one trial judge told us: "We're where the action is. We often have to 'shoot from the hip' and hope you're doing the right thing. You can't ruminate forever every time you have to make a rul-ing. We'd be spending months on each case if we ever did that." (Virtually all of the judges interviewed for this study were promised anonymity.)

Decision making by the appeals courts and the supreme courts is different in several important respects. By the time a case reaches the appellate levels, the record and facts have already been established. The jurists' job is to review dispas-sionately the transcript of a trial that has already occurred, to search for legal errors that may have been committed by others. Few snap judgments are required. And although the appeals courts and a supreme court may occasionally hear oral argu-ments by attorneys, they do not examine witnesses and they are removed from the drama and confrontations of the trial courtroom. Another difference in the deci-sion-making process between the trial and appellate levels is that the former is largely individualistic, whereas the latter is to some degree the product of group de-liberation.

Despite the acknowledged differences between trial and appellate judge decision making, all American jurists have many factors in common. We shall examine sev-eral studies that have sought to explain why judges in general think and act as they do, using Richardson and Vines's basic analytic framework. The thrust of these scholarly attempts at explanation has differed. Some view judges as judicial com-puters who take in a volume of facts, law, and legal doctrines and spew out "cor-rect" rulings—determinations that are virtually independent of the judges' values and characteristics as human beings. Other researchers tend to explain judicial de-cision making in terms of the personal orientations of the judges themselves. A de-cision is seen not so much as the product of some unbiased, exacting thought process that judges learn in law school but as being affected by the judge's life expe-riences, prejudices, and overall social values. As with most explanatory theories of human behavior, each of these approaches has its fair share of the truth, but none accounts for the whole story of the activity in question.

The Legal Subculture

In examining the legal subculture as a source of trial judge decision making, fo-cusing on a number of specific questions is useful. What are the basic rules, practices, and norms of this subculture? Where do judges learn these principles, and what groups or institutions keep judges from departing from them? How often and under what circumstances do judges respond to stimuli other than those from the traditional legal realm?

The Nature of Legal Reasoning

In a popular television series of the 1970s, *The Paper Chase,* the formidable Professor Kingsfield promises his budding law students that if they work hard and turn their mush-filled brains over to him, he will instill in them the ability "to think like a lawyer." How do lawyers and judges think when they deliberate in their professional capacities? One classic answer to this question is that "the basic pattern of legal reasoning is reasoning by example. It is a three-step process described by the doctrine of precedent as follows: (1) similarity is seen between cases; (2) the rule of law inherent in the first case is announced; and (3) the rule of law is made applicable to the second case." [2]

For example, the cases of *Lane v. Wilson* and *Gomillion v. Lightfoot* had similar arguments and factual situations.[3] In the former case a black citizen of Oklahoma brought suit in federal court alleging that he had been deprived of the right to vote. In 1916 the legislature of that state had passed a law, ostensibly designed to give formerly disenfranchised black citizens the right to vote, that required them to register—but the registration period was only twelve days. (White voters were for all practical purposes exempted from this scheme through the use of a "grandfather clause.") If blacks did not sign up within that short interval, never again would they have the right to vote. The Oklahoma legislature clearly realized that a twelve-day period was wholly inadequate for blacks to mount a voter registration drive and that the vast majority would not acquire the franchise. The plaintiff in this case did not get on the registration rolls in 1916. When he was thereafter forbidden to vote, he brought suit claiming the Oklahoma registration scheme to be unconstitutional. The Supreme Court agreed with the plaintiff. In striking down the statute, it set forth this principle, or rule of law: "The Fifteenth Amendment nullifies sophisticated as well as simple-minded modes of discrimination."[4]

Two decades later another black citizen, Charles Gomillion, brought suit in the federal courts alleging a denial of his right to vote as secured by the Fifteenth Amendment. Here an Alabama statute altered the Tuskegee city boundaries from a square to a twenty-eight-sided figure, allegedly removing "all save only four or five of its 400 Negro voters while not removing a single white voter or resident." Although not denying the right of a legislature to alter city boundaries "under normal circumstances," the Court saw through this thinly disguised attempt by the Alabama legislature to deny the suffrage to the black citizens of Tuskegee. Reasoning that the situation in *Gomillion* was analogous to that in the Oklahoma case, the Court used the precedent of *Lane v. Wilson* to strike down the Alabama law: "It is difficult to appreciate what stands in the way of adjudging a statute having this inevitable effect invalid in light of the principles of which this Court must judge, and uniformly has judged, statutes that, howsoever speciously defined, obviously discriminate against colored citizens. 'The Fifteenth Amendment nullifies sophisticated as well as simple-minded modes of discrimination.' *Lane v. Wilson*." This is one example of the judicial reasoning process—of thinking like Professor Kingsfield's lawyer. Two cases are compared because the facts or principles are similar; a rule of law gleaned from the first case is applied to the second. This step-by-step process is the essence of proper and traditional legal reasoning.

Adherence to Precedent

A related value held by trial and appellate judges is a commitment to follow precedents, decisions rendered on similar subjects by judges in the past. The sacred doctrine of stare decisis ("stand by what has been decided") is a cardinal principle of the common law tradition. In a series of interviews, William Kitchin asked federal district judges to rate the importance of "clear and directly relevant" precedents in their decision-making process. Precedent attained a score of 90–44 on a 100-point scale, whereas the judge's "personal, abstract view of justice in the case" was ranked only 60–69.[5] As for appellate court judges, one study of appeals courts in the Second, Fifth, and District of Columbia Circuits concluded that "adherence to precedent remains the everyday, working rule of American law, enabling appellate judges to control the premises of decision of subordinates who apply general rules to particular cases."[6] The U.S. Supreme Court, although technically free to depart from its own precedents, does so seldomly, for when "the Court reverses itself or makes new law out of whole cloth—reveals its policy-making role for all to see—the holy rite of judges consulting a higher law loses some of its mysterious power."[7]

Ideally, adherence to past rulings gives predictability and continuity to the law and reduces the dangerous possibility that judges will decide cases on a momentary whim or with an individualistic sense of right and wrong. Not all legal systems have placed such emphasis on stare decisis, however. In early Greek times, for example, the judge-kings decided each case on the basis of what appeared fair and just to them at the moment. When a judge-king resolved a dispute, the judgment was assumed to be the result of direct divine inspiration.[8] The early Greek model is thus the antithesis of the common law tradition. However, strict adherence to past precedent may be something of a legal fiction. Judges can and do distinguish among various precedents in creating new law. This helps to keep the law flexible and reflective of changing societal values and practices. Many scholars have argued that the readiness of common law judges occasionally to discard or ignore precedents that no longer serve the public has contributed to the survival of the common law tradition.

Constraints on Trial Judge Decision Making

Another significant element of the legal subculture is found under the heading of what one prominent scholar has called the "great maxims of judicial self-restraint." [9] These maxims derive from a variety of sources—the common law, statutory law, legal tradition—but each serves to limit and channel the decision making of state and federal judges. Because we have already discussed these various principles in detail, we shall merely reiterate here a few of the major themes of judicial self-restraint.

Before a judge will agree to consider a lawsuit, a definite case or controversy at law or in equity must exist between bona fide adversaries under the Constitution. The case must concern the protection or enforcement of valuable legal rights or the punishment, prevention, or redress of wrongs directly related to the litigants. Allied with this maxim is the principle that U.S. judges may not render advisory opinions; that is, rulings on abstract, hypothetical questions. (This rule is not followed as strictly in many state systems.) Also, all parties to a lawsuit must have standing, or a substantial personal interest infringed by the statute or action in question.

The rules of the game also forbid jurists to hear a case unless all other legal remedies have been exhausted. In addition, the legal culture discourages the judiciary from deciding political questions, or matters that ought to be resolved by one of the other branches of government, by another level of government, or by the voters. Judges are also obliged to give the benefit of the doubt to statutes and to official actions when their constitutionality is being questioned. A law or an executive action is presumed to be constitutional until proven otherwise. (Some judges adhere to this principle on economic issues but not on matters of civil rights and civil liberties, believing that in these matters the burden of proof is on the government.) In this same realm, judges feel bound by the norm that if they must invalidate a law, they will do so on as narrow a ground as possible or will void only that portion of the statute that is unconstitutional.

Finally, America's jurists may not throw out a law or an official action simply because they personally believe it to be unfair, stupid, or undemocratic. For a statute or an official deed to be invalidated, it must be clearly unconstitutional. Judges do not always agree about what is a clearly unconstitutional act, but most acknowledge that broad matters of public policy should be determined by the people through their elected representatives—not by the judiciary.

The Impact of the Legal Subculture: An Example

Because the principles that make up the legal subculture—reasoning, precedent, and restraint—tend to be abstract, it is useful to illustrate them with a real-life example. *Evers v. Jackson Municipal Separate School District* was an uncomplicated 1964 school integration case in which a group of black children and their parents sought to enjoin the "district and its officials from operating a compulsory biracial school system."[10] The facts and controlling precedents were clear: (1) Jackson, Mississippi, was overtly maintaining a segregated public school system; (2) the U.S. Supreme Court had ruled a decade previously in *Brown v. Board of Education* that such segregation was unconstitutional; and (3) the U.S. Court of Appeals for the Fifth Circuit, which has jurisdiction over Mississippi, had handed down a string of rulings ordering the integration process to go ahead.

The federal trial judge in *Evers*, Sidney Mize, did not like the commands he heard from the legal subculture. Appointed to the federal bench in 1937, Mize was an unabashed segregationist, as his written opinion in this case clearly shows. After discussing a score of alleged physical and mental differences between blacks and whites, Mize argued further that

in the case of Caucasians and Negroes, such differences may be directly confirmed by comparative anatomical and encephalographic measurements of the correlative physical structure of the brain and of the neural and endocrine systems of the body. The evidence was conclusive to the effect that the cranial capacity and brain size of the average Negro is approximately ten per cent less than that of the average white person of similar age and size, and that brain size is correlated with intelligence.[11]

On an ostensibly more positive and benign note, Judge Mize also argued, "From the evidence I find that separate classes allow greater adaptation to the differing educational traits of Negro and white pupils, and actually result in greater scholastic accomplishments for both."[12]

It seems clear where this decision was headed. But wait: Enter the legal subculture. After fourteen single-spaced printed pages of argument against the integration of the Jackson schools, Mize yielded to the requirements of legal reasoning, respect for precedent, and judicial self-restraint. Almost sheepishly he concluded his decision with these unexpected words:

Nevertheless, this Court feels that it is bound by what appears to be the obvious holding of the United States Court of Appeals for the Fifth Circuit that if disparities and differences such as that reflected in this record are to constitute a proper basis for the maintenance of separate schools for the white and Negro races it is the function of the United States Supreme Court to make such a decision and no inferior federal court can do so.[13]

Mize then quietly enjoined the school district and its officials from operating a compulsory biracial school system. The legal subculture tiptoed to victory.

Wellsprings of the Legal Subculture

The institutions that instill and maintain the legal values in the United States are "the law schools, the bar associations, the judicial councils, and other groups that spring from the institutionalization of the 'bench and the bar.' "[14]

"The purpose of law school," a scholar wrote, "is to change people; to turn them into novice lawyers; and to instill in them a nascent self-concept as a professional, a commitment to the value of the calling, and a claim to that elusive and esoteric style of reasoning called 'thinking like a lawyer.' "[15] The world just does not look the same to someone on whom law school has worked its indoctrinating magic. Facts and relationships in the human arena that formerly went unnoticed suddenly become "compelling" and "controlling" to the fledgling advocate. Likewise other facets of reality that previously had been important in one's world view are now dismissed as "irrelevant and immaterial."

Besides the indoctrination that occurs in law school, the values of the legal subculture are maintained by the state and national bar associations and by a variety of professional-social groups whose members are from both bench and bar—for example, the honorary Order of the Coif.[16] The values and practices of jurists are handed down from one generation to another. Thus the traditions and tenets of the American legal subculture are well tended by powerful support groups. They are rightly accorded ample deference if one is to understand judicial decision making in America.

The Limits of the Legal Subculture

Despite the taut nature of judicial reasoning and the importance of stare decisis and of judicial self-restraint, the legal subculture does not totally explain the behavior of American jurists. If objective facts and obvious controlling precedents were the only stimuli to which jurists responded, then the judicial decision-making process would be largely mechanical and all judicial outcomes would be predictable. Yet even the legal subculture's most loyal apologists would concede that judges often distinguish among precedents and that some judges are more inclined toward self-restraint than others.

To understand the thinking of judicial decision makers and the evolution of the law, more than law school curricula and the canons of the bar associations must be considered. One of the first great minds to realize this was Justice Oliver Wendell Holmes Jr., who over a century ago wrote that

the life of the law has not been logic; it has been experience. The felt necessities of the time, the prevalent moral and political theories, intuitions of public policy, avowed or unconscious, even the prejudices which judges share with their fellow-men have had a good deal more to do than syllogism in determining the rules by which men should be governed. The law embodies the story of a nation's development through many centuries, and it cannot be dealt with as if it contained only the axioms and corollaries of a book of mathematics. In order to know what it is, we must know what it has been, and what it tends to become. . . . The very considerations which judges most rarely mention, and always with an apology, are the secret root from which the law draws all the juices of life. I mean, of course, considerations of what is expedient for the community concerned.[17]

By about the 1920s a whole school of thought had developed that argued that judicial decision making was as much the product of human, extralegal stimuli as it was of some sort of mechanical legal thought process. Adherents of this view, who were known as judicial realists, insisted that judges, like other human beings, are influenced by the values and attitudes learned in childhood. As one of these realists put it, a judge's background "may have created plus or minus reactions to women, or blonde women, or men with beards, or Southerners, or Italians, or Englishmen, or plumbers, or ministers, or college graduates, or Democrats. A certain facial twitch or cough or gesture may start up memories, painful or pleasant."[18]

Since the late 1940s, the study of the personal, extralegal influences on decision making has become more rigorous. Often calling themselves judicial behavioralists, modern-day advocates of the realist approach have improved on it in two ways. First, they have tried to test empirically many of the theories and propositions advanced by the realist school. Second, they have attempted to relate their findings to more scientifically grounded theories of human behavior. Thus, whereas a realist might have asserted that a Democratic judge would probably be more supportive of labor unions than a Republican jurist, a judicial behavioralist might go a step further by taking a generous random sample of labor union-versus-management decisions and statistically determining whether Democratic judges are significantly more likely to back the union position than their GOP counterparts. Thus it is one thing to intuitively ascribe a cause for human behavior; it is another to subject an assertion to careful empirical analysis.

The Democratic Subculture

The legal subculture has an impact on American jurists. Evidence shows that popular, democratic values—manifested in a variety of ways through many different mediums—have an influence as well. Some scholars have argued that the only reason courts have maintained their significant role in the American political system is that they have learned to bend when the democratic winds have blown. That is, judges have tempered rigid legalisms with commonsense popular values and have maintained "extensive linkages with the democratic subculture."

Very often, legal elites such as bar associations and judicial councils are more noticeable spokesmen for the federal judiciary than are the spokesmen of the democratic subculture. However, representatives of the democratic subculture, such as members of political parties, members of social and economic groups, and local state political elites, can also be observed commenting on controversial questions. In matters like staffing the courts, determining their structure and organization, and fixing federal jurisdiction, democratic representatives have access through Congress and through other institutions that are influential in establishing judicial policy. Although Congress provides a main channel to the federal courts, access for democratic values is also obtained through the President, the attorney general, and through nonlegal officials who deal with the judiciary. In addition, the location of federal courts throughout the states and regions renders them unusually susceptible to local and regional democratic forces.[19]

In discussing the democratic subculture, our focus will be on the influences most often observed by students of the American court system—political party identification, localism, public opinion, and the legislative and executive branches of government.

The Influence of Political Party Affiliation

Do judges' political party affiliations affect the way they decide certain cases? The question is straightforward enough, but those who reply to it are by no means unanimous in their response. To most attorneys, judges, and court watchers among the general public, the question rings with outright impertinence, and their answer is usually something like this: After taking the sacred judicial oath and donning the black robe, a judge is no longer a Republican or a Democrat. Former affiliations are (or at least certainly should be) put aside as the judge enters a realm in which decisions are the product of evidence, sound judicial reasoning, and precedent as opposed to such a base factor as political identification. Or, as Donald Dale Jackson quipped in his perceptive book *Judges*, "Most judges would sooner admit to grand larceny than confess a political interest or motivation."[20]

Despite the cries of indignation from those who contend that the legal subculture explains virtually all judicial decision making, a mounting body of evidence strongly suggests that judges' political identification does affect their behavior on the bench.[21] Studies have shown that other personal factors—such as religion, gender, race, prejudicial career, and the level of prestige of their law school education—may also play a role. However, only political party affiliation seems to have any significant and consistent capacity to explain and predict the outcome of judicial decisions.[22] One prominent student of American politics explains why there may be a cause-and-effect relationship between judges' party allegiance and their decisional patterns:

> If judges are party identifiers before reaching the bench, there would be a basis for believing that they—like legislators—are affected in their issue orientations by party.... Furthermore, judges are generally well educated and the vote studies show that the more educated tend to be stronger party identifiers, to cast policy preferences in ideological terms, to have clearer perceptions of issues and of party positions on those issues, to have issue attitudes consistent with the positions of the party with which they identify, and to be more interested and involved in politics. For judges, even more than for the general population, party may therefore be a significant reference group on issues.[23]

Federal District Court Judges. Given the relationship between party affiliation and court decision making, the following observation should come as no surprise: As a whole, Democratic trial judges on the U.S. district courts are more liberal than their Republican colleagues. In a study of more than sixty-one thousand published district court decisions reached between 1932 and 1998, Democratic judges took the liberal position 48 percent of the time whereas Republican jurists did so in only 39 percent of the cases.[24] Thus, for almost seventy years, the Democrats' ratio of liberal-to-conservative opinions has been 1.44 times greater (more liberal) than the Republican ratio.[25] Although the overall differences cannot be called overwhelming, neither can they be dismissed as inconsequential.

As the data in Table 10-1 suggest, differences between Republicans and Democrats depend considerably on the type of cases. In analyzing partisan voting patterns in twenty-six separate case categories, differences between judges from the two parties were greatest for cases concerning the right to privacy (for example, abortion, gay and lesbian rights), support for affirmative action programs involving race and gender, and disputes about state and local government efforts to regulate the economic lives of their citizens. Partisan differences were modest or nonexistent in disputes between union members and their union hierarchy, when cases involved rent control and excess profits, and in cases when the secretary of labor (or the National Labor Relations Board) was suing a labor union.

All these facts and figures would become more meaningful if one could enter into the minds of typical Republican and Democratic judges and view the world from their perspectives. Barring that, however, the partial contents of interviews with a lifelong member of each of the two parties is revealing. The two jurists, sitting in the same city and on the same day, discussed a subject that in recent decades has divided Republican from Democratic judges—their philosophy of criminal justice and, more specifically, their views about sentencing convicted felons. The rank-and-file Democrat (appointed by Lyndon B. Johnson) said in part:

> Most of the people who appear before me for sentencing come from the poorer classes and have had few of the advantages of life. They've had an uphill fight all the way and life has constantly stepped on them. . . . I come from a pretty humble background myself, and I know what it's like. I think I take all this into consideration when I have to sentence someone, and it inclines me towards handing down lighter sentences, I think.

One hour later a lifelong Republican (appointed by Richard M. Nixon) addressed the same issue but with a different twist at the end:

> When I was first appointed, I was one of those big law-and-order types. You know—just put all those crooks and hippies in jail and all will be right with the world. But I've changed a lot. I never realized what poor, pathetic people there are who come before us for sentencing. My God, the terrible childhoods and horrendous backgrounds that some of them come from! Mistreated when they were kids and kicked around by everybody in the world for most of their lives. Society has clearly failed them. As a judge there's only one thing you can do: send them to prison for as long as the law allows because when they're in that bad a state there's nothing anyone can do with them. All you can do is protect society from these poor souls for as long as you can.

Although we would not contend that all Republican and all Democratic trial judges think precisely in these terms, we believe that something of the spirit of partisan differences is captured in these two quotations.

Federal Appeals Court Judges. As for partisan variations in the voting patterns of U.S. appeals court judges, here, too, evidence shows that the judges' (prior) party affiliation tempers their decision making to some degree.[26] Studies conducted during the 1960s by Sheldon Goldman and others concluded that "on balance, the findings underscore the absence of a sharp ideological party cleavage in the United States but also give support to the contention that the center of gravity of the Dem-

TABLE 4-1   Liberal Decisions of Federal District Judges in Order of Magnitude of Partisan Differences for Twenty-Six Types of Cases, 1932–1998

Type of case	Overall	Democrat	Republican	Partisan difference	Odds ratio [a]
Right to privacy	51%	70%	37%	33%	4.02
Affirmative action programs (race and gender)	57	72	49	23	2.71
Local economic regulation	66	77	57	20	2.51
Race discrimination	46	56	34	22	2.45
Women's rights	51	59	43	16	1.96
Freedom of religion	50	57	42	15	1.87
Criminal convictions	37	43	30	13	1.78
Fourteenth Amendment	37	43	31	12	1.70
Freedom of expression	56	63	50	13	1.68
Rights of the disabled	47	54	42	12	1.65
Age discrimination	35	41	31	10	1.57
U.S. habeas corpus pleas	27	27	21	6	1.57
Environmental protection	62	67	58	9	1.47
U.S. commercial regulation	69	72	65	7	1.41
Criminal court motions	30	34	27	7	1.39
Secretary of labor or NLRB versus employer	64	67	60	7	1.39
Voting rights cases	49	52	45	7	1.34
Alien petitions	41	43	36	7	1.32
Union versus company	51	54	48	6	1.28
Employee versus employer	37	40	35	5	1.27
Secretary of labor or NLRB versus union	67	65	59	6	1.26
Indian rights and law	49	52	47	5	1.24
State habeas corpus pleas	25	27	23	4	1.23
Union members versus union	43	45	41	4	1.18
Rent control, excess profits	61	61	58	3	1.14
Secretary of labor or NLRB versus union	58	57	57	0	0.98

SOURCE: Unpublished data collected by Robert A. Carp, Ronald Stidham, and Kenneth Manning.

NOTE: NLRB = National Labor Relations Board.

[a] The odds ratio, also called the cross-product ratio, is a measure of the relationship between two dichotomous variables. Specifically, it is a measure of the relative odds of respondents from each independent variable category being placed in a single dependent variable category.

ocratic party is more 'liberal' than that of the Republican party."[27] These early studies showed that partisan differences tended to be greatest on economic issues. GOP jurists were more likely than their Democratic counterparts to oppose government efforts to regulate the economy and to support business in its judicial tussles with labor. More recently, however, the field of battle has switched from the economic realm to that of the rights of criminal defendants and civil rights and liberties. Studies show that Democratic judges on the whole tend to be more supportive of the rights of criminal defendants and of those seeking to expand First and Fourteenth Amendment freedoms.[28]

For example, a 1990 study of voting patterns among appellate court judges was conducted for decisions made en banc—by all or a specified number of the judges in a circuit court of appeals instead of by the usual three-judge panels. This study focused primarily on partisan differences in cases dealing with criminal justice and civil liberties issues. The researchers found that support for criminal appellants by the Democrats (in effect, the Jimmy Carter appointees) was 58.9 percent, whereas for Republican appointees the figures were significantly lower—19.9 percent for Nixon's judicial team and 22.3 percent for Ronald Reagan's. Likewise, the Carter Democrats supported the civil liberties petitioners 67.1 percent of the time, whereas Nixon's cohort did so 38.5 percent of the time and Reagan's team took the stance in only 29.8 percent of the cases.[29]

U.S. Supreme Court Justices. Does political party affiliation affect the way members of the U.S. Supreme Court decide some of their cases? Although scholars have found this to be a hard subject to investigate, the evidence suggests a mild but positive yes. The research hurdle stems, in part, from the fact that the Court has nine justices, and generalizing about the behavior of groups this small is virtually impossible. Moreover, numerous political parties have been represented on the Court in its more than two-century history, and the definitions of *Federalist, Democrat, Whig, Republican, liberal,* and *conservative* have varied so over time that generalizations become difficult. For example, prior to the 1920s most mainstream Democrats opposed civil rights for blacks. Since that era most champions of the civil rights movement have been Democrats. In the jargon of the trade, the variables are so numerous and the *n*'s (number of justices) are so small that statistically significant observations are extremely difficult to make.

Despite the methodological problems involved, some judicial scholars have sought to explore this subject. In a comprehensive study of the relationship between party affiliation and the liberal-conservative voting patterns of the justices in the twentieth century, one scholar found that between 1903 and 1939 party identification was "clearly a good cue for selecting judicial decision-makers with the proper values." That is, on matters of support for the economic underdog, Democratic justices were more liberal than their Republican colleagues. Since 1940 the greater liberalism of Democratic Court members has extended as well to matters of civil rights and liberties, thereby reaffirming "the concept that judges are not random samples of their group." But even this scholar concedes, as did those who studied partisan voting by the appeals court and trial court judges, that the relationships are weak.

The inability to predict at high rates of probability is not surprising when one considers the assumptions that must be made and the variety of other influences on the Court such as political and environmental pressures, social change, precedent, reasoned argument, intra-court social influences and idiosyncrasy.[30]

A major study of partisan voting patterns on the Supreme Court focused on criminal justice cases. Among other things, the researchers found that "Democratic control of the Court and the White House, coupled with a high proportion of the Court's docket devoted to criminal issues, results in significantly higher support levels for criminal defendants than under the condition of the Republicans occupying the presidency and a majority of the Supreme Court seats with a relatively low priority placed on criminal justice appeals."[31] Still, some scholars urge caution before making a flat-out pronouncement about the relationship between the justices' backgrounds and their subsequent voting patterns. For example, one prominent researcher has argued that previous studies may be time-bound; that is, during some time periods decisional differences among the justices might be explained by background characteristics, whereas during others background is only a modest predictor of behavior.[32] When faced with such conflicting and tentative studies, it is clear that the final chapter of a book on this subject is yet to be written.

Partisanship in State Courts. The federal courts are not the only arena in which Republican and Democratic jurists sometimes square off against one another. Partisan voting patterns often occur as well among the men and women who sit on the trial and appellate court benches. Still, the evidence at the state level is weaker, for three general reasons. First, the state courts have not been studied as extensively and systematically as have the federal courts. This may be either because some political scientists have held the (mistaken) view that state judiciaries are less important than their federal counterparts or because many state court decisions are unpublished and therefore much more difficult to acquire and study. Second, partisanship among state jurists is not strongly uniform across the country. In some states, for instance, judicial selection is truly bipartisan (or nonpartisan) and both political parties may support the same candidates. Also, many state judges do not have extensive relationships with a political party. Though they may have partisan identifications, they might not see judicial questions as being reflective of their party's ideology. Finally, America still has a number of one-party states in which virtually all judges bear the same party label. Thus it would make little sense to study partisan differences among judges in states such as Mississippi or West Virginia, where almost all the jurists are Democrats. Still, keen levels of partisanship have been documented in some jurisdictions—particularly in the states with big cities.

Michigan is a state in which partisan voting patterns among the judges, especially on the state supreme court, have been noteworthy. Studies have shown that on labor-management issues, for example, Democrats on the bench were significantly more likely to support the side of the worker in unemployment compensation cases and in issues dealing with workers' compensation (on-the-job injuries). Democratic judges are also more likely to support criminal defendants seeking a new trial, to favor government efforts to regulate business, and to side with persons who sue business enterprises—all consistent with the voting behavior of Democrats on the federal bench.[33]

In a study of partisan conflict on a California intermediate court of appeals, significant differences were found between Democrats and Republicans in both criminal and civil cases.[34] Studying issues such as votes in criminal justice cases, labor-management disputes, debtor/creditor disagreements, and consumerism, the author concluded that "as previous research . . . would have predicted, the results are in the expected direction, with Republican panels significantly more likely to reach conservative outcomes than Democratic panels."[35]

Illinois, Iowa, Maryland, New York, and Pennsylvania are examples of other states for which researchers have reported meaningful partisan differences between Republican and Democratic judges.[36]

A Note on Partisan Voting in Foreign Courts. Partisan voting behavior by jurists in other nations is not an unknown phenomenon, but it is more difficult to pinpoint for several reasons. First, in virtually no other countries do judges run for elective office in an openly partisan manner as they do in those American states that elect judges. Also, in these foreign nations potential judicial candidates are more likely to eschew active partisan politics prior to their appointment to the bench. Thus, identifying a judge's party affiliation and correlating it with a particular substantive voting pattern is more difficult. Nevertheless, many studies suggest that a judge's background, which is highly corrected with his or her political orientation, does meaningfully affect the jurist's decisions on the bench.[37] Likewise other studies have identified the existence of clear ideological voting patterns of appellate court judges on foreign courts, and these ideological values can usually be traced to a political party within that country.[38]

An Appraisal. The political party affiliation of the judges and justices can make a difference in the way they decide cases. Of all the background variables studied, it seems to be the most compelling and consistent. But a word of caution is in order. Although evidence of partisan influence on judicial behavior is convincing, it by no means suggests that Democrats always take the liberal position on all issues whereas Republicans always opt for the conservative side. Rather, the issue is tendencies; that is, when the decision is a close call, a Democrat on the bench tends to be more liberal than a GOP judge. When controlling precedents are absent or ambiguous or when the evidence in the case is about evenly divided, Democrats more than Republicans are inclined to be supportive of civil rights and liberties, to support government regulation that favors the worker or the economic underdog, and to turn a sympathetic ear toward the pleas of criminal defendants.

The Impact of Localism

A wide range of influences are included in the term *localism*, and we shall regard it as a broad second category of factors that affect federal and state judicial decision making. An accumulating body of literature suggests that federal judges are influenced by the traditions and mores of the region in which their courts are located or, in the case of Supreme Court justices, by the geographic area in which they were reared. For trial and appeals court judges, geographical differences define both the legal and the democratic subcultures as well as the nature of the questions they must decide. Historically, such judges have had strong ties with the state and the circuit in which their courts are situated, and on many issues judicial decision making reflects the parochial values and attitudes of the region. As two leading students of the subject have noted:

A persistent factor in the molding of lower court organization has been the preservation of state and regional boundaries. The feeling that the judiciary should reflect the local features of the federal system has often been expressed by state officials most explicitly. Mississippi Congressman John Sharp Williams declared that he was "frankly opposed to a perambulatory judiciary, to carpetbagging Nebraska with a Louisianian, certainly to carpetbagging Mississippi or Louisiana with somebody north of Mason and Dixon's line."[39]

Why should judges in one district or circuit decide cases differently from their colleagues in other localities? Why should a Supreme Court justice make decisions differently from colleagues who hail from other parts of the United States?[40] Richardson and Vines have put the matter succinctly:

Since both district and appeals judges frequently receive legal training in the state or circuit they serve, the significance of legal education is important. If a federal judge is trained at a state university, he is exposed to and may assimilate state and sectional political viewpoints, especially since state law schools are training grounds for local political elites. . . . Other than education, different local environments provide different reactions to policy issues, such as civil rights or labor relations. Indeed, throughout the history of the lower court judiciary there is evidence that various persons involved in judicial organization and selection have perceived that local, state, or regional factors make a difference and have behaved accordingly.[41]

Moreover, trial and appellate judges tend to come from the district or state in which their courts are located, and the vast majority were educated in law schools of the state or circuit they work in. (For example, two-thirds of all district judges in one study were born in the state where their court is located, and 86 percent of all circuit judges attended a law school in their respective circuits.)[42] Also, the strong local ties of many judges tend to develop and mature even after their appointment to the bench.[43]

In their identification with their regional base, judges are similar to other political decision makers. Public attitudes and voting patterns on a wide range of issues vary from one section of America to another.[44] As for national political officials, evidence exists that regionalism affects the voting patterns of members of Congress on many important issues—for example, civil rights, conservation, price controls for farmers, and labor legislation.[45] Furthermore, sectional considerations have their impact within each political party—for instance, Northern Democrats are more liberal than their Southern counterparts on many significant issues.

Regionalism at the Three Judicial Levels. When President George Washington appointed the first Supreme Court, half of its members were Northerners and half were Southerners. Surely Washington's choice was more than just a symbolic gesture to give a superficial balance to the Court. Washington, who had successfully led a group of squabbling former colonies during the Revolutionary War, understood that the attitudes and mores of his fellow citizens differed widely from one locale to another and that justices would not be immune to these parochial influences. Studies of the early history of the High Court reveal that sectionalism did creep into its decision-making patterns—particularly along North-South lines. For example, a study of Supreme Court voting patterns in the sectional crisis that preceded the Civil War noted that the four justices who were most supportive of Southern regional interests were all from the South, whereas those jurists from the Northern states usually favored the litigants from that region.[46]

In the twentieth century, evidence also supports the belief that where the justices came from tempered their decision making to some degree.[47] A fairly dramatic manifestation of this principle is found in President Nixon's famous "southern strategy." After the appointment of Warren E. Burger as chief justice in 1969,

pressure had been building on Nixon to name a southerner to the Court. Though he had never publicly promised a southern nominee, Nixon's intentions were never seriously doubted. Aware that a judge in the South enjoyed a prestige unrivaled in any other section of the country, Nixon advisors believed that he could do southerners no higher favor than to appoint one of their own to the highest court in the land. Even before Nixon assumed office, he had successfully identified with the southern cause. "The one battle most white southerners feel they are fighting is with the Court and Nixon has effectively identified himself with that cause," wrote election analyst Samuel Lubell. "Only Nixon can change the makeup of the Court to satisfy southern aspirations."[48]

Nixon then nominated Clement Haynsworth Jr. of South Carolina, who was turned down by the Senate. Next he sent forth the name of G. Harrold Carswell of Florida, but this nomination met the same fate as Haynsworth's. An angry Nixon then stated, "As long as the Senate is constituted the way it is today, I will not nominate another southerner."[49]

Although political leaders and much of the general public believe that a relationship exists between the justices' regional backgrounds and their judicial decisions, scholars have had difficulty in documenting this phenomenon. First, links between the justices' regional heritage and their subsequent voting behavior are very difficult to pinpoint, and they exist at most for probably a few regionally sensitive issues. Also, after Supreme Court justices are appointed and move to Washington, over time they may take on a more national perspective, loosening to a significant degree the attitudes and narrow purview of the region in which they were reared and educated. For example, in his early days in Alabama, Hugo Black had been a member of the Ku Klux Klan, but after his judicial appointment in 1937, Justice Black became one of the most articulate advocates of civil rights ever to sit on the Supreme Court.

Some evidence exists that regionalism pervades the federal judicial system at the appeals court level as well. A 1981 study noted regional differences on such important questions as rights of the consumer, pleas by criminal defendants, petitions by workers and by blacks, public rights in patent cases, and immigration litigation. The author of this study concluded that "regionalism is an inescapable adjunct of adjudicating appeals in one of the oldest regional operations of federal power in existence." He observed that although the appeals courts may adhere to national standards, such norms are nevertheless "regionally enforced. In the crosswinds of office and constituencies, Courts of Appeals may mediate cultural values—national and local, professional and political—in federal appeals."[50] In a recent study of regional variations in the voting of court of appeals judges, Susan Haire noted, for example, that "in search and seizure cases, Western judges were more liberal than their counterparts in the East (including the South) whereas in race-based employment discrimination cases Western judges adopted positions that were more conservative than their colleagues in the East."[51]

Federal district judges appear to reflect their sectional heritage in decisional patterns even more distinctly than their colleagues on the appellate bench. In an analysis of trial judge decision making between 1933 and 1987, one research team compared the ratio of liberal to conservative opinions for Northern and Southern judges (see Table 10-2). The Northerners were 1.2 times more liberal than their colleagues in the South. However, North-South differences have declined in recent years. Between 1969 and 1977 the ratio was 1.41, but in the interval between 1978 and 1987 it declined to a mere 1.07—the smallest ratio of all the time periods studied. East-West differences among the district judges have been almost negligible for all the time periods studied since 1933. On questions of criminal justice, judges in the North have historically been somewhat more liberal, although this trend has reversed itself since 1977. In cases that pertain to civil rights and liberties, Northern jurists have been on the liberal side more often since 1969, although this was not the case in earlier time spans. Finally, on issues concerning government regulation of the economy and labor, judges in the North were more liberal prior to 1978, but since that time the North-South split has been negligible. A 1990 study showed that in the more conservative South, federal district judges were almost 70 percent more likely to take an anti-abortion stance in their decisions than their colleagues in the North. This was found to be consistent with the values of the region as measured by public opinion polls and other data.[52]

Regional differences within the parties have also been observed over the years—mainly between judges in the North and South. In the past half century, Northern Democrats have been the most liberal group of judges. This group is followed by Southern Democrats, Northern Republicans, and then Southern Republicans. The difference between Southern Republicans and Northern Democrats is 14 percentage points; that is, Northern Democrats are 40 percent more liberal than Southern Republicans.[53]

Regional influences of judges' voting behavior are by no means a uniquely American phenomenon. For example, even in a small country such as Norway, what region the judges come from often affects the way they vote in certain types of cases. One early study found that for violations of the conscientious objector laws, the

TABLE 4-2   Liberal Decisions of Federal District Judges, Controlled for Region, 1933–1987

	1933–1953	1954–1968	1969–1977	1978–1987	All years
All cases					
North	46	42	47	46	45
South	43	37	38	44	41
α	1.14	1.22	1.41	1.07	1.20
East	46	42	43	43	43
West	44	39	44	47	44
α	1.08	1.08	0.90	0.83	0.93
Criminal justice					
North	26	23	31	31	28
South	27	21	24	35	26
α	0.93	1.12	1.40	0.85	1.12
East	23	23	27	28	25
West	29	23	30	35	29
α	0.66	0.94	0.89	0.72	0.81
Civil rights and liberties					
North	39	39	53	48	47
South	45	42	45	41	43
α	0.79	0.88	1.39	1.30	1.20
East	39	39	51	44	44
West	42	41	49	46	46
α	0.80	0.86	1.00	0.90	0.92
Labor and economic regulation					
North	58	64	61	55	58
South	49	55	55	54	53
α	1.48	1.40	1.30	1.01	1.22
East	62	65	61	53	59
West	51	58	58	55	55
α	1.59	1.32	1.08	0.93	1.18

SOURCE: Unpublished data collected by Robert A. Carp, Ronald Stidham, and C. K. Rowland.

NOTE: All figures except the odds ratio are given in percentages.

likelihood of being convicted varied from a low of 3 percent if the judge was located in the Western Military District (Vestlandet) to a high of 54 percent if the jurist was from the Northern District (Nordland).[54]

Variances in Judicial Behavior among the Circuits. Not only does judicial decision making vary from one region of the land to another, but studies also reveal that, for numerous reasons, each of the circuits has its own particular way in which its appellate and trial court judges administer the law and make decisions. One reason is that circuits tend to follow sectional lines that mark off historical, social, and political differences. Another reason is that the circuit courts of appeals tend to be idiosyncratic, and thus the standards and guidelines they provide the trial judges will reflect their own approach.[55] In a recent study of variations in the behavior of appellate judges from one circuit to another, the "findings . . . strongly suggest judges' decisional tendencies are shaped by the circuit." In her analysis Haire found "meaningful policy differences" in such fields as search and seizure cases, obscenity rulings, and employment discrimination lawsuits.[56] Similarly, the behavior of U.S. trial judges has been observed to vary on a circuit-by-circuit basis. In the First Circuit, for example, which covers several New England states, 50 percent of the judges' decisions have been liberal. In the Fourth Circuit (Maryland, North and South Carolina, Virginia, and West Virginia), only 37 percent of the judges' decisions have been liberal.[57]

Variances in Trial Judge Behavior among the States. At first blush it may appear strange to argue that U.S. judicial decisions vary significantly by state, because the state is not an official level of the federal judicial hierarchy, which advances from district to circuit to nationwide system. Still, direct and indirect evidence suggests that each state is unique in the way its federal judges administer justice. There are several reasons that this is so. First, a state, like a circuit or a region, is often synonymous with a particular set of policy-relevant values, attitudes, and orientations. One would automatically expect, for instance, that on some issues U.S. trial and appellate judges in Texas would act differently from Massachusetts jurists, not so much because they are from different states but because they are from different political, economic, legal, and cultural milieus. Second, many judges regard their states as meaningful boundaries and behave accordingly. For example, a U.S. trial judge in Louisiana told us: "One thing I frequently discuss with the other judges here is sentencing matters. Judge X has been a big help with this. I wouldn't want to hand down a sentence which is way out of line with what the other judges are doing here in this state for the same crime."[58] Comments from a jurist indicate that the same phenomenon occurs in the U.S. Eighth Circuit. For instance, in Iowa the federal trial judges

were anxious that their sentencing practices be reasonably similar, particularly where the facts of a case were almost identical. They . . . believed that if a person committed a federal crime in Iowa, the criminal should expect nearly equal treatment regardless of whether he was tried in the Northern or Southern federal districts of the state. This mutual belief is nicely illustrated in these remarks made by Judge Graven to Judge Riley in 1954:

"I have coming before me at Sioux City for sentencing on December 14 one . . . who apparently was splitting $20 [bills] and passing them. I am informed that there is a similar charge against him in the Southern District which is being transferred to this District under Rule 20 and that it is expected that that charge will also be disposed of at Sioux City on December 14th.

"I note that you have two defendants who were associates of Mr. _____ coming up before you for sentencing. Since all the defendants committed the same crimes and presumably have much the same background, I would not want my sentence of Mr. _____ to be out of line with the sentence you impose. If you impose your sentences before December 14th at 10:00 a.m., I wish you would let me know what your sentences are."[59]

Third, note the impact upon federal judicial behavior of diversity of citizenship cases—suits that constitute a quarter of the district courts' civil business and about a sixth of civil appeals to circuit courts. Because the Supreme Court requires the lower courts to apply state instead of federal law in such cases, it behooves U.S. trial judges to keep abreast of and be sensitive to the latest developments in state law. The effect may be the same for circuit judges as well. For example, when three-judge appellate panels are appointed for diversity of citizenship cases, the tendency is to name circuit judges from states whose law governs. As one scholar observed: "A 'slight local tinge' thus colored diversity opinions as part of a general tendency of members to defer to colleagues most knowledgeable about the subject."[60]

Quantitative studies of federal trial judges' voting behavior substantiate the proposition that meaningful differences are evident on a state-by-state basis. Such differences have been increasing since the late 1960s. Also, both circuits that cross North-South boundaries (the Sixth and the Eighth) and the district courts in the border and Southern states are markedly more conservative than those in the other states.[61] This suggests that local and regional values—as personified by the state— have a greater influence on trial judge decision making than do those of the circuit as a whole.

Localism and the Behavior of State Judges. If regional factors leaven the bread of federal judicial decisions, then this phenomenon is even more pervasive for state jurists. State judges, even more than their federal counterparts, tend to be local folks—born, bred, educated, and socialized in the locale in which they preside. Whether they be elected directly by the people or appointed as a result of their political connections with the governor or the local political machine, state judges are likely to mirror the values and attitudes of their environment. A study by Martin A.

Levin, who compared and contrasted judges and justices in Minneapolis and Pittsburgh, provides a fitting example.[62]

In Minneapolis the state trial judges are elected on a nonpartisan ballot, and in practice the political parties have almost no role in the selection of judges. "The socialization and recruitment of [the] . . . judges reflect this pattern of selection. Most of these judges [as the majority of the local population] have Northern European-Protestant and middle-class backgrounds, and their pre-judicial careers have been predominantly in private legal practice. . . . Such career experiences seem to have stimulated these judges to be interested more in 'society' than in the defendant." Minneapolis's conservative, middle-class environment, from which its judges come, is reflected in the law-and-order, no nonsense grist of the judicial mill.

This pre-judicial experience, reinforced by their lack of party or policy-oriented experiences and their middle-class backgrounds, seems to have contributed to the legalistic and universalistic character of their decision-making and their eschewal of policy and personal considerations. In their milieu, rules were generally emphasized, especially legal ones, and these rules had been used to maintain and protect societal institutions. Learning to "get around" involved skill in operating in a context of rules. The judges' success seems to have depended more on their objective achievements and skills than on personal relationships.[63]

The environment of the Pittsburgh jurists is in stark contrast. The highly partisan (Democratic) judges reflect the working-class, ethnic group-based values of the political machine that put them on the bench. These jurists were likely to have held public office before becoming judges, and they were thus much more people-oriented than their counterparts in Minneapolis. They often felt that their own "minority ethnic and lower-income backgrounds and these government and party experiences had developed their general attachment to the problems of the 'underdog' and the 'oppressed.' " Levin concludes this about the judicial behavior reflected by the local environment and recruitment process:

Their political experiences and lack of much legalistic experience apparently contributed to the highly particularistic and nonlegalistic character of their decision-making, their emphasis on policy considerations, and their use of pragmatic criteria. . . . Personal relationships, especially with constituents, were emphasized, and focused on particular and tangible entities. Success depended largely on the ability to operate within personal relationships. It depended on *whom* one knew, rather than on *what* one knew. Abstractions such as "the good of society as a whole" seem to have been of little concern.[64]

Although social science still needs to develop more systematic empirical evidence for the relationship between the local environment and the output of state courts, these two brief case studies are indicative of the kind of phenomena we are describing.

The Impact of Public Opinion

If one were to approach a typical judge or justice and ask whether public opinion affected the decisions made from the bench, the jurist might respond with a fair measure of indignation. The answer might be something like this: "Look, as a judge with a lifetime appointment, I'm expected to be free from the pressures of public opinion. That's part of what we mean when we say that we're a 'government of laws—not of men.' When I decide a case, I look at the law and the facts. I don't go out into the streets and take some sort of public opinion poll to tell me what to do."

Yet to some degree and on certain issues, American judges do seem to temper their decision making with public opinion. Intuitive reasons for asserting some role for public opinion are severalfold. First, judges as human beings, as parents, as consumers, and as residents of the community are themselves part of public opinion. Putting on a black robe may stimulate a greater concern for responsible, objective decision making, but it does not void a judge's membership in the human race. As one judicial scholar has noted, "Since judges, both appointed and elected, usually have been born and reared locally and recruited from a local political system, it seems likely that public opinion would have an effect, especially in issues that are locally visible and controversial. In addition . . . many judges seem to consider themselves independent judicial officials who represent local populations in the courts. Consequently, judges may feel that they ought to take local values into account."[65] Even a conservative and strict constructionist such as Supreme Court Chief Justice William Rehnquist has acknowledged this in a revealing statement:

Judges, so long as they are relatively normal human beings, can no more escape being influenced by public opinion in the long run than can people working at other jobs. And, if a judge on coming to the bench were to decide to hermetically seal himself off from all manifestations of public opinion, he would accomplish very little; he would not be influenced by current public opinion, but instead would be influenced by the state of public opinion at the time he came to the bench.[66]

The following is an example of a judge's keen sensitivity to local public opinion. When the media reported that U.S. district judge William Overton was involved in rendering a decision that overturned Arkansas's creation-science law, the judge received more than five hundred letters, most of them highly critical. (The Arkansas law required that the teaching of evolution in schools be accompanied by the teaching of creation science, a theory that life is of recent, supernatural, sudden origin, as related in the book of Genesis. Overton's position was that the law violated the principle of separation of church and state.) The judge was so overwhelmed by the outpouring of negative public opinion that he took the unusual step of making the letters available to reporters and to the University of Arkansas at Little Rock. "How many monkeys are in your family tree?" asked one angry letter writer from Richmond, Virginia. "Repent!" And from Benton, Arkansas, came a clipping that included a picture of three persons who filed suit, and the sender wrote: "I hope the souls of you and these 3 goons rot in Hell for eternity."[67]

Second, in many instances public opinion is supposed to be an official factor in the decision-making process. For example, in the implementation of the famous *Brown v. Board of Education* school desegregation ruling, the Supreme Court refused to set strict national guidelines for how its decision was to be carried out. Instead, individual federal district judges were to implement the High Court decision based on the judges' determination of local moods, conditions, and traditions.[68] Likewise, when the Supreme Court ruled that federal courts could hear cases concerning malapportionment of state legislatures, it refused to indicate how its decision was to be carried out. Instead it was, in effect, left to the lower federal courts to implement the ruling in accordance with the way they viewed local needs, conditions, and the state political climate.[69] A further example may be found in the obscenity rulings of the Burger Court, in which the justices determined that the courts should use community values and attitudes in determining what materials are obscene.[70]

Thus, not only is it impossible for judges to rid themselves of the influence of public opinion, but in many important types of cases judges are obliged to consider the attitudes and values of the public. This does not mean they go out and take opinion polls whenever they face a tough decision, but public opinion is often one ingredient in the decision-making calculus.

Third, both federal and state judges are aware that ultimately their decisions cannot be carried out unless a reasonable degree of public support exists for them. As Lawrence Baum has noted, "Justices care about public regard for the Court, because high regard can help the Court in conflicts with the other branches of government and increase people's willingness to carry out its decisions."[71] It has been an open secret for a long time that when the Court is about to hand down a bombshell decision likely to be unpopular among many groups of Americans, the author of the majority opinion takes great pains to word the decision in such a way as to generate popular support for it—or at least to salve the wounds of those potentially offended by it. Examples of High Court decisions in which the author is thought to have written as much for the public at large as for the usual narrow audience of lawyers and lower-court judges include the following: *Marbury v. Madison,* in which the Court claimed for itself the right to declare acts of Congress unconstitutional; *Brown v. Board of Education,* which called for an end to racial segregation in the public schools; *Roe v. Wade,* in which the Court upheld a woman's right to an abortion; and *United States v. Nixon*—the Watergate case—in which the justices ordered the president of the United States to yield to the authority of the courts.[72]

The empirical evidence for the impact of public opinion is suggestive but hardly conclusive, in part because relatively few comprehensive studies of the phenomenon have been conducted and because the proposition is difficult to prove. While many of the earliest studies of this subject came up with conflicting conclusions, more recent and exhaustive investigations have begun to map a real, albeit imperfect, relationship between public opinion and jurists' decisional patterns.[73] In 1993 two Supreme Court researchers concluded that popular sentiment "exercises important influence on the decisions of the Court even in the absence of changes in the composition of the Court or in the partisan and ideological make up of Congress and the presidency."[74] However, they qualified their findings by noting that there was a fairly lengthy lag time—three to seven years—between a change in the public mood and a corresponding alteration in justices' voting behavior.[75] Likewise these voting changes tended to be concentrated among only a handful of justices.[76]

The most recent team of researchers to address this phenomenon came up with a set of conclusions that were more emphatic and contained fewer qualifications about the link between public mood changes and Supreme Court decisional patterns. Roy B. Flemming and B. Dan Wood discovered that "public opinion *directly* affects decisions by individual members of the Court" and that "the result holds across various issue areas, is not restricted to only a few justices, and that the justices' responses are relatively quick with a lag of only one term."[77] Equally interesting and significant, however, are studies that indicate that at the lower federal court levels (that is, the appeals and trial courts) no evidence whatever could be found to connect the voting patterns of the judges to public mood—either the national mood or even to public opinion shifts in the judges' own states. These studies suggest that the Supreme Court may be singular and unique and that its decision-making environment makes the justices particularly susceptible to shifts in the public mood, conditions that do not apply to lower appellate and trial court judges.[78] Further studies will have to resolve this apparent enigma about why lower federal court jurists appear to be immune from shifts in the public mood while U.S. Supreme Court justices are not. Research is now also under way to determine whether shifts in public opinion affect the decision making of federal appeals court judges as well as U.S. trial jurists.

Researchers have also explored this phenomenon at the state level. For example, a study of California state courts found that sentencing in marijuana cases often changed in severity soon after a popular referendum was held on reducing criminal penalties for personal use of the drug. For example, judges who had given light sentences prior to the referendum sometimes gave harsher sentences if the local vote was in favor of maintaining criminal penalties. Conversely, harsh-sentencing jurists sometimes became more lenient when the vote indicated that the public favored reducing the penalties.[79]

Given that in a majority of the states judges must periodically run for election, they probably are more attuned to public opinion than federal judges, with their lifetime tenure. One study of elected state supreme court justices found that "to appease their constituencies, justices who have views contrary to those of the voters and the court majority, and who face competitive electoral conditions will vote with the court majority instead of casting unpopular dissents on politically volatile issues."[80] Likewise a more recent study involving state supreme court justices' voting behavior in death penalty cases found a clear link between their voting patterns and voter sentiment about capital punishment. The authors noted that "while Democrats and Republicans generally exhibit behavior patterns that are quite distinct, these distinctions are blurred by variables related to retaining office. Having to face voters more frequently, thereby risking the chance of being removed from office, encourages justices in state supreme courts, who otherwise might vote consistently to overturn death sentences instead, to manifest conservative voting patterns in these cases."[81]

The following more down-to-earth example illustrates a state judge's greater grass-roots political awareness and also the greater degree to which elected jurists interact with the local environment. On November 28, 1988, Jack Hampton, a state district court judge in Dallas, Texas, gave a thirty-year prison sentence to a defendant who had been convicted of murdering two gay men. The killer, Richard Bednarski, had testified in court that he and some friends went to a central Dallas park to "pester homosexuals" and ended up killing two of them in what authorities called an execution-style slaying. (Bednarski placed a gun in one victim's mouth and pulled the trigger; he then shot the other man several times.) Because of the heinous and unprovoked nature of the crime and because Hampton is known as a "hanging judge" who usually gives life sentences for murder, the *Dallas Times Herald* decided to interview the judge about his lighter-than-usual sentence. During the interview Judge Hampton said that the murder victims more or less got what they asked for, because they were "queers" who "wouldn't have been killed if they hadn't been cruising the streets picking up teenage boys."[82]

Immediately after the interview was published, public protests were staged by human rights groups, local church leaders, and various gay rights organizations. Protest rallies were held, including one attended by five hundred people at the City Hall Plaza, where letters of support were read from Sen. Edward M. Kennedy of Massachusetts and Texas state treasurer Ann Richards. Also, formal complaints were filed with the Texas Commission on Judicial Conduct, calling for Hampton to be disciplined. In reply, this elected judicial official issued a four-paragraph letter to a group of eight Methodist ministers. Judge Hampton said he wished "to apologize" for his "poor choice of words that appeared in a recent newspaper story." He promised that in his court "everyone is entitled to and will receive equal protection."

Was the judge's public apology in response, at least in part, to his perception of public opinion and the effect that it might have on his bid for reelection? This might be surmised from a later statement made by the judge when he was asked about possible political fallout from the incident: "If it makes anybody mad, they'll forget it by 1990" (when Judge Hampton was up for reelection).[83]

This particular incident is not typical of the behavior of state judges, but it demonstrates the degree to which locally elected judicial officials respond to the tides of public opinion. Very rarely do lifetime judicial appointees, such as federal judges, feel the need to justify their sentencing behavior in interviews with the local press or to issue public apologies when public opinion turns critical of their behavior. For better or worse, public opinion does affect judicial behavior, and this is particularly true when judges must be accountable directly to the electorate.

Thus, despite the traditional notion of the blindfolded justice weighing only the facts in a case and the relevant law, common sense and statistical evidence support the assertion that jurists do keep their eyes (and ears) open to public opinion.

The Influence of the Legislative and Executive Branches

A final set of stimuli that the democratic subculture may bring to bear on the behavior of American judges is the executive and the legislative branches.

Congress and the President. Perhaps the most obvious link between the values of the democratic subculture and the output of the federal courts is that the people elect the president and members of the Senate, and the president appoints judges and justices with the advice and consent of the Senate. The chief executive and certain key senators greatly influence what kind of men and women will sit on the bench, but even after judges have been appointed, the president and Congress may have an impact on the content and direction of judicial decision making.

First, to a large degree the jurisdiction of the federal trial and appellate courts is determined by the Congress of the United States. Congress has the authority to decide which types of issues may become appropriate matters for judges to resolve. For example, when Congress passed the Civil Rights Acts of 1964, Title VII and its subsequent amendments greatly expanded the rights of women to be free from gender discrimination in the workplace. In doing so Congress in effect expanded the jurisdiction of the federal courts to hear a large number of disputes that previously had been outside the purview of the federal judiciary. And the evidence suggests that the courts have not been idle in expanding the power Congress gave them.[84] Conversely, Congress may restrict the jurisdiction of the federal courts. In response to popular dissatisfaction with many court rulings on busing, abortion, school prayer, and so on, Congress has considered passage of a number of bills designed to restrict the right of the courts to render decisions on these subjects.[85] Even if Congress does not pass such legislation, the threat to do so may cause the federal courts to pull in their horns when it comes to deciding cases in ways that are not in accord with the will of the president or Congress.

Second, judicial decision making is likely to be bolder and more effective if it has the active support of at least one other branch of the federal government, and ideally both of them.[86] School integration is a case in point. When the federal courts began to order desegregation of the public schools after 1954, they met with considerable opposition—primarily from those parts of the country most affected by the Supreme Court ruling in the *Brown* case. It is doubtful whether the federal courts could have overcome this resistance without the support given them (sometimes reluctantly) by the president and Congress. For example, in 1957 Arkansas governor Orville Faubus sought to obstruct a district judge's order to integrate Little Rock's Central High School. President Dwight D. Eisenhower then mobilized the National Guard and in effect used federal bayonets to implement the judge's ruling. President John F. Kennedy likewise used federal might to support a judge's decision to admit a black student to the University of Mississippi in the face of massive local resistance. Congress also lent its hand to federal desegregation rulings. For instance, it voted to withhold federal aid to school districts that refused to comply with district court desegregation decisions. Surely White House and congressional support emboldened the Supreme Court and the lower judiciary to carry on with their efforts to end segregation in the public schools.

Sometimes presidential and congressional actions may lead rather than just implement judicial decision making. One study analyzed the impact on trial judge behavior of the 1937 Supreme Court decisions that permitted much greater government regulation of the economy.[87] As expected, federal district judge support for government regulation increased markedly after the Supreme Court gave its official blessing to the government's new powers. However, it was also learned that district court backing for labor and economic regulation had been building before the Supreme Court's decisions: Pro-regulation decisions by U.S. trial judges increased from 44 percent in 1936 to 67 percent in 1937—a change of 23 percentage points. The authors attributed this at least in part to the fact that prior to 1937 the president and Congress, in response to public opinion, were strongly pushing legislation that favored an expanded federal role in labor and economic regulation.[88]

Thus the Supreme Court and the lower courts are not, and cannot be, immune to the will of Congress and of the chief executive as they go about their judicial business. Not only does the president, with the advice and consent of the Senate, select all members of the federal judiciary, but to a large degree the Congress also prescribes the jurisdiction of the federal courts and often the qualifications of those who have standing to sue in these tribunals. Moreover, many court decisions cannot be meaningfully implemented without the support of the other two branches of government—a fact not lost on the judges and justices themselves. Sometimes, too, the courts appear to follow the lead of the president and Congress on various public policy matters. Whichever set of circumstances is the case, the legislative and executive branches of government clearly constitute an important source of nonjudicial influence on court behavior.

The State Legislature and the Governor. Just as the legislative and executive branches affect judicial decision making at the national level, so, too, do their counterparts at the state and local levels. In almost half of the jurisdictions the popularly elected governor (or the state legislature) makes the selection of the state judges, and a policy link likely exists among the value sets of the voters, the appointing officials, and the judges who render subsequent decisions. More specifically, the authors of one study found three major ways that the political branches affect the role of the state courts.[89]

First, legislation sponsored by the governor or passed by the legislature regulates the sorts of claims that can be adjudicated in state courts and also brought to the state appellate courts. For example, class action suits may be easily brought in state judicial tribunals. (Such suits facilitate access to the courts by allowing large numbers of potential litigants with individually small claims to band together, thereby reducing or eliminating entirely the financial costs of seeking redress.) Actions by the legislature determine who may bring such suits and under what circumstances. The evidence suggests that the states vary greatly in this area. Some states make it very easy to initiate such suits whereas in others access to the courts in this fashion is very difficult.[90]

Second, actions by the legislature (which may or may not be part of the governor's political agenda) determine the authority of the state supreme court to regulate its workload and focus on important cases. For example, it is generally accepted that for most cases litigants should have the right to appeal trial court decisions. In states that have an ample number of intermediate appellate courts this right to appeal is readily available. However, in states without sufficient numbers of intermediate appeals courts or in states where the supreme court is forced by law to deal with a succession of relatively minor disputes, the chances of litigants having their cases heard by the supreme court are slim. This fact is significant in itself in terms of the distribution of justice, but it is important for another reason. In states where the supreme court is forced by the legislature into overwork on judicial trivia, the court does not have time to devote much attention to cases that raise important policy questions. For instance, after the legislature in North Carolina created intermediate courts of appeals, a study concluded that such action enabled the state high court to assume "a position of true leadership in the legal development of the state."[91] Thus actions by the legislature (supported or opposed by the governor) may determine whether the supreme court plays a major or minor role in policy questions important to the state.

Finally, because a prime function of courts is to enforce existing legal norms, the sorts of issues that state courts address depend to a large degree on the substantive law of the state. For instance, seventeen state constitutions contain "little ERAs" (equal rights amendments); ten states specifically protect the right to privacy; and some states guarantee a right to quality of the environment.[92] Thus, a judge in a state in which good air quality is guaranteed will have a much greater opportunity and right to issue an injunction against a polluter than one in a state where such a right is not legally provided. An example of a legislature's taking a subject matter out of the hands of its state judges occurred in Hawaii after its Supreme Court ruled in 1993 that same-sex couples could marry. Shortly after the court's decision the legislature began a process to modify its state's constitution to deny marriage licenses to same-sex couples, thereby overruling the state supreme court and taking the subject matter out of its jurisdiction[93]. The point here is that judges render decisions within the existing constitutional and legal environment of their respective states.

Such an environment is largely the product of political decisions made by the governor and the legislature as representatives of the electorate.

In sum, the output of the state courts, as that of federal tribunals, is to a significant degree the result of the political values and policy goals of the chief executive and the legislative branch of government.

The Subcultures as Predictors

There is scholarly divergence over the question of whether judicial decision making is essentially the product of facts, laws, and precedent (the legal subculture model) or whether the various extralegal factors carry more weight (the realist-behavioralist view). In other words, are court decisions better explained by understanding the facts and law that impinge upon a given case or by knowing which newspaper the judge reads in the morning or how the judge voted in the last election?

The clue to answering the question lies in knowing what kind of case the judge is being asked to decide. The vast majority of federal trial judges' cases and much appellate judicial business involve routine norm enforcement decisions. In cases in which the law and the controlling precedents are clear, the victor will be the side that is able to marshal better evidence to show that its factual case is stronger. In other words, in the lion's share of cases, the legal subculture model best explains and predicts judicial decision making. When traditional legal cues are ambiguous or absent, however, judges are obliged to look to the democratic subculture for guidance in their decision making.

When the Legal Evidence Is Contradictory

It is probably fair to say that in a majority of cases the facts, evidence, and controlling precedents distinctly favor one side. In such instances the judge is clearly obliged to decide for the party with the stronger case. Not to do so would violate the judge's legal training and mores; subject a trial or appeals court judge to reversal by a higher court, an event most jurists find embarrassing; and render the Supreme Court vulnerable to the charge that it was making up the law as it went along—an impression not flattering to the High Court justices. However, judges often find themselves in situations in which the facts and evidence are about equally compelling on both sides, or in which a roughly equal number of precedents sustain a finding for either party. As one U.S. trial judge in Houston told us:

There are days when you want to say to the litigants, "I wish you guys would've settled this out of court because I don't know what to do with you." If I grant the petition's request, I can often modify the relief requested [in an attempt to even out the decision], but still one side has got to win and one side has got to lose. I could cite good precedents on either side, and it's no good worrying about the appeals court because there's no telling what they would do with it should the judge's decision be appealed.

The following is an example in which a U.S. trial judge was forced to decide a case by his own lights (that is, using his democratic subculture values) when the cues from the legal subculture were clearly contradictory or nonexistent. Judge Robert E. Coyle, who holds court in the Eastern District of California (Fresno), was presented with a case that stemmed from an employment discrimination complaint filed with the Equal Employment Opportunity Commission (EEOC). Alicia Castrejon had been employed by the Tortilleria La Mejor of Farmersville, California, and claimed in her suit that she had been dismissed from her job because of previous complaints filed with the EEOC against her employer.

The legal issue was whether Castrejon had the right to file a suit in the first place because she was an undocumented immigrant. When Congress passed the Immigration Reform and Control Act of 1986, which prohibits employment of undocumented workers, it did not specify in the act whether immigrants who have applied for amnesty are protected in the period when their applications are being processed. Castrejon had filed for amnesty, but her application had not been acted on at the time she filed her employment discrimination complaint.

The judge looked to the Department of Labor and to the EEOC for some legal guidance on the matter of the interim rights of undocumented residents. Both of these federal agencies maintained that workers are covered by federal labor and antidiscrimination laws even if they are here illegally. But the judge learned that many employers had been interpreting the Immigration Reform and Control Act of 1986 to mean that illegal immigrants are not protected, and they were able to point to a 1987 ruling by a federal district judge in Alabama. That decision dismissed an undocumented immigrant's claim for minimum wages and overtime because, the judge said, that would conflict with the congressional act of 1986. The legal subculture was giving Judge Coyle few cues as to the "right" answer, and the existing cues were contradictory. Furthermore, in deciding this case, the judge had to tap attitudes and values derived from his democratic subculture and to put much of his legal subculture orientation on hold.

After sitting on the case for more than two years, the judge finally issued a ruling in February 1991 that had significant immediate impact for hundreds of thousands of immigrants. For reasons known fully only to Judge Coyle, he ruled that undocumented workers do have the right to pursue discrimination suits against an employer—regardless of legal residency status. In his decision the judge acknowledged the seeming incongruity of discouraging illegal immigration while at the same time allowing undocumented workers to seek legal recourse against discrimination on the job: "We doubt, however, that many illegal aliens come to this country to gain the protection of our labor laws. Rather it is the hope of getting a job—at any wage—that prompts most illegal aliens to cross our borders." [94]

In situations such as the one just described, judges have little choice but to turn to their personal value sets to determine how to resolve the cases. Decision making is affected by local attitudes and traditions or by the judge's perception of the public mood or the will of the current Congress or state legislature or administration.

Since the advent of the Burger Court in 1969, and continuing throughout the Rehnquist Court, an inordinate number of the Supreme Court's decisions have been regarded as "ideologically imprecise and inconsistent," often sustained by weak, five-to-four majorities. This state of affairs has increased the likelihood that trial and appellate judges will respond to stimuli from the democratic rather than the legal subculture. That is, the confusion created by the Court in setting forth ambiguous or contradictory guidelines has meant that judges in the lower federal and state courts—and perhaps even members of the Supreme Court—have been forced to rely on (or have felt free to give vent to) their own personal ideas about how the law should read. As one study concluded, "With the decline of the fact-law congruence after 1968 the . . . [lower courts] became more free to take their decision-making cues from personal-partisan values rather than from guidelines set forth by the Higher Court." [95]

When a Case Concerns New Areas of the Law

Researchers also set aside the legal subculture model and turn to the democratic subculture approach when jurists are asked to resolve new types of policy questions for which statutory law and appellate court guidelines are virtually absent. Since about 1937 most new and uncharted areas of the law (at least at the federal level) have been in the realms of civil liberties and criminal justice rather than in the area of labor and economic regulation. Since 1937 the federal courts have leaned toward self-restraint and deference to the elected branches when it comes to ordering the economic lives of the American people.[96] Moreover, in recent decades Congress has legislated, often with precision, in the areas of economic regulation and labor relations, and this has further restricted the discretion of judges in these fields. As a result, the noose of the legal subculture has been drawn tightly around trial judges' necks, and little room is left for creative decision making or for responding to the tug of the heart instead of the clear command of the law. Thus, since New Deal days the legal subculture, not the democratic subculture, has been the better predictor of trial and appellate judge decision making in labor and economic regulation cases.

Since the 1930s the opposite trend has been observable for issues of criminal justice and civil rights and liberties:

The "great" and controversial decisions of the Stone, Vinson, Warren, and Burger Courts [as well as the Rehnquist Court] focused primarily on issues of civil liberties and of the rights of criminal defendants, and it is precisely those sorts of issues which evoked the greatest partisan schisms among the justices. Research has shown that . . . [the lower courts] were by no means immune to the debates and divisions which racked the nation's High Court; they, too, seem to have split along "political" lines more often on criminal justice and on civil rights matters than they did with other sorts of cases.[97]

The ambiguity (or perhaps the constant state of flux) of the law on matters such as the rights of criminal defendants, First Amendment freedoms, and equal protection of the law has given the federal jurists greater opportunity to respond than in the labor and economic realms, where their freedom of action has been more circumscribed. Put another way, since the 1930s the democratic subculture model has become increasingly important as a predictor of judicial behavior on Bill of Rights matters.[98]

A series of interviews with a wide range of district and appellate court judges lends further credence to this notion. In William Kitchin's study, the trial judges were asked about their willingness to "innovate"; that is, their inclination to make new law in areas where appellate court or congressional guidelines were ambiguous or nonexistent. After asking why judges create new law through judicial innovation, Kitchin noted:

One answer is that the courts innovate because other branches of government ignore certain significant problems which, to individual judges, cry out for attention. Accordingly, the individual district judge innovates in an attempt to fill a legal vacuum, as one judge commented, "The theory is that judges should not be legal innovators, but there are some areas in which they have to innovate because legislatures won't do the job. Race relations is one of these areas. . . ." Other areas mentioned as needing judicial innovation because of legislative inaction were housing, equal accommodations, and criminal law (especially habeas corpus).[99]

Another study of decisional patterns and variations in U.S. district judge decision making showed that "the subjects that . . . [the Kitchin study] found to represent the greatest areas of freedom in judicial decision making are the very same subjects that we find to maximize partisan voting differences among the district judges. In situations where judges are more free to take their decision-making cues from sources other than appellate court decisions and statutes, they are more likely to rely on their personal-partisan orientations."[100]

A relatively new area of the law in which appellate court and congressional guidelines are few and thus lower-court judges must fend for themselves is the definition of obscenity. Prior to 1957 no Supreme Court decisions of note had been handed down on the matter of obscenity. In that year the nation's high court ruled that obscenity was not protected by the First Amendment and said that it could be defined as material that dealt with sex "in a manner appealing to prurient interest."[101] Seven years later, the Supreme Court said that in determining what appealed to the prurient interest of the average person, hypothetical "national standards" were to be used.[102] However, nine years after that the Court changed its mind and ruled that "state community standards" could be employed."[103] But what is obscenity? No one seems to know with any greater certainty today than Justice Potter Stewart did in 1964 when he confessed that he could not intelligibly define obscenity but that "I do know it when I see it."[104] As U.S. District Judge José Gonzalez in 1990 wrote in determining that an album by the controversial Miami-based rap group 2 Live Crew was obscene, "It is an appeal to 'dirty' thoughts and the loins, not to the intellect and mind." (The 2 Live Crew's attorney defended the album as "art" and said, "Put in its historical context, it is a novel and creative use of sound and lyrics.")[105] Given the reluctance or the inability of Congress and the Supreme Court to define obscenity, America's trial and appellate judges have little choice but to look to their own personal values and perceptions of the local public need to determine what kinds of books, films, art, and plays the First Amendment protects in their respective jurisdictions.

Another lively new area of the law that is currently bedeviling federal judges is the subject of sexual harassment. Ever since Congress added sexual harassment to the list of items prohibited in the workplace by Title VII of the Civil Rights Act of 1964, federal jurists have had a difficult time defining what sexual harassment means. Obvious examples are clear enough (a boss explicitly telling a female employee that sexual favors were required for a pay raise), but the gray areas are taxing judges' minds. For example, a U.S. trial judge in Los Angeles was recently asked to rule that there was sexual harassment in an office because women's breasts were being compared among female workers and sexual toys were being given as presents. The judge ruled that according to his lights, while the office in question had been turned into a "bawdy sorority," federal law did not provide a "cause of action for embarrassment."[106]

But confusion in this new realm by no means ends with trying to define traditional forms of sexual harassment. The federal courts are now trying to determine whether same-sex harassment can be understood to mean a violation of one's civil rights. For instance, in May 1997 a U.S. appeals court in Atlanta considered a case involving a waiter at a hotel restaurant whose maitre d' had made sexual advances to him. This court said that such activity did come within the strictures of the 1964 Civil Rights Act, although other courts have clearly ruled to the contrary.[107] Even here the confusion and uncertainty does not end. What about sexually oriented horseplay among straight men? A suit is currently being pressed in a federal courtroom in Denver against the United Parcel Service of America by Michael Garcia, a heterosexual maintenance mechanic. Garcia is claiming that his boss "tried to un-nerve him by prodding him from behind with a radio antenna and touching him in front of co-workers." The company has claimed in similar cases that this amounted to no more than "locker-room" antics—not harassment—to which Garcia responded that "I've played many sports in my time and I've never seen that kind of action in any locker rooms I've been in."[108] What is the judge going to do in this case? With the legal subculture virtually silent in this realm, the jurist is going to have to look to the democratic subculture to find an answer.

Judicial innovation in new legal realms or in the absence of appellate court or legislative guidelines is by no means confined to federal jurists; the phenomenon is just as significant at the state court level. For example, in 1992 the Tennessee Supreme Court had to decide the novel question of whether a state can force a man to become a father. The case revolved around a couple whose marriage had ended in a divorce. Prior to the divorce, however, the couple had placed in frozen storage seven of the woman's eggs that had been fertilized with the man's sperm—"children in vitro" as the courts came to call them. The woman wished to secure the right either to have the eggs implanted in her womb or to donate them to an anonymous childless couple. Her former husband objected, and the question became grist for the Tennessee judicial mill. Are embryos human beings with independent rights? Could the man be forced to become a father without his consent? With no clear legislative or judicial precedents to guide it, the state's high court eventually ruled in favor of the former husband: "The state's interest in the potential life of these pre-embryos is not sufficient to justify any infringement upon the freedom of these individuals to [decide] whether to allow a process to continue that may result in such a dramatic change in their lives as becoming parents."[109] This case is a vivid reminder that judicial policy making in new legal realms is by no means the exclusive activity of the federal courts.

The Judge's Role Conception

In the discussion of which better explains judicial decision making—the rules of the legal subculture or stimuli from the democratic subculture—one additional factor must be considered: how judges conceive of their judicial role. Judicial scholars often talk about three basic decision-making categories regarding whether judges should make law when they decide cases. Lawmakers are those who take a broad view of the judicial role. These jurists, often referred to as activists or innovators, contend that they can and must make law in their decisions, because the statutory law and appellate or Supreme Court guidelines are often ambiguous or do not cover all situations and because legislative intent is frequently impossible to determine. In Kitchin's study of federal district judges, 14 percent were classified in this category, whereas in an investigation of appeals court judges, 15 percent were associated with this role.[110]

At the other end of the continuum are the law interpreters, who take a narrow, traditional view of the judicial function. Sometimes called strict constructionists, they do not believe that judges should substitute judicial wisdom for the rightful power of the elected branches of government to make policy. They tend to eschew making innovative decisions that may depart from the literal meaning of controlling precedents. In the Kitchin study, 52 percent of the U.S. trial judges were found to be law interpreters, whereas only 26 percent of the appeals court judges were so designated.[111] This finding is consistent with the fact that federal district judges are more concerned with routine norm enforcement, whereas the appellate judges' involvement—and their perception of it—is with broader questions of judicial policy.

Midway between the law interpreters and the lawmakers are judges known as pragmatists or realists, who believe that on occasion they are obliged to make law, but that for most cases a decision can be made by consulting the controlling law or appellate court precedents. Studies have indicated that a third of federal district judges assume this moderate role, whereas a full 59 percent of their appellate court colleagues do so.[112] Comparing federal jurists with state judges, one scholar has noted, "A slightly greater number of federal than state judges take the pragmatist or realist views, possibly because they have more opportunities to make innovative decisions."[113]

Thus, whether judicial decisions are better explained by the legal model or by the democratic model depends not only on the nature of the cases and the state of the controlling law and precedents; but also to some degree on how the individual judges evaluate these factors. In virtually every case that comes before them, judges have to determine how much discretion they have and how they wish to exercise it. This is a subjective process, and, as one research team put it, "activist judges will find more discretion in a given fact situation than will their more restrained colleagues."[114]

Summary

Federal and state judges make hundreds of millions of decisions each year, and scholars have sought to explain the thinking behind these decisions. Two schools of thought provide two explanations. One theory is based on the rules and procedures of the legal subculture. Judges' decisions, according to this model, are the product of traditional legal reasoning and adherence to precedent and judicial self-restraint. Another school of thought, the realist-behavioralist approach, argues that judges are influenced in their decision making by such factors as party affiliation, local values and attitudes, public opinion, and pressures from the legislative and executive branches. In the vast majority of cases, the legal subculture model is the more accurate predictor of judicial decision making. However, stimuli from the democratic subculture often become useful in accounting for judges' decisions (1) when the legal evidence is contradictory or equally compelling on both sides; (2) if the situation concerns new areas of the law and significant precedents are absent; and (3) when judges are inclined to view themselves more as activist lawmakers than as law interpreters.

NOTES

1. Richard J. Richardson and Kenneth N. Vines, *The Politics of Federal Courts* (Boston: Little, Brown, 1970). Although Richardson and Vines developed their model primarily for federal courts, we feel that their hypotheses and conclusions are equally true for state judges.

2. Edward H. Levi, *An Introduction to Legal Reasoning* (Chicago: University of Chicago Press, 1948), 1–2.

3. *Lane v. Wilson*, 307 U.S. 268 (1939); and *Gomillion v. Lightfoot*, 364 U.S. 339 (1960).

4. *Lane v. Wilson*, 307 U.S. 275 (1939).

5. William Kitchin, *Federal District Judges* (Baltimore: Collage Press, 1978), 71.

6. J. Woodford Howard Jr., *Courts of Appeals in the Federal Judicial System: A Study of the Second, Fifth, and District of Columbia Circuits* (Princeton, N.J.: Princeton University Press, 1981), 187.

7. Walter F. Murphy, *Elements of Judicial Strategy* (Chicago: University of Chicago Press, 1964), 204.

8. Henry Sumner Maine, *Ancient Law* (Boston: Beacon Press, 1963), 3–19.

9. Henry J. Abraham, *The Judicial Process*, 4th ed. (New York: Oxford University Press, 1980), chap. 9.

10. *Evers v. Jackson Municipal Separate School District*, 232 F. Supp. 241 (1964).

11. Ibid., 247.

12. Ibid., 249.

13. Ibid., 255.

14. Richardson and Vines, *The Politics of Federal Courts*, 8–9.

15. Steven Vago, *Law and Society*, 5th ed. (Englewood Cliffs, N.J.: Prentice-Hall, 1997), 354.

16. For a good, current bibliography on this subject, see ibid., chap. 9.

17. Oliver Wendell Holmes Jr., *The Common Law* (Boston: Little, Brown, 1881), 1–2.

18. Jerome Frank, *Courts on Trial: Myth and Reality in American Justice* (Princeton, N.J.: Princeton University Press, 1950), 151.

19. Richardson and Vines, *The Politics of Federal Courts*, 10.

20. Donald Dale Jackson, *Judges* (New York: Atheneum, 1974), 18.

21. One recent study noted that, between 1959 and 1998, 140 books, articles, dissertations, and conference papers reported empirical data showing a link between judges' political party affiliation and their judicial behavior. Daniel R. Pinello, "Linking Party to Judicial Ideology in American Courts: A Meta-Analysis," *Justice System Journal* 20 (1999): 219–254.

22. Some studies suggest that age, socioeconomic status, and religion may influence some judges in some of their cases, but the associations are weak. See, for example, Sheldon Goldman, "Voting Behavior on the United States Courts of Appeals Revisited," *American Political Science Review* 69 (1975): 491–506; John R. Schmidhauser, "The Justices of the Supreme Court: A Collective Portrait," *Midwest Journal of Political Science* 3 (1959): 1–57; and Donald Leavitt, "Political Party and Class Influences on the Attitudes of Justices of the Supreme Court in the Twentieth Century," paper delivered at the annual meeting of the Midwest Political Science Association, Chicago, 1972. Other studies suggest that these background factors have virtually no explanatory power—for example, Howard, *Courts of Appeals in the Federal Judicial System*, chap. 6. For a more detailed discussion of this subject and a literature review, see C. K. Rowland and Robert A. Carp, *Politics and Judgment in Federal District Courts* (Lawrence: University Press of Kansas, 1996), chap. 2.

23. David W. Adamany, "The Party Variable in Judges' Voting: Conceptual Notes and a Case Study," *American Political Science Review* 63 (1969): 59.

24. These figures are based on unpublished data collected by Robert A. Carp, Ronald Stidham, and Kenneth Manning.

25. For a more extensive discussion of the odds ratio and methodology used in this study, see Rowland and Carp, *Politics and Judgment in Federal District Courts*, 180–181.

26. For a good review of the early literature on this subject, see Goldman, "Voting Behavior on the United States Courts of Appeals Revisited," 491, note 2. See also Howard, *Courts of Appeals in the Federal Judicial System*, chap. 6.

27. Sheldon Goldman, "Voting Behavior on the United States Courts of Appeals, 1961–1964," *American Political Science Review* 60 (1966): 384.

28. See, for example, Donald Songer, "Consensual and Nonconsensual Decisions in Unanimous Opinions of the United States Courts of Appeals," *American Journal of Political Science* 26 (1982): 225–239; Donald Songer and Sue Davis, "The Impact of Party and Region on Voting Decisions in the United States Courts of Appeals, 1955–1986," *Western Political Quarterly* 43 (1990): 317–334; and Ronald Stidham, Robert A. Carp, and Donald R. Songer, "The Voting Behavior of President Clinton's Judicial Appointees," *Judicature* 80 (1996): 16–21.

29. Christopher E. Smith, "Polarization and Change in the Federal Courts: *En Banc* Decisions in the U.S. Courts of Appeals," *Judicature* 74 (1990): 137.

30. Leavitt, "Political Party and Class Influences on the Attitudes of Justices of the Supreme Court in the Twentieth Century," 18–19.

31. Lee Epstein, Thomas G. Walker, and William J. Dixon, "The Supreme Court and Criminal Justice Disputes: A Neo-Institutional Perspective," *American Journal of Political Science* 33 (1989): 838.

32. S. Sidney Ulmer, "Are Background Models Time-Bound?" *American Political Science Review* 80 (1986): 957–967.

33. S. Sidney Ulmer, "The Political Party Variable in the Michigan Supreme Court," *Journal of Public Law* 11 (1962): 352–362; and Malcolm M. Feeley, "Another Look at the 'Party Variable' in Judicial Decision-Making: An Analysis of the Michigan Supreme Court," *Polity* 4 (1971): 91–104.

34. Philip L. Dubois, "The Illusion of Judicial Consensus Revisited: Partisan Conflict on an Intermediate State Court of Appeals," *American Journal of Political Science* 32 (1988): 946–967.

35. Ibid., 953–954.

36. For a good, current bibliography of the literature on partisan voting patterns among state judges, see ibid., 965–967.

37. Donald P. Kommers, "The Federal Constitutional Court in the West German Political System," in *Frontiers of Judicial Research*, eds. Joel B. Grossman and Joseph Tanenhaus (New York: John Wiley, 1969), 73–132; Fred L. Morrison, "The Swiss Federal Court: Judicial Decision Making and Recruitment," in *Frontiers of Judicial Research*, eds. Joel B. Grossman and Joseph Tanenhaus (New York: John Wiley, 1969), 133–162; and Glendon Schubert, "The Dimensions of Decisional Reponse: Opinion and Voting Behavior of the Australian High Court," in *Frontiers of Judicial Research*, eds. Joel B. Grossman and Joseph Tanenhaus (New York: John Wiley, 1969), 163–195.

38. See, for example, Glendon Schubert and David J. Danelski, eds., *Comparative Judicial Behavior: Cross-Cultural Studies of Political Decision-Making in the East and West* (New York: Oxford University Press, 1969); Matthew E. Wetstein and C. L. Ostberg, "Search and Seizure Cases in the Supreme Court of Canada: Extending an American Model of Judicial Decision Making across Countries," *Social Science Quarterly* 80 (1999): 757–774; and J. Mark Ramseyer and Eric B. Rasmusen, "Skewed Incentives: Paying for Politics as a Japanese Judge," *Judicature* 83 (2000): 190–195.

39. Richardson and Vines, *The Politics of Federal Courts*, 71.

40. For a more elaborate discussion of this phenomenon, see Robert A. Carp and C. K. Rowland, *Policymaking and Politics in the Federal District Courts* (Knoxville: University of Tennessee Press, 1983), chap. 4.

41. Richardson and Vines, *The Politics of Federal Courts*, 73.

42. Ibid., 72.

43. For example, see Robert A. Carp and Russell Wheeler, "Sink or Swim: The Socialization of a Federal District Judge," *Journal of Public Law* 21 (1972): 359–393. See also Robert A. Carp, "The Influence of Local Needs and Conditions on the Administration of Federal Justice," paper delivered at the annual meeting of the Southwestern Political Science Association, Dallas, 1971.

44. See, for example, Angus Campbell, Philip E. Converse, Warren E. Miller, and Donald E. Stokes, *The American Voter* (New York: Wiley, 1960); Everett Carll Ladd Jr. and Charles D. Hadley, *Transformations of the American Party System*, 2d ed. (New York: W. W. Norton, 1978); V. O. Key Jr., *Public Opinion and American Democracy* (New York: Knopf, 1967); and Robert S. Erikson and Kent L. Tedin, *American Public Opinion: Its Origins, Content, and Impact*, 5th ed. (Boston: Allyn Bacon, 1995).

45. Barbara Hinckley, *Stability and Change in Congress* (New York: Harper and Row, 1978); Randall B. Ripley, *Congress: Process and Policy*, 2d ed. (New York: W. W. Norton, 1978); V. O. Key Jr., *Politics, Parties, and Pressure Groups*, 5th ed. (New York: Crowell, 1964), especially chaps. 9 and 24; and J. H. Fenton, "Liberal-Conservative Divisions by Sections of the United States," *Annals* 344 (1962): 122–127.

46. John R. Schmidhauser, "Judicial Behavior and the Sectional Crisis of 1837–1860," *Journal of Politics* 23 (1961): 615–640. To be more precise, Schmidhauser found that justices' party affiliations and their geographic orientations were highly interrelated. Because the four justices who were most supportive of

Southern regional interests were all Southern Democrats, and because the two justices with the strongest pro-Northern voting patterns were Northern Whigs, Schmidhauser concluded that the effects of party and region were virtually inseparable.

47. Leavitt, "Political Party and Class Influences on the Attitudes of Justices of the Supreme Court in the Twentieth Century."

48. James F. Simon, *In His Own Image* (New York: David McKay, 1973), 103–104.

49. Ibid., 123.

50. Howard, *Courts of Appeals in the Federal Judicial System*, 55, 79, 156.

51. Susan Brodie Haire, "Judges' Decisions in the United States Courts of Appeals: A Reassessment of Geographic Patterns in Judicial Behavior," Ph.D. dissertation, University of South Carolina, 1993, 160.

52. Steve Alumbaugh and C. K. Rowland, "The Links Between Platform-Based Appointment Criteria and Trial Judges' Abortion Judgments," *Judicature* 74 (1990): 161.

53. Based on unpublished data collected by Robert A. Carp, Ronald Stidham, and C. K. Rowland.

54. Vilhelm Aubert, "Conscientious Objectors before Norwegian Military Courts," in *Judicial Decision-Making*, ed. Glendon Schubert (New York: Free Press of Glencoe, 1963), 206–207.

55. For example, see Goldman, "Voting Behavior on the United States Courts of Appeals, 1961–1964," 370–385.

56. Haire, "Judges' Decisions in the United States Courts of Appeals," 163 and chap. 5.

57. Based on unpublished data collected by Robert A. Carp, Ronald Stidham, and C. K. Rowland.

58. Carp and Wheeler, "Sink or Swim," 376.

59. Carp, "The Influence of Local Needs and Conditions on the Administration of Federal Justice," 17–18.

60. Howard, *Courts of Appeals in the Federal Judicial System*, 234.

61. For example, see Carp and Rowland, *Policymaking and Politics in the Federal District Courts*, 106–116.

62. This discussion is based on material taken from Martin A. Levin, *Urban Politics and the Criminal Courts* (Chicago: University of Chicago Press, 1977).

63. Ibid., 136–142.

64. Ibid., 142–147.

65. Henry R. Glick, *Courts, Politics, and Justice*, 3d ed. (New York: McGraw-Hill, 1993), 321.

66. As quoted in William Mishler and Reginald S. Sheehan, "The Supreme Court as a Countermajoritarian Institution? The Impact of Public Opinion on Supreme Court Decisions," *American Political Science Review* 87 (1993): 89.

67. "Arkansas Judge Who Struck Down Creation-Science Law Condemned in Hundreds of Letters," *Houston Chronicle*, August 6, 1982, 1:9.

68. *Brown v. Board of Education*, 349 U.S. 294 (1955).

69. *Baker v. Carr*, 369 U.S. 186 (1962).

70. *Miller v. California*, 413 U.S. 15 (1973).

71. Lawrence Baum, *The Supreme Court*, 5th ed. (Washington, D.C.: CQ Press, 1995), 151. For a good discussion of this subject, see David G. Barnum, "Supreme Court and Public Opinion: Judicial Decision Making in the Post–New Deal Period," *Journal of Politics* 47 (1985): 652–666.

72. The full citations are as follows: *Marbury v. Madison*, 1 Cranch 137 (1803); *Brown v. Board of Education*, 347 U.S. 483 (1954); *Roe v. Wade*, 410 U.S. 113 (1973); and *United States v. Nixon*, 418 U.S. 683 (1974).

73. For examples of these earlier studies, see Glen T. Broach et al., "State Political Culture and Sentence Severity in Federal District Courts," *Criminology* 16 (1978): 373–382; and Ronald Stidham and Robert A. Carp, "Trial Courts' Responses to Supreme Court Policy Changes: Three Case Studies," *Law and Policy Quarterly* 4 (1982): 215–235.

74. Mishler and Sheehan, "The Supreme Court as a Countermajoritarian Institution?" 96.

75. Ibid., 87–101; and Mishler and Sheehan, "Popular Influence on Supreme Court Decisions: A Response to Helmut Norpoth and Jeffrey A. Segal," *American Political Science Review,* 88 (1994): 716–724.

76. Mishler and Sheehan, "The Supreme Court as a Countermajoritarian Institution?" 87–101.

77. Roy B. Flemming and B. Dan Wood, "The Public and the Supreme Court: Individual Justice Responsiveness to American Policy Moods," *American Journal of Political Science* 41 (1997): 468–498.

78. See, for example, Ashlyn Kuersten, Kenneth L. Manning, and Robert A. Carp, "The Political Context of Lower Court Decision Making," paper delivered at the annual meeting of the Southern Political Science Association, Savannah, Georgia, 1999; and Kenneth L. Manning, Ashlyn K. Kuersten, and Robert A. Carp, "Public Opinion and the Political Context of Lower Court Decision Making," paper delivered at the annual meeting of the American Political Science Association, Washington, D.C., 2000.

79. James H. Kuklinski and John E. Stanga, "Political Participation and Government Responsiveness: The Behavior of California Superior Courts," *American Political Science Review* 73 (1979): 1090–1099.

80. Melinda Gann Hall, "Electoral Politics and Strategic Voting in State Supreme Courts," *Journal of Politics* 54 (1992): 427.

81. Paul R. Brace and Melinda Gann Hall, "The Interplay of Preferences, Case Facts, Context, and Rules in the Politics of Judicial Choice," *Journal of Politics* 59 (1997): 1223.

82. "Dallas Judge Apologizes for 'Poor Choice of Words,'" *Montrose Voice,* December 23, 1988, 5.

83. "Overheard," *Newsweek,* January 2, 1989, 13.

84. For example, in 1998 the Supreme Court ruled that an employee could recover damages under Title VII against an employer who had had sexually harassed her even through she suffered no adverse job-related consequences. *Burlington Industries v. Ellerth,* 524 U.S. 742 (1998).

85. However, many constitutional scholars argue that the right of the federal courts to hear such cases stems directly from Article III of the Constitution and that therefore Congress could not legally curtail court jurisdiction over these subjects except by initiating an amendment to the Constitution.

86. See, for example, Stephen L. Wasby, *The Impact of the United States Supreme Court* (Homewood, Ill.: Dorsey Press, 1970), especially 255–256; and Harrell R. Rodgers Jr. and Charles S. Bullock III, *Coercion to Compliance* (Lexington, Mass.: Heath, 1976).

87. *National Labor Relations Board v. Jones and Laughlin Steel Corp.,* 301 U.S. 1 (1937); and *West Coast Hotel Co. v. Parrish,* 300 U.S. 379 (1937).

88. Stidham and Carp, "Trial Courts' Responses to Supreme Court Policy Changes," 218–222.

89. G. Alan Tarr and Mary Cornelia Aldis Porter, *State Supreme Courts in State and Nation* (New Haven, Conn.: Yale University Press, 1988), chap. 2.

90. Ibid., 45.

91. Roger D. Groot, "The Effects of an Intermediate Appellate Court on the Supreme Court Product: The North Carolina Experience," *Wake Forest Law Review* 7 (1971): 548–572.

92. Tarr and Porter, *State Supreme Courts in State and Nation,* 51.

93. Meki Cox, "Hawaii Starts Benefits to Gay Couples," *Houston Chronicle,* July 9, 1997, A5.

94. This example is based on Jim Carlton and Amy Dockser Marcus, "Undocumented Worker's Suit Is Upheld," *Wall Street Journal,* February 25, 1991, B5. THE CASE CITATION IS *E.E.O.C. v. TORTILLERIA LA MEJOR,* 758 F. Supp. 585 (E.D. Cal. 1991).

95. Carp and Rowland, *Policymaking and Politics in the Federal District Courts,* 37.

96. However, on matters of local economic regulation, voting differences among judges are still sharp (see Table 10-1). Only at the national level have federal judges tended to refrain from substituting their own views for those of elected officials.

97. Carp and Rowland, *Policymaking and Politics in the Federal District Courts,* 39.

98. At the state level, whether high court ambiguity is thought to be greater on civil rights and liberties issues or in the labor and economic realm varies from one jurisdiction to another. Note the several areas discussed in Chapter 4, under the heading "Jurisdiction and Policy Making of State Courts," in which state courts have taken the lead in bringing about policy-making innovations.

99. Kitchin, *Federal District Judges*, 104.

100. Carp and Rowland, *Policymaking and Politics in the Federal District Courts*, 40.

101. *Roth v. United States* and *Alberts v. California*, 354 U.S. 476 (1957).

102. *Jacobellis v. Ohio*, 378 U.S. 184 (1964).

103. *Miller v. California*, 413 U.S. 15 (1973).

104. *Jacobellis v. Ohio*, 378 U.S. 184 (1964) at 197.

105. Laura Parker, "Federal Judge in Florida Rules 2 Live Crew Album Is Obscene," *Houston Chronicle*, June 7, 1990, A11.

106. Ann Davis, "When Ribaldry among Men Is Sex Harassment," *Wall Street Journal*, June 5, 1997, B1.

107. "Same-Sex Harassment: Is It Illegal and Under What Circumstances?" *Wall Street Journal*, June 3, 1997, A1.

108. Davis, "When Ribaldry among Men Is Sex Harassment."

109. Helene Cooper, "Tennessee Court Refuses to Give Custody of 7 Embryos to Mother," *Wall Street Journal*, June 2, 1992, B8.

110. Kitchin, *Federal District Judges*, 107.

111. Ibid.

112. Ibid.

113. Glick, *Courts, Politics, and Justice*, 335.

114. Carp and Rowland, *Policymaking and Politics in the Federal District Courts*, 14.

SUGGESTED READINGS

Burton, Steven J. *An Introduction to Law and Legal Reasoning.* Boston: Little, Brown, 1985. Explains what it has traditionally meant to "think like a judge"; explores the judicial reasoning process.

Carter, Lief H. *Reason in Law,* 5th ed. New York: HarperCollins, 1998. A short, excellent discussion of how judges think and reason; offers a good explication of the legal subculture.

Gates, John B., and Charles Johnson. *The American Courts: A Critical Assessment,* Part III. Washington, D.C.: CQ Press, 1991. A collection of essays by prominent political scientists on the various influences on judicial decision making.

Goldman, Sheldon, and Austin Sarat, eds. *American Court Systems: Readings in Judicial Process and Behavior,* 2d ed. White Plains, N.Y.: Longman, 1989. A reader containing contemporary approaches to explaining why judges think and act the way they do.

Richardson, Richard J., and Kenneth N. Vines. *The Politics of Federal Courts: Lower Courts in the United States.* Boston: Little, Brown, 1970. A classic discussion of the influences of both the legal subculture and the democratic subculture on judicial decision making.

Rowland, C. K., and Robert A. Carp. *Politics and Judgment in Federal District Courts.* Lawrence: University Press of Kansas, 1996. A comprehensive study of decision making at the federal district court level, based on a large data sample.

Schubert, Glendon. *Judicial Behavior: A Reader in Theory and Research.* Chicago: Rand McNally, 1964. A classic reader in judicial decision making; excellent essays introduce each chapter.

Tanenhaus, Joseph, and Walter F. Murphy. *The Study of Public Law.* New York: Random House, 1972. Systematically discusses the history of public law and examines the various approaches to its study.

CHAPTER 5

Decision Making in Collegial Courts

The Supreme Court is the ultimate interpreter of the U.S. Constitution, state constitutions, and national and state legislation. The decision making of these jurists is a product of both the legal and democratic subcultures.

✎ In the past Congress largely mandated which cases the U.S. Supreme Court would and would not hear, but today the High Court justices have almost complete control over their own docket. Is it a good idea that the Supreme Court should control its own agenda—not even having to offer an explanation for its refusal to hear almost 99 percent of the cases appealed to it?

✎ When appellate court justices get together to discuss a case and to decide its outcome, are their deliberations on a high and lofty plane, or are their motivations and actions no different than any group of ordinary citizens acting as an organized committee?

✎ Some chief justices have been powerful and highly influential men while others are barely remembered by legal historians. How can this be, given that their official, formal powers have remained largely identical for the past two hundred years?

✎ Are patterns of appellate judge behavior similar throughout the world, or are the decision-making patterns of America's collegial court jurists unique?

UNTIL NOW WE HAVE TREATED decision making by American judges at all levels as if it were essentially the product of the same two influences—the legal and the democratic subcultures. To a substantial degree this is a valid approach to take. After all, jurists on multijudge appellate courts adhere to the same legal reasoning process as do their colleagues on the trial court bench. Lower-court judges may be influenced in close cases by their political party affiliation just as members of the appeals courts are. But before an analysis of judicial decision making can be complete, one vital difference must be recognized between trial courts and the state and federal appellate courts. The former render decisions that are largely the product of a single individual, whereas the latter, as collegial courts, make decisions through group interaction. As one former trial judge, now a member of an appellate court, said:

> The transition between a district judge and circuit judge is not an easy one, primarily because of, shall I say, the autocratic position occupied by the district court judge. He is the sole decider. He decides as he sees fit, and files the decision in a form as he sees fit. A Court of Appeals decides by committee. One of the first traumas I had was when opinions were sent back by the other judges asking me to add this sentence, change that, etc., to get concurrence. I admit at the beginning I resisted that. It was pride. I learned it was a joint project, but it was a very difficult thing. I see the same in others.[1]

What are the extra ingredients that go into a decision made by the nine-member Supreme Court or by a three-judge state appellate panel? What is the essence of the dynamics of multijudge decision making that distinguishes it from a judgment made by a single jurist? We shall discuss several theoretical approaches that have attempted to get a handle on this slippery subject. Although we shall continue to address these phenomena as they affect both state and federal judges, we shall not treat the several judicial systems as separate entities. This is because there is no reason to believe that the variables and forces we are exploring here affect state jurists differently from federal judges. For example, when we contend that the corporate decision of a collegial court is often the product of personal interaction among its judges, there is no reason to believe that such interpersonal variables differ to any significant degree whether the court in question is the U.S. Supreme Court or the highest tribunal of a given state.[2] An increasing amount of comparative data about appellate jurists in other countries reveal that some patterns of collegial court behavior may be international in nature.

Cue Theory

As long as trial and appeals courts have jurisdiction over a case, the judges must render some type of decision on the merits. They have little discretion about the

composition of their dockets. If the judges view a particular case as presenting a trivial question, they will not spend time agonizing over it, but they are still obliged to
provide some kind of formal ruling on the substance of the matter. Not so with the
Supreme Court. Of the approximately eight thousand petitions presented to the
Court each year, the justices agree to hear only a few hundred on the merits—and in
recent years fewer than a hundred of these carry with them full-blown written opinions. Since the enactment of Public Law 100–352 in 1988, the Supreme Court has had
almost complete control over its own docket. That is, the justices decide which issues
they want to tackle in a given term and which ones are not ripe for adjudication or
must be summarily dismissed for "want of a substantial federal question." The importance of this is that what the Supreme Court decides not to rule on is often as significant as the cases it does summon forth for its scrutiny. (Great variance exists in
the amount of control that the state supreme courts have over their dockets.)[3]

In other countries few courts have the kind of control over its docket possessed
by the U.S. Supreme Court. For example, the highly important and prestigious European Court of Justice is required to hear all cases referred to it, however unimportant. To circumvent this legal requirement it has developed a number of mechanisms to avoid dealing with what would otherwise be a crushing and impossible
workload. For example, the court (as most foreign judicial tribunals and lower U.S.
federal courts) divides itself into chambers. Panels of three or five judges sit together to hear a particular case. Or, when the law requires that the full court hear a case,
the court may sit with a quorum of eleven judges instead of all fifteen.[4]

Judicial scholars have sought to identify the reasons some petitions are culled for
special attention and the rest never receive those important four votes that are
needed for the Supreme Court to grant certiorari and decide the case. A pioneering
study of this question was conducted by a research team during the early 1960s.[5]
Analysts began by examining the Court's official reasons for granting certiorari as
set forth in Rule 17, which specifies that the Court might hear a case if (1) an appeals
court has decided a point of local law in conflict with local decisions, (2) a court of
appeals has departed from "the usual course of judicial proceedings," (3) a conflict
is perceived between a lower-court decision and a Supreme Court precedent, (4) a
conflict exists on a point of law among the various federal circuits, or (5) the Court
feels it must have the final word on a particularly important question.

The research team tested these official reasons by comparing the cases for which
certiorari was granted with those in which review was denied. The official reasons
did not prove to be an accurate or useful guide to the Court's decision making. For
example, in over 50 percent of the cases that were selected for review, the Court's of-

ficial reason for its actions was that the cases were "important"—however that was defined. The researchers thought they could do better. They set out to identify certain key characteristics of those cases for which review was and was not granted. They hoped to develop some predictive statements that were more precise and reliable than Rule 17. The result was cue theory.

Cue theory is based on the assumption that the Supreme Court justices have neither the time nor the desire to wade through the myriad of pages in the thousands of petitions presented to them each year. Therefore, they presumably must have developed some sort of shortcut to help them select the petitions. The justices must, the researchers hypothesized, look for cues in each petition—readily identifiable characteristics that trigger a positive response in the justices as they skim through the cumbersome assemblage of legal documents. After all, people have their own particular cue theories as they go about their daily lives. Someone would not read through a four-page circular on a local store's white sale, for instance, if he or she already had an ample supply of bedding material. Just as people look for cues in sorting through the daily mail, so, too, do justices on the Supreme Court as they sort through the daily arrival of petitions for certiorari. At least this is what the research team reasoned.

The results of the team's hypotheses and investigations were encouraging. Of the several possible cues they tested for, three were found to contain substantial explanatory power. In order of importance they were (1) whether the U.S. government was a party to a case and was asking for Court review, (2) whether a civil rights or civil liberties issue was debated, and (3) whether there was dissension among the judges in the court that had previously heard the case (or disagreement between two or more courts and government agencies). If a case contained all three cues, there was an 80 percent chance that certiorari would be granted; if none were present, the chance dropped to a mere 7 percent. Clearly the researchers had developed a useful model to explain this one aspect of Supreme Court behavior.

During the past three decades judicial scholars have further tested, elaborated on, and revised cue theory. Some studies have found a relationship between the way the justices voted on a grant of certiorari and their eventual vote on the merits of the case at conference.[6] Additional studies have suggested that a fourth cue has considerable explanatory power—the ideological direction of the lower-court decision.[7] In comparing selected periods of the Warren Court (1967–68 and 1968–69 terms) and the Burger Court (1976–77 and 1977–78 terms) on certiorari voting, the analysts reached several conclusions. First, during the liberal Warren Court era, the justices were more likely to review economic cases that had been decided in a conservative manner by the lower court—especially when the U.S. government was seeking Court review.[8] Second, and conversely, the more conservative Burger Court tended to review liberal lower-court economic decisions. Third, the Burger Court was readier to scrutinize a civil libertarian position taken by a lower court than a lower-court decision limiting civil liberties.

A study of the first three terms of the Rehnquist Court reveals the presence of a new hybrid strategy for granting certiorari. Unlike the Warren and Burger Courts, the Rehnquist Court has not engaged in much "error correction" activity; that is, overturning lower-court decisions with which it disagrees. Instead, it has chosen to affirm a tremendous percentage of conservative lower-court decisions with which it is in ideological harmony, thereby underscoring the values inherent in these cases. It is also more likely to accept cases that concern issues on which lower-court judges had rendered conflicting decisions. The researchers conceded that they could only speculate as to why the Rehnquist Court had switched gears in this decision-making area.[9]

Cue theory, then, is one predictor of High Court voting behavior. One contemporary judicial scholar has summarized the certiorari behavior of the Court during the past several decades:

When the civil rights movement was building in importance (1950s), the Supreme Court, under the leadership of Chief Justice Earl Warren, paid special attention to cases involving civil liberties violations, and during the 1960s various underdog appellants, such as aliens, minorities, criminal defendants, laborers, and other have-nots, were more successful than others in getting *certiorari*. However, as the Supreme Court has shifted toward the conservatives, upperdogs such as governments at all levels and businesses have received more attention by the Supreme Court.[10]

Small-Group Analysis

As applied to the judiciary, most small-group research is based on the thesis that judges want to influence the judgments of their colleagues and to be on the winning side as often as possible. This school of thought assumes that judges' positions are not written in stone from the start but are susceptible to moderation or even to a 180-degree turn on occasion. More specifically, scholars believe that a good deal of interaction takes place among justices from the time a case is first discussed in conference to the moment the final decision is rendered in open court some weeks or months later. One researcher has referred to the appellate judges' openness to change as "fluidity."[11]

The way judges relate to one another affects their behavior on the court. Examination of the personal papers of members of the Supreme Court, interviews with appellate court jurists, and reminiscences of former law clerks all reveal the impact of group dynamics on voting behavior and on the content of written opinions.[12] Two characteristics in particular seem to carry weight when justices seek to influence their colleagues—personality and intellect. Judges who are considered to be warm, good-hearted, fair-minded, and so on seem able to put together winning coalitions and to hammer out compromises a bit more effectively than colleagues who have a reputation for condescension, self-righteousness, hostility, or vindictiveness.[13] As one researcher put it after interviewing supreme court justices in Louisiana, Massachusetts, New Jersey, and Pennsylvania:

Generally, the judges believed it is important for court members to moderate their own personal idiosyncrasies in order to maintain as much harmony in the group as possible. Such things as arrogance, pride, sense of superiority, and loss of temper were condemned. . . . A pleasing personality . . . can be particularly important on collegial courts because the judges interact on a continuous basis: they operate as a small, permanent committee.[14]

This reflection on human nature should come as no surprise. A student who had served on his university's multimember student court gave us an illustration of this phenomenon, and though a student tribunal is certainly not a state or federal appellate court, we think the dynamics are similar:

We had this guy on the court . . . who was one of these people that you just kind of naturally take to. I mean, he had a good sense of humor and was real decent and outgoing. I don't think he was that much of a "brain" or anything, but you always felt that he honestly wanted to do the right thing. Well, when we were split on some case—especially on matters of what punishment to hand down—and he suggested a way out, I think we all listened pretty carefully to what he thought was fair. He was just that sort of person.

The other personal attribute that is part of small-group dynamics is the knowledge and intellectual capacity of the individual judge.[15] A justice with a superior intellect or wide experience in a particular area of the law has a good deal more clout than a jurist who is seen as an intellectual lightweight. As one appeals court judge observed:

Personality doesn't amount to so much as opinion-writing ability. Some judges are simply better than others. Some know more, think better. It would be strange if among nine men all had the same ability. Some simply have more respect than others. . . . That's bound to be so in any group. The first thing, is the judge particularly broad and experienced in the field? A couple of judges are acknowledged masters in admiralty. What they think carries more weight. I don't have much trouble being heard on criminal law or state government. I've been there. Ex-district judges on Courts of Appeals certainly carry more weight in discussion of trial procedures, instructions to juries, etc. Every judge is recognized for a particular proficiency obtained before or after his appointment. It saves enormous spadework and drudgery [to assign opinions accordingly]. No one could develop an expertise in all these fields.[16]

The techniques or strategies that justices use in their conscious (or even unconscious) efforts to maximize their impact on multijudge courts can be grouped into three general categories: persuasion on the merits, bargaining, and threat of sanctions. Although the tactics overlap and are inherently interrelated, their central focuses are different.

Persuasion on the Merits

The persuasion on the merits strategy means that, because of their training and values, judges are open to persuasion based on sound legal reasoning bolstered by legal precedents. Unless judges have taken a hard-and-fast position from the start, most can be swayed by an articulate and well-reasoned argument from a colleague with a differing opinion.

One study of the Supreme Court concluded that the justices

can be persuaded to change their minds about specific cases as well as about broad public policies, and intellectual persuasion can play an important role in such shifts. . . . Time and time again positions first taken at conference are changed as other Justices bring up new arguments. Perhaps most convincing in demonstrating the impact of intellectual factors are the numerous instances on record in which the Justice assigned the opinion of the Court has reported back to the conference that additional study had convinced him that he and the rest of the majority had been in error.[17]

For example, Justice Robert Jackson, hardly a wilting violet when it came to holding fast to a judicial point of view, once commented: "I myself have changed my opinion after reading the opinions of the other members of this Court. And I am as stubborn as most. But I sometimes wind up not voting the way I voted in conference because the reasons of the majority didn't satisfy me."[18]

Judges on state appellate courts appear to be just as willing to have their positions altered by arguments seasoned by precedent and sound judicial reasoning. After interviews with supreme court justices in four states, one scholar observed:

When differences become evident, members of the court may attempt to persuade other judges to adopt their view by vigorously presenting their position or arguing the merits of their way of analyzing the case. Because of different amounts of influence exerted by the chief justice or by judges who have special personal status on the court, certain members of the court may be "persuaded" to abandon their own position and adopt the views of others.[19]

The persuasion on merits phenomenon cannot be pushed too far, however. If the facts and legal arguments are straightforward, a justice may not be open to change. And judges who are deeply committed to a specific point of view or whose egos are sufficiently great will probably be impervious to legal arguments inconsistent with their own views. For instance, Thurgood Marshall and (later in his career) Harry A. Blackmun were profoundly and morally opposed to the principle of capital punishment and often said so in their opinions. It is doubtful that any amount of legal reasoning or any calling up of "sacred precedents" could alter their belief that executions constitute "cruel and unusual punishment" by contemporary standards.

Bargaining

Bargaining may be a strange word to use in talking about the personal interactions of judges on collegial courts. When students first hear the term, they often think of the vote-trading technique called logrolling that legislators sometimes use. For example, one lawmaker might say to another, "If you vote for a new federal dam in my district, I'll vote to build a couple of new post offices in yours." Is this what happens with judges, too? Is there evidence that they sometimes say to one another, "If you vote for me in this case, I'll decide with you in one of your 'pet cases'"? No, there is virtually no such evidence. Bargaining does take place, but it is more subtle and does not involve vote swapping. Although some bargaining occurs in the give-and-take that goes on in conference, when the initial votes are taken, most attention is focused on the scope and contents of the majority (or even the dissenting) opinion. A recent study of the phenomenon concluded that "in 58.8% of [the cases studied] members of the majority conference coalition bargained with the opinion author" and that, in the authors' opinion, "our results therefore suggest that justices are indeed rational actors—systematically making judgments about the most efficacious tactic to secure favored outcomes."[20]

To understand how the bargaining process works, it is important to realize that usually much more is at stake in the outcome of a decision than merely whether party A or party B wins. Judges also have to discuss such questions as these: How broad should the decision be? Should they suggest in their written opinion that this case is unique, or should they open the gates and encourage other suits of this nature? Should they overturn what appears to be the controlling precedent or should they "distinguish around" it and let the precedent stand? Should they base their decision on constitutional grounds or should they allow the victor to win on more technical and restrictive grounds? In other words, most decisions at the appellate level are not zero-sum games in which the winner automatically takes all. Important supplementary issues almost always have to be talked about or bargained for.

Two landmark cases of the 1970s provide a good example. In 1973 the Supreme Court handed down a joint decision on the matter of abortion.[21] To most citizens the only issue the Court had to decide was whether abortion was legal. Although that may have been the bottom-line question, many other issues were at stake, and the bargaining over them among the majority justices was intense.[22] What is human life and when does it begin? Should the decision rest on the Ninth Amendment or should it be based on the due process clause of the Fourteenth Amendment? Does a fetus have any constitutional rights? Is it a greater health risk to a woman to have an abortion or to deliver a child after carrying it to full term? Can a woman decide to have an abortion on her own or does a physician have to concur? If the latter, how many doctors need concur? And this by no means completes the list.

For the abortion cases the justices spent over a year trying to hammer out a decision that would be acceptable to a majority. Draft opinions were sent around, altered, and changed again as the official opinion writer, Justice Harry Blackmun, tried to accommodate all views—or at least not to offend someone in the majority so strongly that he would join the dissenters. Bob Woodward and Scott Armstrong noted in *The Brethren: Inside the Supreme Court* that the law clerks "in most chambers were surprised to see the Justices, particularly Blackmun, so openly brokering their decision like a group of legislators."[23] But the law clerks themselves were not immune to the bargaining process. In the Supreme Court's cafeteria, law library, and gymnasium the clerks asked one another whether "your Justice" could go along with this or that compromise or related that "my Justice" would never support an opinion containing such and such an offensive clause.

Bargaining of this nature is just as common on state collegial courts as it is at the national level. This statement by one state supreme court justice is quoted by a scholar who regards it as typical:

You might say to another judge that if you take this line out, I'll go along with your opinion. You engage in a degree of compromise and if it doesn't hurt the point you're trying to make in an opinion, you ought to agree to take it out. . . . The men will write an opinion and circulate it. And then the other judges will write a letter or say at conference, can you change this or that, adjust the language here, etc. . . . Your object is to get a unanimous court. That's always best.[24]

In a significant portion of appellate court cases, then, bargaining is the name of the game—it is one way in which a group of jurists, in a unanimous or majority opinion, is able to present a united front. The author of one classic study that focused on the Supreme Court has observed:

For Justices, bargaining is a simple fact of life. Despite conflicting views on literary style, relevant precedents, procedural rules, and substantive policy, cases have to be settled and opinions written; and no opinion may carry the institutional label of the court unless five Justices agree to sign it. In the process of judicial decision-making, much bargaining may be tacit, but the pattern is still one of negotiation and accommodation to secure consensus. Thus how to bargain wisely—not necessarily sharply—is a prime consideration for a Justice who is anxious to see his policy adopted by the Court. A Justice must learn not only how to put pressure on his colleagues but how to gauge what amounts of pressure are sufficient to be "effective" and what amounts will overshoot the mark and alienate another judge. In many situations a Justice has to be willing to settle for less than he wants if he is to get anything at all. As [Louis] Brandeis once remarked, the "great difficulty of all group action, of course, is when and what concession to make."[25]

Appellate judges do most of their face-to-face bargaining at the three-judge conferences and then iron out the details of the opinion later, using the telephone and short memos. As with Supreme Court decision making, a threat to dissent can often result in changes in the way the majority opinion is drafted.

When a conservative minority sought to amend a middle-of-the-road compromise by which the 5th circuit achieved unanimity in the Mississippi school case, for example, a former legislator reportedly threatened to bolt to the left. "They came back into the fold in a hurry," a colleague remarked. "So you see, the judicial process is like legislation. All decisions are compromises."[26]

Threat of Sanctions

Besides persuasion on the merits and bargaining, there is one other tactic that jurists use in their efforts to maximize their impact on the multimember appellate tribunals—the threat of sanctions. Basically a judge or justice can invoke three sanctions against colleagues: the vote, the willingness to write a strong dissenting opinion, and the threat to "go public."

The Judge's Vote. The threat to take away one's vote from the majority, and thus dissent, may cause the majority to alter its views. For example, Justice Horace Gray in 1889 sent this message to Justice Samuel Miller:

After a careful reading of your opinion in *Shotwell v. Moore*, I am very sorry to be compelled to say that the first part of it . . . is so contrary to my conviction, that I fear, unless it can be a good deal tempered, I shall have to deliver a separate opinion on the lines of the enclosed memorandum. I am particularly troubled about this, because, if my scruples are not removed, and Justices [Stephen J.] Field, [Joseph P.] Bradley and [Lucius Q. C.] Lamar adhere to their dissent, your opinion will represent only four judges, half of those who took part in the case.[27]

His back against the wall because of his narrow majority, Justice Miller was obliged to yield to his colleague's costly "scruples."

For the most part the potential effect of a threat to dissent from the majority depends on how small that majority is. Thus if the initial vote among a three-judge appellate panel were three-to-zero, the threat of one member to dissent would not be all that serious; there would still be a two-to-one majority. Conversely, if at a preliminary Supreme Court conference there were a five-to-four vote, the threat by one of those five to defect would be of concern to the remaining four. At the end of the 1993–1994 term, Justice Anthony M. Kennedy had voted with the majority in thirteen of the Court's fourteen cases decided by a five-to-four vote. His support in close cases was likely much sought after.

The newly acquired judicial papers of Thurgood Marshall provide a colorful example of how pivotal one justice's vote can be. In January 1989 the Court decided to take the case of *Webster v. Reproductive Health Services*, which dealt with the constitutionality of Missouri's law that severely restricted abortions.[28] Many Court observers believed that a viable conservative majority on the Court could strike down the 1973 *Roe v. Wade* and *Doe v. Bolton* decisions that established the constitutional right to an abortion. Justice Marshall's informal tally sheet dated April 28 indicated five tentative initial votes to uphold the law: Justices William H. Rehnquist, Byron R. White, Antonin Scalia, Kennedy, and Sandra Day O'Connor. Rehnquist assigned the majority opinion to himself, and Justice Harry Blackmun penned a bitter dissent in which he said in part that the right to abortion "no longer survives."

"Over the course of two months, in flurries of court memos, the justices traded views and language. Throughout, O'Connor remained the pivotal swing vote. But she couldn't bring herself to join Rehnquist. Within days of the end of the term O'Connor changed her mind. She signaled her switch when she wrote that *Roe* was 'problematic,' rather than 'outmoded,' as she had said in an earlier draft."[29]

Still, "on June 27, Rehnquist circulated his fourth draft. The document still said, 'Chief Justice Rehnquist delivered the opinion of the Court,' traditional wording indicating that he had not given up his hopes of getting O'Connor's support. Then something definitive happened to the Rehnquist majority. On June 28, O'Connor and Blackmun submitted drafts referring to the Rehnquist opinion as a 'plurality,' rather than a majority."[30] The next day Rehnquist circulated his final draft in which, for the first time, he called his opinion the "judgment" of the Court instead of the majority opinion, meaning in effect that the Missouri law would be upheld but there would be no reversal of *Roe v. Wade.* This illustration shows vividly how important a single justice's vote can be when the Court is split evenly between one ideological camp and another.

Sometimes, however, the impact of one's vote is not merely a function of how divided the court is. On occasion the perceived need for unanimity may be so strong that any justice's threat to vote against the prevailing view may have a disproportionate effect. For example, prior to the 1954 *Brown v. Board of Education* decision, a majority on the Supreme Court opposed segregation in the schools. Chief Justice Earl Warren and the other liberals believed, though, that a simple majority was not enough to confront the backlash expected if segregation were struck down. Only a unanimous Court, they felt, could have any chance of seeing its will prevail throughout the nation. Therefore, the liberal majority bided its time during the early 1950s until the moment came when all nine justices were willing to take on the malignant giant of racial segregation.

A more recent example occurred when President Bill Clinton, former governor of Arkansas, wished to postpone the sexual harassment suit brought against him by former Arkansas state employee Paula Jones. He argued that the president should be immune from such troublesome and time-consuming litigation during his tenure in the White House. Otherwise, he and his attorneys argued, the chief executive would be plagued by scores of such suits brought by publicity-seeking troublemakers who would detract from his ability to devote his full time and energies to the task of governance. A district court judge rejected the president's motion to dismiss the case entirely, but the jurist did agree to postpone the case until the end of Clinton's presidency. Both parties were unhappy with the trial court's rulings and both appealed. A panel of the Eighth Circuit Court of Appeals ruled against the president in a split vote, and Clinton appealed to the U.S. Supreme Court.

The High Court's decision was unanimous, and it went against the president. Speaking for the majority, Justice John Paul Stevens said in part: "We think the District Court may have given undue weight to the concern that a trial might generate unrelated civil actions that could conceivably hamper the President in conducting the duties of his office. If and when that should occur, the court's discretion would permit it to manage those actions in such fashion (including deferral of trial) that interference with the President's duties would not occur. But no such impingement upon the President's conduct of his office was shown here."[31] Besides the importance of the decision itself, what is equally important is that the decision was unanimous; even the president's two Supreme Court appointees (Ruth Bader Ginsburg and Stephen G. Breyer) voted against him. A unanimous vote coming from the deeply divided Rehnquist Court underscored the legal principle involved in the case, and it quashed any notion that partisan politics was a variable in the decision. The defection of just a single vote, while not changing the outcome, would have detracted from the decisive impact of a totally unified court.

State judges, too, may feel the need for unanimity in certain types of cases. For example, one New Jersey Supreme Court justice told a researcher: "We did have a case where we felt a unanimous opinion was necessary. No one felt strongly about a dissent, so no dissents were made. . . . A religious case, for example, needs a unanimous decision. Courts don't try to be divisive on this." [32]

Thus although the impact of the threat to abandon the majority is usually in direct proportion to the closeness of the vote, occasions arise when a majority will pay top dollar to keep any judge or justice from breaking ranks. That is, the majority may accommodate the contents and scope of its majority opinion to suit the demands of the minority justices to get those justices to join the final opinion and make it unanimous.

The Willingness to Write a Strong Dissent.   There are dissents and there are dissents. Appellate court jurists who intend to vote against the majority must decide whether to write a lengthy, assertive dissenting opinion or merely to dissent without opinion. If jurists are not regarded by other justices—or by the public at large—as being prestigious or articulate, their threat to write a dissenting opinion may be taken with the proverbial grain of salt. If, however, potential dissenters are respected jurists with a reputation for a keen wit or for often being right in the long run, the situation is different. The other judges may be willing to alter their views to accommodate potential dissenters' positions or at least to dissuade them from attacking the majority position. As one Court observer has noted:

There are factors which push the majority Justices, especially the opinion writer, to accept accommodation. An eloquent, tightly-reasoned dissent can be an upsetting force. [Harlan F.] Stone's separate opinions during the thirties pointed up more sharply the folly of the conservative Justices than did any of the attacks on the Court by elected politicians. The majority may thus find it profitable to mute criticism from within the Court by giving in on some issues.[33]

Thus the second sanction—the threat to write a dissenting opinion—depends on the circumstances for its effectiveness. Sometimes it may be regarded as no more than a nuisance or the fruit of judicial egomania. On other occasions it may be viewed as likely to weaken the impact of the majority opinion.

In state courts the impact of a threat to author a strong dissent is smaller simply because dissents are more infrequent at that level. Consensus and unanimity are norms in most of the state appellate tribunals, whereas this is clearly not the case at the federal level. Since the 1943 term at least 50 percent of Supreme Court decisions have produced dissents. However, using data from the early to mid-1960s, researchers have found that fewer than ten state supreme courts produced dissents in 20 percent or more of their cases, and only the high courts in Michigan, New York, and Pennsylvania produced dissents at or above the 40 percent mark.[34]

Not all countries value the concept of dissenting opinions, which some regard as a threat to the concepts of legal clarity and national harmony. In these nations dissents are not published. Historical examples have been Italy and Switzerland, although anyone interested in how the Swiss judges voted would be free to attend the conferences and listen to what the judges said and watch how they voted. In Germany and Japan dissenting and concurring opinions by their constitutional court judges had at one time been strictly forbidden although by the early 1970s both nations began to adopt the American practice of publishing such opinions.[35]

The Threat to "Go Public." On rare occasions an appellate judge may use the ultimate weapon against colleagues—public exposure. Such strong medicine is usually administered only when a jurist believes a colleague (or a group of judges) has violated the basic rules of the game. The judge then threatens to hang out the dirty linen for all to see. For example, one appeals court judge told how, as a newcomer to the bench, he had threatened public exposure to force a senior colleague to withdraw an opinion filed without his consent, a possibility he had been warned against by another judge on the court: "It was my first sitting as a circuit judge," he recalled. "It was not a major case. But there was strong give and take!"[36]

In 1967 Judges John Danaher and Warren E. Burger (soon to be Chief Justice Burger) accused three of their appellate court colleagues of consciously attempting to foist on the Washington, D.C., Circuit a minority position on criminal procedures.[37] Ironically, some four years later it was Burger who was threatened with public exposure by a Supreme Court colleague who felt that Burger was trying to turn his minority status on a case into a majority position.

The incident occurred as follows. When the vote had been taken at conference on the abortion cases (*Roe v. Wade*, considered jointly with *Doe v. Bolton*), Chief Justice Burger was in the minority. According to Supreme Court practice, this would have meant that the senior member of the majority—in this case William O. Douglas—would have been assigned to speak for the Court. Ignoring Court protocol, Burger assigned the official opinion writing to his alter ego Harry Blackmun. This enraged Douglas. But the pot did not boil over until several months later when Burger lobbied from his minority status to have the case postponed until the next term. (Douglas wanted the decision to be handed down immediately.) These extracts from *The Brethren* capture something of the drama of the confrontation:

This time Douglas threatened to play his ace. If the conference insisted on putting the cases over for reargument, he would dissent from such an order, and he would publish the full text of his dissent. Douglas reiterated the protest he had made in December about the Chief's assigning the case to Blackmun, Burger's response and his subsequent intransigence. . . . Douglas . . . continued: "When, however, the minority seeks to control the assignment, there is a destructive force at work in the Court. When a Chief Justice tries to bend the Court to his will by manipulating assignments, the integrity of the institution is imperiled."

Douglas's pen then became more acid:

Borrowing a line from a speech he had given in September in Portland, Douglas then made it clear that, despite what he had said earlier, he did in fact view the Chief and Blackmun as Nixon's Minnesota Twins. "Russia once gave its Chief Justice two votes; but that was too strong even for the Russians."[38]

Douglas was ultimately prevailed upon to refrain from publishing this petulant opinion.

The threat to go public is probably a less potent weapon at the state level than it is for federal judges—particularly Supreme Court justices—because state appellate courts are generally much less visible to the general public except in the most unusual and controversial cases. Thus if a judge on a typical state appellate court threatened to go public and reveal to the populace some irregularity to which he or she had been subjected, the jurist might be told, "So, who cares?"

Despite the availability of several sanctions, they are usually invoked with varying degrees of hesitation—lest a judge or justice acquire a reputation for intransigence. For example, with regard to a justice's willingness to write a dissenting opinion, one perceptive scholar has noted:

Although dissent is a cherished part of the common law tradition, a Justice who persistently refuses to accommodate his views to those of his colleagues may come to be regarded as an obstructionist. A Justice whose dissents become levers for legislative or administrative action reversing judicial policies may come to be regarded as disloyal to the bench.[39]

Or, putting it in more human terms, one appeals court judge observed that "you have to keep on living with each other. In the next case the situations may be reversed."[40]

The Special Role of the U.S. Chief Justice, the U.S. Chief Judges, and State Supreme Court Chief Justices

The heads of the multijudge federal and state appellate tribunals have a number of special duties and responsibilities. Their respective roles constitute one more ingredient in the recipe for small-group interaction.

The Chief Justice of the United States.   The Constitution makes only passing reference to this official whose stature has come to loom so large in the eyes of the American people. Despite the constitutional slight, the chief justice can have considerable impact on the decision-making process. The key seems to be whether the chief justice possesses the capacity and the will to use the formal and informal powers that have accrued to the office during the past two centuries.

The chief justice's greatest potential for leadership is at the conference, where the cases are discussed and where the initial votes are taken among the justices. Because the chief has the primary responsibility for setting the agenda of the conference and traditionally is the first to offer an opinion about each case, the potential for influencing both the format and the tone of the deliberation is significant. David J. Danelski has identified two types of roles for justices at conference: social leader and task leader. The social leader "attends to the emotional needs of his associates by affirming their values as individuals and as Court members, especially when their views are rejected by the majority. Ordinarily he is the best liked member of the Court. . . . In terms of personality, he is apt to be warm, receptive and responsive." The task leader, however, is the intellectual force behind the conference deliberations, focusing on the final decision and trying to keep the Court consistent with itself. Danelski describes how the two roles complement each other:

As presiding officer of the conference, the Chief Justice is in a favorable position to assert task and social leadership. His presentation of cases is an important task function. His control of the conference's process makes it easy for him to invite suggestions and opinions, seek compromises, and cut off debate which appears to be getting out of hand, all important social functions.[41]

One observer, commenting on the transition from the Burger to the Rehnquist Court, has noted these differences in leadership styles:

Differences are already apparent during oral arguments. Rehnquist is sharper, more thoughtful, more commanding and wittier than his predecessor in the center chair. And from the far right of the bench, Scalia almost bubbles over with energy and questions for counsel. No less revealing is that in the week before the start of the 1986–87 term on the first Monday in October, Rehnquist managed to get the justices to dispose of over 1,000 cases (granting 22 and denying or otherwise disposing of the rest). He did so in only two days, whereas it usually took Burger more than twice as long to get through about the same number.[42]

Not only does Rehnquist seem to possess the task leadership skills that provide the intellectual stimulus of his chief justiceship, but evidence shows his social leadership skills as well. One study noted that

Mr. Rehnquist's consensus-building is aided by the more friendly and informal style he has imposed at the court, which is for many a stark and pleasing contrast with the stiff and formal manner of former Chief Justice Warren Burger. Observers say this comfortable style, along with a powerful intellect, has made Mr. Rehnquist far more influential at the high court than Mr. Burger ever was. "The fact that he is agreeable, affable, well-liked, low-keyed, has made him a more effective leader as the court begins to emerge with what looks to be a conservative working majority," says A. E. Dick Howard, a University of Virginia Law School professor.[43]

In the past the chief justice has also had a key role in setting up what is called the discuss list—special petitions selected out of the many to which the Court will give full consideration. The chief's law clerks helped with this task, but the chief guided their judgment. In the Burger and Rehnquist Courts the chief justice played much less of a role in establishing the discuss list. At the present time a majority of the justices pool their law clerks and give a single clerk the authority to summarize a particular petition for all the justices who participate in the pool. However, not all members of the Court participate in this practice—for example, the moderately liberal Justice Stevens has his clerks screen all petitions and write memos only on those they deem important enough for him to consider. Whether the chief justice chooses to play a major or minor role in this process, the activity is important because it determines which cases the Court will consider as a group and which are to be summarily dismissed.[44]

The final power of the chief justice is the assignment of opinions; that is, designation of who will write the official decision of the Court.[45] This task falls to the chief justice only if he is in the majority when the vote on a case is taken at conference; otherwise the most senior justice in the majority selects the opinion writer. The chief justice has the greatest control over an opinion when he assigns it to himself, and traditionally he has retained many important cases for that reason.[46] In such cases as *Marbury v. Madison, Brown v. Board of Education,* and *United States v. Nixon,* the chief justice used his option to speak as the official voice of the Court.

The chief justice who chooses not to write the opinion may assign it to that member of the majority whose views are closest to the dissenters', with the hope that some of the minority may subsequently switch their votes to the majority view.[47] Or, as has most often been the case in recent decades, the chief justice will assign the opinion to an ideological alter ego so that the grounds for the decision will be favorable to his own. A 1996 study of opinion assignments made by Chief Justice Rehnquist indicated that he has utilized this power for institutional rather than policy reasons. For example, he has had an eye for evenly distributing the workload and for assigning opinions to justices who have an expertise in the subject matter of the case. He has not been motivated as keenly as other chief justices to assigning opinions to those whose ideologies are closest to his own. The authors of this study concluded: "Our model suggests that each justice's efficiency, expertise, and the number of majority opinion assignments by other justices—and not ideological compatibility—are the factors that shape Rehnquist's decisions. The only instance where Rehnquist demonstrates a bias related to ideology is when the initial majority coalition cannot afford to lose a single vote."[48]

Determining who will speak for the court has policy-making implications in other countries as well. For example, in a comprehensive study of the Supreme Court in India, one author noted that the person chosen to write the Court's opinion has an inordinate capacity for influencing public policy. He then adds: "This is especially true if the chief justice subscribes to that particular philosophy, and continues to appoint the same justice(s) to hear a certain type of case."[49]

Despite the considerable influence that a chief justice may have on the Court's small group, the crucial factor seems to be whether the chief has both the capacity and the desire to exert such potential authority. For example, the first great chief justice, John Marshall, possessed both these traits, and they helped fill the intellectual vacuum of the Court during the early 1800s:

Marshall, like the majority of justices in the court's history, was an experienced politician. . . . He guided the Court in a series of sweeping decisions . . . through force of personality and a talent for negotiation. Justice William Johnson, a Jefferson appointee, grumbled to his patron about Marshall's dominance. Wondering why Marshall invariably wrote the Court's opinions, Johnson reported to Jefferson that he had "found out the real cause. [William] Cushing was incompetent. [Samuel] Chase could not be got to think or write. [William] Paterson was a slow man and willingly declined trouble, and the other two judges [Marshall and Bushrod Washington] you know are commonly estimated as one judge."[50]

Although John Marshall had the skill and the desire to influence the Court, not all of his successors possessed these traits. For instance, the nation's chief justice between 1941 and 1946, Harlan Fiske Stone, had neither the talent nor the will for either task leadership or social leadership. As his biographer sadly wrote of him, "He was totally unprepared to cope with the petty bickering and personal conflict in which his court became engulfed."[51]

The Chief Judges of the U.S. Appeals Courts   As with the chief justice, the leadership potential of the administrative circuit heads is determined, in part, by their intellectual and negotiating skills and by their desire to put them to use. In reality, however, their potential effect on their respective circuits is probably less than the potential impact of the chief justice on the Supreme Court. First, because most appellate court decisions are made by three-judge panels on a rotating basis, the chief judge is not likely even to be a part of most circuit decision making. Second, the circuits are more decentralized than the Supreme Court. Finally, the chief judge is not nearly so prominent a figure in the eyes of the public or of other government decision makers. As one former chief judge said about the job: "The only advantage is that the title sounds more imposing if you are speaking in public or writing an article. Otherwise it's a pain in the ass."[52]

Much of a chief judge's work is administrative (such as docketing cases, keeping financial records, adjusting the caseloads), but administration and policy making are not mutually exclusive endeavors. The chief judge of the former U.S. Fifth Circuit once acknowledged: "So many times judicial problems slop over into administrative problems and vice versa" that the real questions are when and where this effect occurs. Commenting on the influence of the chief judges, one observer has said:

As with strong presidents [or as with strong chief justices, he might have added] . . . the spillover depends on the personality of the chief and the countervailing force of experienced colleagues. The impact of chief judges was most noticeable on freshmen and the composition of three-judge district courts. ("If all the judges are new, he'll pack a wallop out of proportion to one vote.") Southern judges made no bones about packing three-judge district courts in race relations cases. ([The liberal] "[Elbert P.] Tuttle was not about to set up a three-judge court with [segregationists such as Benjamin F.] Cameron and [William H.] Cox on it; this occurs no more.") Of all administrative powers, plainly the most potent instruments of policy leadership involve the assignment of work.[53]

The State Supreme Court Chief Justices.   To some extent the powers and leadership potential of state chief justices mirror those of the U.S. chief justice, but significant differences also exist, between the federal and state levels as well as from one state to another. At the national level, the chief justice is appointed by the president with the advice and consent of the Senate. In some states—Michigan, for example—the chief justice is chosen by fellow associate justices; in Texas and Ohio the chief justices are elected directly by the people.

The states also differ in regard to whether the chief justice has the most power in the assignment of opinions. Only four states, including Hawaii, follow closely the opinion assignment practice of the U.S. Supreme Court. In more than a quarter of the states the chief justice assigns opinions in all cases, whether he or she is in the majority or not.[54] Well over half of the states use an automatic method of opinion assignment whereby a justice either draws cases by lot or, more often, receives them by rotation. In less than half of the twenty states that use the rotating system, the assignments hold only if the justice to whom the case is assigned is in the majority.

On the effectiveness of the chief justice under the different opinion assignment methods, one scholar has concluded:

A chief justice who is an extraordinary leader can make the court perform more effectively and efficiently by using selective opinion assignment. A court without an extraordinary leader may be better served by a rotational method of assignment. . . . Nondiscretionary methods best maintain social cohesion, but the chief justice's discretion in assigning opinions can best accomplish the efficient disposition of the workload.[55]

As with the U.S. chief justice, however, nothing inherent in the office guarantees that a chief justice will be an active and effective leader. Intellect, personality, political skills, and a fair degree of happenstance still interact and blend in mysterious ways to create chief justices whom court watchers term either "great" or "ineffectual." On the positive side, there have been people such as Arthur Vanderbilt, who became chief justice of the New Jersey Supreme Court in 1948. As one scholar observed of him:

Once installed as chief justice . . . he had to contend with a set of judges who had served under the old constitution and did not fully share either his vision or his aims. Nevertheless, Vanderbilt provided impetus and direction to the movement for judicial reform in the state, and, as chief justice, he secured the gains of the reform movement, gave the court stature, and ensured it the independence it needed to play a major role in the governance of the state. Despite the obvious differences, the comparison that springs to mind is with John Marshall, who—like Vanderbilt—assumed the leadership of a relatively moribund court and transformed it.[56]

Likewise one can point to Howell Heflin, chief justice of the Alabama Supreme Court, whose dynamic leadership and political skills during the 1970s brought about much-needed judicial reforms in the state and effective leadership on the court.[57]

On the negative side, many examples can be cited of persons who came to the state high court bench with great potential but who lacked the ability or the political savvy (and perhaps the luck) to provide leadership when confronted by opposition or political lethargy. For instance, when Frank D. Celebrezze headed the Ohio Supreme Court during the early 1980s, he blatantly politicized the court until he was driven from office by the voters in the 1986 election. One observer summarized the unhappy period of his chief justiceship:

> Squabbles on the Celebrezze court were important because, owing to the Celebrezze agenda, the court was important. The irony of Celebrezze's stewardship is that as his court attained prominence, his actions, so visible on so many fronts, brought the court as an institution into disrepute. During [Celebrezze's term as chief justice] Ohioans perceived their court as a "circus." [58]

Evidence of Small-Group Interaction

We have argued that small-group dynamics include persuasion on the merits between individual judges, bargaining among the appellate jurists, and the threat of sanctions—a judge changing his or her vote, a willingness to write a strong dissent, and (at least for federal judges) the threat to go public. We have also contended that supreme court chief justices and chief judges of the appeals courts can potentially affect the decision making of their respective small judicial groups. The evidence we have cited for this so far has largely been anecdotal or subjective, but some more rigorous empirical data are available to back up our arguments.

One study compared U.S. Supreme Court justices' initial votes at conference with the final votes as they appeared in the published reports for the years 1946 to 1956.[59] Any change in the two sets of votes was attributed to small-group interaction. The findings reveal several things. First, there were vote changes in about 60 percent of all cases. Most of these changes occurred when a justice who had not participated in the first vote or who had been a dissenter opted to join the majority position.

But when one considers all votes for all cases, the justices changed positions only 9 percent of the time. In such instances of vote change, the initial majority position lost out in only 14 percent of the cases. A study of conference and final votes underestimates the extent of small-group interaction, because plenty of such interaction takes place prior to the initial conference vote.[60] The most recent study of fluidity on the Supreme Court not only confirmed that it is an ongoing phenomenon, but also revealed that most of the vote changes stem from justices who move from the minority to the majority positions rather than vice versa. The authors of the study suggested that "the majority opinion author has little incentive to be responsive to the suggestions of a dissenter. Since the majority opinion becomes the law of the land, justices who wish to shape the law have an incentive to be part of the majority. Consistent with this theory is the fact that justices who initially voted with the majority switched only 4.6% of the time, and justices who initially dissented switched 18.1% of the time."[61]

Many other empirical studies that deal with the federal appeals courts and with state supreme courts likewise suggest the importance of small-group dynamics as a factor in judicial decision making.[62]

Although how many final outcomes are determined by small-group dynamics is unclear, they are a major factor in the drawing up of the majority opinion and in setting forth its perimeters and corollaries. Scholars still lack a precise measure of the impact of small-group interaction, but it seems fair to say that it is considerable. Attempts to be more precise—both theoretically and empirically—about the output of appellate court decision making have resulted in the development of several analytic approaches that have attempted to explain and analyze this phenomenon with greater and more quantifiable precision. The first and primary of these is attitude theory, and the others are variations of what is called the rational choice model.

Attitude Theory

Many judicial scholars have been dissatisfied with small-group analysis, arguing that the fruits of such exploration are barely worth their efforts. Although not denying that personal interactions make a difference in some cases and perhaps play a key role in a handful of decisions, they contend that the richest ore for explaining judicial behavior can be found in other mines. A decision-making model that claims greater explanatory power deals with the discovery of the justices' basic, judicially relevant attitudes and with the coalitions, or blocs, formed by jurists who share similar attitudes.[63] This approach rests on the assumption that judges—particularly appellate jurists—view cases primarily in terms of the broad political and socioeconomic issues they raise and that they generally respond to these issues in accordance with their own personal values and attitudes. The official reasons the justices give for their decisions (found in their published opinions) are regarded as mere rationalizations. For example, suppose that Judge X strongly believes that the government should never tamper with freedom of the press. If a case comes before the court in which censorship is the central issue, then Judge X will go with his convictions and vote on the side of the news media. His written opinion may be full of impressive legal citations, quotations from eminent law reviews, or lofty discussions of the importance for democracy of a maximum of freedom of expression. But all this, the attitude scholars contend, is only a rationalization after the fact. The real reason for Judge X's vote was that he strongly dislikes the concept of government censorship.

The attitude theorists do not claim that their decision-making models explain everything, and they do not deny that judges must often decide cases against the grain of their personal values. For instance, a justice may be a strong environmentalist, but if a pro-environment petitioner has absolutely no standing to sue, the justice is unlikely to yield to the tug of the heart. Nevertheless, supporters of the judicial attitude approach contend that it can explain a significant portion of judicial behavior and that it is well worth the research time and effort that such studies require.

Specific questions about this approach arise: Where do judicial attitudes originate? How does one learn about a judge's attitudes? What are some of the limitations of the attitudinal model?

First, appellate jurists acquire their relevant attitudes from the same sources that people in general do—from parents and friends, from educational institutions, from the media, from political activities, and so on. Thus, an overlap clearly exists between the attitude theorists and those who study judicial background characteristics. The difference is that the latter want to know from what source the justices acquire their values, whereas the former concentrate on measuring the effects of judges' values—regardless of their origin—on collegial decision making. The attitude scholars acknowledge that some beliefs change during a jurist's tenure on the bench, but still they postulate "that attitudes are 'relatively enduring.' " [64]

Second, judges unfortunately have shown no willingness to answer the sort of in-depth questionnaires that might reveal judicially significant attitudes—particularly on matters that relate to issues that may come before them in court. Likewise judges are reluctant to give speeches, grant interviews, or write articles that bare their judicial souls. Judges consider such behavior inappropriate, and many resist making it easy for reporters and social scientists to suggest a link between their personal values and the way they decide cases.

Third, one criticism of this approach has focused on the source of the attitude theorists' data: the contents of the written opinions that are used to categorize judges' primary values. A justice who writes a strong opinion attacking government interference with the free operation of the marketplace is said to have a conservative economic attitude. This sort of approach has opened the researchers to the charge that they have created a tautology: A justice writes several conservative economic opinions, is classified as an economic conservative, and, lo and behold, aggregate analysis of his or her voting patterns reveals that the judge is a conservative on economic issues. Such theorists respond that this criticism is unfair because the patterns they have uncovered have proved to be consistent over time and susceptible to duplication by other researchers using similar methodologies. Furthermore, the best and most recent study based on attitude theory successfully formulated and applied three separate and independent ways in which to eliminate the circular reasoning problem: using facts derived from lower court records of cases decided by the U.S. Supreme Court, conducting content analysis of editorials appearing in publications prior to a justice's confirmation, and employing the justices' prior voting behavior as a predictor of votes in subsequent cases.[65]

Another shortcoming is that the attitudinal model has not been used successfully to explain and predict lower court behavior, and some scholars have even argued that the model is inherently inapplicable to trial judge decision making.[66] As the dean of the attitudinal model, Professor Harold Spaeth, acknowledges,

Lower courts do operate in an environment distinctly different from that of the Supreme Court. These differences may cause lower-court judges to decide on bases other than their personal policy preferences. They may be electorally accountable and as a result render decisions that enhance their reelection. Others may seek higher positions—either inside or outside the judiciary—and color their decisions accordingly. Most courts are subject to appellate review. Judges thereon may decide according to their superiors' dictates rather than their own preferences. And with the exception of some state supreme courts, judges do not have control of their dockets as the justices do. Hence, their decision making may involve run-of-the-mill litigation in which policy matters are either absent or not amenable to discretion because a jury decides or because matters are open and shut.[67]

The fact that attitude theory may be timebound is another criticism that its supporters concede. Virtually all research has focused on recent decades instead of the past, and during many periods in the Supreme Court's history the vast majority of all decisions were unanimous, and thus there would be no variance to measure or explain. Finally, critics of attitude theory note that it has been applied only to the justice's final vote—the one specified in the reports of the Court's decisions. Its thrust thus misses the important matters of coalition formation and opinion writing.

Despite these limitations, attitude theory is still regarded by most judicial behavioralists as the most elegant and persuasive model for predicting appellate judge behavior. Students of foreign collegial court systems have used it effectively to explain decision making on these tribunals. For example, a recent study of voting on search and seizure cases by justices on the Canadian Supreme Court found that the attitudinal model "correctly predicts 77 percent of the judicial decisions, providing a 25 percent improvement . . . over the null model. More important, many of the same factual variables that prove significant in the U.S. cases are significant in Canada as well." The researchers further concluded that Canadian "justices [as their American counterparts] rely on the predisposed attitudes they have toward particular factual circumstances to guide their decisions."[68] And earlier studies using the attitudinal model found it highly instructive in explaining the voting patterns of justices in countries as diverse as Australia, Canada, India, Japan, and the Philippines.[69]

Rational Choice Theory

The rational choice model by no means rejects the basic assumptions of attitude theory. Rational choice theorists generally agree that appellate court jurists are primarily motivated by their personal, deeply felt attitudes about public policy and vote accordingly in their judicial decisions. But the rational choice school contends that there is more to it than that, and that the attitudinal position is somewhat simplistic and shortsighted. They contend that goal-directed justices operate in what they term "strategic" or "inter-dependent decision-making contexts." The justices realize that the fate of their policy goals often depends on the values of other decision makers, such as their colleagues on the bench, the president, and members of Congress. The justices must often then include in their calculus not only what they personally want as a case outcome but also how such an outcome might be affected by the decisions of these other actors. As two key scholars associated with the rational choice approach put it:

"If justices are 'single-minded seekers of legal policy' [as the attitude theorists contend], would those justices not care about the ultimate state of that policy? To rephrase the question, why would justices who are policy maximizers take a position they know Congress would overturn? To argue that justices would do this—merely vote their attitudes—is to argue that the Court is full of myopic thinkers, who consider only the shape of policy in the short term. It is also to argue that justices do not consider the preferences of other political actors and the actions they expect others to take when they make their decisions and simply respond to stimuli before them. Such a picture does not square with much important writing about the Court . . . or with the way many social scientists now believe that political actors make decisions."[70]

And these and other scholars have found empirical evidence to support the basic tenets of the rational choice approach.[71]

As with all explanatory models, there are variations on a theme, and rational choice is no exception. Some exponents of this model argue, for example, that when it comes to congressional responses to Supreme Court decisions, the justices do more than merely act to minimize the possibility of a conflict with Congress (which might result in a congressional override of the Court's decision). These theorists note that the Court often calls for and invites congressional action to help secure the policy goals that the justices desire. One study found clear evidence of this phenomenon and concluded that:

> Our most striking finding concerned the ideological position of the justices who joined in the Court's majority opinion. The strong statistical impact of this variable suggests that one motivation for invitations to override is a concern with achieving both good law and good policy. More specifically, one response to a perceived conflict between the two is for justices to follow the law as they see it while asking Congress to supplant their choice with good policy as they see it.[72]

Rational choice theory, then, is not a rejection of the attitudinal model but argues that attitude theorists are too narrow in their approach. The rational choice school suggests that justices often consider in their decision making the possible responses of other political actors—sometimes even going so far as to invite some of these other actors to modify or supplement the High Court's decisions.

Summary

We began this chapter with the observation that decision making by judges on collegial appellate courts is in some key ways different from decision making by judges acting alone on trial benches. Because of these differences scholars have devised theories and research techniques to capture the special reality of decision making by jurists on federal and state multijudge appellate courts. We took a close look at the discretionary review process of the Supreme Court and noted that the issues it decides not to rule on are often as substantively important as those cases it selects for full review. In this context we discussed the importance of cue theory— the attempt by scholars to learn the characteristics of those few cases chosen from the many for Supreme Court consideration.

We then focused on several separate theoretical approaches to explain the decision making of multijudge courts: small-group analysis, attitude theory, and the rational choice model. (In our discussion we often noted the similarity of patterns between United States courts and those of other countries and also those instances where the American experiences seem to be unique.) Each of these theoretical models has its own working assumptions and research techniques that are used to glean the explanatory data. Although it is tempting to speculate on which of these several approaches provides the best insights into appellate court behavior, it is probably fairest to say that the jury of judicial scholars is still out. An increasing belief in recent years has been that models representing a combination of these and other approaches provide much greater explanatory power than any of them taken alone.[73]

NOTES

1. From an interview with an appeals court judge as quoted in J. Woodford Howard Jr., *Courts of Appeals in the Federal Judicial System* (Princeton, N.J.: Princeton University Press, 1981), 135.

2. However, for a discussion of the causes of dissent in state supreme courts and of how such causes may differ from those at the federal level, see Paul Brace and Melinda Gann Hall, "Neo-Institutionalism and Dissent in State Supreme Courts," *Journal of Politics* 52 (1990): 54–70.

3. Alabama, for example, imposes a burdensome original jurisdiction on its Supreme Court, and Arizona requires its high court to hear appeals in a wide variety of cases. However, Florida has given its Supreme Court broad discretion in case selection. See G. Alan Tarr and Mary Cornelia Aldis Porter, *State Supreme Courts in State and Nation* (New Haven, Conn.: Yale University Press, 1988), 49.

4. For a good discussion of the workings of the European Court of Justice, see Sally J. Kenney, "The European Court of Justice: Integrating Europe through Law," *Judicature* 81 (1998): 250–255.

5. Joseph Tanenhaus, Marvin Schick, Matthew Muraskin, and Daniel Rosen, "The Supreme Court's Certiorari Jurisdiction: Cue Theory," in *Judicial Decision-Making*, ed. Glendon Schubert (New York: Free Press, 1963), 111–132.

6. See, for example, S. Sidney Ulmer, "The Decision to Grant Certiorari as an Indicator to Decision 'On the Merits,' " *Polity* 4 (1972): 429–447. Nevertheless, in a later study Ulmer found that despite the inordinate willingness of the High Court to hear cases brought by the U.S. government, such willingness did not translate into subsequent support for the government's position—at least in civil liberties cases. See S. Sidney Ulmer, "Governmental Litigants, Underdogs, and Civil Liberties in the Supreme Court: 1903–1968 Terms," *Journal of Politics* 47 (1985): 899–909.

7. See, for example, Donald R. Songer, "Concern for Policy Outputs as a Cue for Supreme Court Decisions on Certiorari," *Journal of Politics* 41 (1979): 1185–1194; and S. Sidney Ulmer, "Selecting Cases for Supreme Court Review: An Underdog Model," *American Political Science Review* 72 (1978): 902–910.

8. Virginia C. Armstrong and Charles A. Johnson, "Certiorari Decisions by the Warren and Burger Courts: Is Cue Theory Time Bound?" *Polity* 15 (1982): 141–150.

9. Jeffrey A. Segal and Harold J. Spaeth, "Rehnquist Court Disposition of Lower Court Decisions: Affirmation Not Reversal," *Judicature* 74 (1990): 84–88.

10. Henry R. Glick, *Courts, Politics, and Justice*, 3d ed. (New York: McGraw-Hill, 1993), 280.

11. J. Woodford Howard Jr., "On the Fluidity of Judicial Choice," *American Political Science Review* 62 (1968): 43–57.

12. See, for example, Walter F. Murphy, *Elements of Judicial Strategy* (Chicago: University of Chicago Press, 1964); Bob Woodward and Scott Armstrong, *The Brethren: Inside the Supreme Court* (New York: Simon and Schuster, 1979); Howard, *Courts of Appeals in the Federal Judicial System*; and Alpheus T. Mason, *Harlan Fiske Stone: Pillar of the Law* (New York: Viking, 1956).

13. In the parlance of judicial scholars, this is referred to as the social leadership function. See David J. Danelski, "The Influence of the Chief Justice in the Decisional Process," in *Courts, Judges, and Politics*, 3d ed., ed. Walter F. Murphy and C. Herman Pritchett (New York: Random House, 1979), 695–703. For an empirical analysis of the phenomena discussed by Danelski, see Stacia L. Haynie, "Leadership and Consensus on the U.S. Supreme Court," *Journal of Politics* 54 (1992): 1158–1169.

14. Henry Robert Glick, *Supreme Courts in State Politics* (New York: Basic Books, 1971), 59.

15. This is termed the task leadership function. See Danelski, "The Influence of the Chief Justice in the Decisional Process."

16. Howard, *Courts of Appeals in the Federal Judicial System*, 230–231.

17. Murphy, *Elements of Judicial Strategy*, 44.

18. As quoted in ibid.

19. Glick, *Supreme Courts in State Politics*, 89.

20. James F. Spriggs II, Forest Maltzman, and Paul J. Wahlbeck, "Bargaining on the U.S. Supreme Court: Justices' Responses to Majority Opinion Drafts," *Journal of Politics* 61 (1999): 503.

21. *Roe v. Wade*, 410 U.S. 113 (1973); and *Doe v. Bolton*, 410 U.S. 179 (1973).

22. Woodward and Armstrong, *The Brethren*, chaps. entitled "1971 Term" and "1972 Term."

23. Ibid., 233.

24. Glick, *Supreme Courts in State Politics*, 66.

25. Murphy, *Elements of Judicial Strategy*, 57.

26. Howard, *Courts of Appeals in the Federal Judicial System*, 209.

27. As quoted in Charles Fairman, *Mr. Justice Miller and the Supreme Court, 1862–1890* (Cambridge, Mass.: Harvard University Press, 1939), 320.

28. *Webster v. Reproductive Health Services*, 492 U.S. 490 (1989).

29. David A. Kaplan, "A Legacy of Strife: Marshall's Papers Shed Light on the Court—and the Library of Congress," *Newsweek*, June 7, 1993, 69.

30. Benjamin Weiser and Bob Woodward, "Roe Decision Nearly Overturned 4 Years Ago, Justice's Files Show," *Houston Chronicle*, May 24, 1993, A2.

31. *Clinton v. Jones*, 520 U.S. 681 (1997).

32. Henry Robert Glick and Kenneth N. Vines, *State Court Systems* (Englewood Cliffs, N.J.: Prentice-Hall, 1973), 79.

33. Murphy, *Elements of Judicial Strategy*, 63–64.

34. Henry R. Glick and George W. Pruet Jr., "Dissent in State Supreme Courts: Patterns and Correlates of Conflict," in *Judicial Conflict and Consensus: Behavioral Studies of American Appellate Courts*, ed. Sheldon Goldman and Charles M. Lamb (Lexington: University Press of Kentucky, 1986), 200.

35. Walter F. Murphy and Joseph Tanenhaus, *The Study of Public Law* (New York: Random House, 1972): 152–153.

36. As quoted in Howard, *Courts of Appeals in the Federal Judicial System*, 209.

37. *Ross v. Sirica*, 380 F.2d 557 (D.C. Cir. 1967).

38. Woodward and Armstrong, *The Brethren*, 187, 188.

39. Murphy, *Elements of Judicial Strategy*, 61.

40. As quoted in Howard, *Courts of Appeals in the Federal Judicial System*, 209.

41. Danelski, "The Influence of the Chief Justice in the Decisional Process," 696.

42. David M. O'Brien, "The Supreme Court: From Warren to Burger to Rehnquist," *PS* 20 (1987): 12.

43. Stephen Wermiel, "Consensus Builder: Rehnquist Emerges as a Skillful Leader of the Court's Majority," *Wall Street Journal*, June 29, 1989, A1.

44. For an excellent discussion of research findings about the discuss list and the U.S. Supreme Court, see Gregory A. Caldeira and John R. Wright, "The Discuss List: Agenda Building in the Supreme Court," *Law and Society Review* 24 (1990): 809–836.

45. For an excellent discussion of this subject, see David W. Rohde and Harold J. Spaeth, *Supreme Court Decision Making* (San Francisco: Freeman, 1976), chap. 8.

46. Lee Epstein and Jeffrey A. Segal, "Measuring Issue Salience," *American Journal of Political Science* 44 (2000): 66–83.

47. However, some research has challenged the "conventional wisdom . . . that assignment of the majority opinion to the marginal member of the minimum winning original coalition might ensure its survival." In a study of the Warren Court the researchers found that "although the marginal justice is substantially advantaged in opinion assignment, coalition maintenance is not thereby enhanced." Saul Brenner and Harold J. Spaeth, "Majority Opinion Assignments and the Maintenance of the Original Coalition on the Warren Court," *American Journal of Political Science* 32 (1988): 72–81. See also Saul Brenner, "Reassigning the Majority Opinion on the United States Supreme Court," *Justice System Journal* 11 (1986): 186–195.

48. Forrest Maltzman and Paul J. Wahlbeck, "May It Please the Chief? Opinion Assignments in the Rehnquist Court," *American Journal of Political Science* 40 (1996): 438.

49. Robert Moog, "Activism on the Indian Supreme Court," *Judicature* 82 (1998): 128.

50. Donald Dale Jackson, *Judges* (New York: Atheneum, 1974), 329.

51. As quoted in Danelski, "The Influence of the Chief Justice in the Decisional Process," 698. For a good discussion of the importance of Harlan F. Stone's leadership style as it affected future chief justiceships, see Thomas G. Walker, Lee Epstein, and William J. Dixon, "On the Mysterious Demise of Consensual Norms in the United States Supreme Court," *Journal of Politics* 50 (1988): 361–389.

52. As quoted in Howard, *Courts of Appeals in the Federal Judicial System*, 228.

53. Ibid., 229. In a few instances the chief judges have been accused of stacking the three-judge panels, which are supposed to operate on a more or less random, rotational basis. For example, see *Armstrong v. Bd. of Educ. of Birmingham*, 323 F.2d 333, 352–361 (5th Cir. 1963); 48 F.R.D. 141, 182 (1969). See also Burton M. Atkins and William Zavoina, "Judicial Leadership on the Court of Appeals: A Probability Analysis of Panel Assignment in Race Relations Cases on the Fifth Circuit," *American Journal of Political Science* 18 (1974): 701–711.

54. Victor E. Flango, Craig R. Ducat, and R. Neal McKnight, "Measuring Leadership through Opinion Assignments in Two State Supreme Courts," in Goldman and Lamb, eds., *Judicial Conflict and Consensus*, 217.

55. Ibid., 218–219.

56. Tarr and Porter, *State Supreme Courts in State and Nation*, 186.

57. Ibid., chap. 3.

58. Ibid., 148. For all the details, see chap. 4.

59. Saul Brenner, "Fluidity on the United States Supreme Court: A Reexamination," *American Journal of Political Science* 24 (1980): 526–535.

60. For a more recent article on this subject, and one that addresses some aspects not included in Brenner's earlier article, see Robert H. Dorff and Saul Brenner, "Conformity Voting on the United States Supreme Court," *Journal of Politics* 54 (1992): 762–775.

61. Forrest Maltzman and Paul J. Wahlbeck, "Strategic Policy Considerations and Voting Fluidity on the Burger Court," *American Political Science Review* 90 (1996): 590–591.

62. For example, see Goldman and Lamb, *Judicial Conflict and Consensus*, pts. 2 and 3; and Glick, *Supreme Courts in State Politics*.

63. For the best statement of attitude theory, along with an excellent summary of the relevant litera-ture, see Jeffrey A. Segal and Harold J. Spaeth, *The Supreme Court and the Attitudinal Model* (New York: Cambridge University Press, 1993). For a sophisticated and up-to-date debate among judicial scholars about the utility of various forms of attitudinal models, see the first six articles in *American Journal of Po-litical Science* 40 (1996): 971–1083.

64. Rohde and Spaeth, *Supreme Court Decision Making*, 75.

65. Segal and Spaeth, *The Supreme Court and the Attitudinal Model*.

66. C. K. Rowland and Robert A. Carp, *Politics & Judgment in Federal District Courts* (Lawrence, Kansas: University Press of Kansas, 1996), especially chaps. 6 and 7.

67. Harold J. Spaeth, "The Attitudinal Model," in *Contemplating Courts*, ed. Lee Epstein (Washington, D.C.: Congressional Quarterly, 1995), 313.

68. Matthew E. Wetstein and C. L. Ostberg, "Search and Seizure Cases in the Supreme Court of Cana-da: Extending an American Model of Judicial Decision Making across Countries," *Social Science Quarterly* 80 (1999): 757, 770.

69. Glendon Schubert and David J. Danelski, eds., *Comparative Judicial Behavior: Cross-Cultural Stud-ies of Political Decision-Making in the East and West* (New York: Oxford University Press, 1969).

70. Lee Epstein and Thomas G. Walker, "The Role of the Supreme Court in American Society: Playing the Reconstruction Game," in *Contemplating Courts*. ed. Lee Epstein (Washington, D.C.: Congressional Quarterly, 1995), 322.

71. For example, see Lee Epstein and Jack Knight, *The Choices Judges Make* (Washington, D.C.: Con-gressional Quarterly, 1998).

72. Lori Hausegger and Lawrence Baum, "Inviting Congressional Action: A Study of Supreme Court Motivations in Statutory Interpretation," *American Journal of Political Science* 43 (1999): 182.

73. For examples of these combined or integrated approaches, see Donald R. Songer and Susan Haire, "Integrating Alternative Approaches to the Study of Judicial Voting: Obscenity Cases in the U.S. Courts of Appeals," *American Journal of Political Science* 36 (1992): 963–982; Paul Brace and Melinda Gann Hall, "Integrated Models of Judicial Dissent," *Journal of Politics* 55 (1993): 914–935; and Carol Ann Traut and Craig F. Emmert, "Expanding the Integrated Model of Judicial Decision Making: The California Jus-tices and Capital Punishment," *Journal of Politics* 60 (1998): 1166–1180.

SUGGESTED READINGS

Cannon, Mark W., and David M. O'Brien, eds. *Views from the Bench: The Judiciary and Constitu-tional Politics*. Chatham, N.J.: Chatham House, 1985. A collection of essays, mainly by ap-pellate judges, about how such jurists ought to carry out their functions and duties.

Epstein, Lee, and Jack Knight. *The Choices Judges Make*. Washington, D.C.: Congressional Quarterly, 1998. This book presents an excellent summary of the several current theoretical approaches to the study of appellate court decision making.

Goldman, Sheldon, and Charles M. Lamb, eds. *Judicial Conflict and Consensus: Behavioral Stud-ies of American Appellate Courts*. Lexington: University Press of Kentucky, 1986. An excellent collection of empirical studies on how appellate courts operate and how they are influ-enced by both internal and external factors.

Howard, J. Woodford Jr. *Courts of Appeals in the Federal Judicial System*. Princeton, N.J.: Prince-ton University Press, 1981. A well-written study of decision making at the level of the U.S. appellate courts; contains both quantitative and anecdotal information.

Murphy, Walter F. *Elements of Judicial Strategy*. Chicago: University of Chicago Press, 1964. Emphasizes the importance of interpersonal interactions on the outcome of collegial court decision making.

O'Brien, David M. *Storm Center*, 5th ed. New York: Norton, 2000. Offers a historical look at and contemporary discussion of the dynamics of decision making by the U.S. Supreme Court.

Perry, H. W., Jr. *Deciding to Decide: Agenda Setting in the United States Supreme Court*. Cambridge, Mass.: Harvard University Press, 1991. Emphasizes the importance of the Supreme Court's decisions with respect to which types of cases it will and will not hear; the author argues that these decisions are as important as the ultimate dispositions of those cases the Court does consider.

Woodward, Bob, and Scott Armstrong. *The Brethren: Inside the Supreme Court*. New York: Simon and Schuster, 1979. A journalistic account of behind-the-scenes interpersonal interactions on the Burger Court.

CHAPTER 6

Implementation and Impact of Judicial Policies

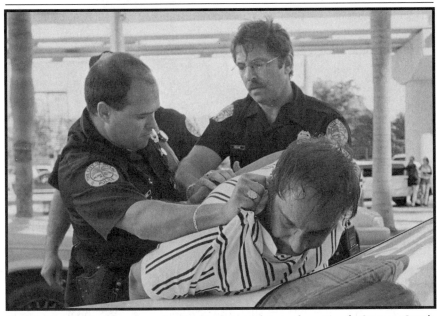

State and local police officers have played an important role in implementing the Supreme Court's ruling that criminal suspects must be advised of their constitutional rights.

✎ Do lower-court judges have too much discretion when implementing decisions of appellate courts?

✎ Should the judicial branch have the ability to develop and implement public policy, or should that power belong exclusively to the executive and legislative branches?

✎ What are the major strengths and weaknesses of the judicial branch in influencing social policies in the United States?

IN THE TWO PREVIOUS CHAPTERS we focused on decision making by judges. In this chapter we extend the discussion to examine what happens after a decision is reached. Decisions made by judges are not self-executing, and a wide variety of individuals—other judges, public officials, even private citizens—may be called upon to implement a court's decisions. We will look at the various actors involved in the implementation process, their reactions to judicial policies, and the methods by which they may respond to a court's decision.

Depending upon the nature of the court's decision, the judicial policy may have a narrow or a broad impact. A suit for damages incurred in an automobile accident would directly affect only the persons involved, and perhaps their immediate families. But the famous *Gideon v. Wainwright* decision has directly affected millions of people in one way or another.[1] In *Gideon* the Supreme Court held that states must provide an attorney for indigent defendants in felony trials. Scores of people—defendants, judges, lawyers, taxpayers—have felt the effects of that judicial policy. As we discuss the implementation process, then, we will also look at the impact judicial policy making has had on society.

The Impact of Higher-Court Decisions on Lower Courts

Americans often view the appellate courts, notably the U.S. Supreme Court, as most likely to be involved in policy making. The trial courts, however, are frequently seen as norm enforcers rather than policy makers. Given this traditional view, the picture that often emerges is one in which the Supreme Court makes a decision that is then implemented by a lower court. In short, some envision a judicial bureaucracy with a hierarchy of courts much like superiors and subordinates.[2] More recent studies, however, have cast doubt on the bureaucracy theory, arguing that "most of the work of the lower courts seems less dependent on the Supreme Court than . . . bureaucracy [theory] would indicate."[3] In other words, lower-court judges have a great deal of independence from the appellate courts and may be viewed as "independent actors . . . who will not follow the lead of higher courts unless conditions are favorable for their doing so."[4] For example, not all federal district judges immediately enforced the Supreme Court's public school desegregation decision.[5] Some judges allowed school districts to engage in a variety of tactics ranging from evasion to postponement of the Supreme Court mandate.[6]

Lower-Court Discretion

Why do the lower-court judges have so much discretion when implementing a higher court's policy? In part, the answer may be found in the structure of the U.S.

judicial system. The judiciary has always been characterized by independence, decentralization, and individualism. Federal judges, for example, are protected by life tenure and traditionally have been able to run their courts as they see fit. Disciplinary measures are not at all common, and federal judges have historically had little fear of impeachment. To retain their positions, the state trial court judges do not have to worry about the appellate courts in their system, either. They simply have to keep the electorate satisfied. In short, lower-court judges have a good deal of freedom to make their own decisions and to respond to upper-court rulings in their own way.

The discretion exercised by a lower-court judge may also be a product of the higher court's decision itself. For example, following the famous school desegregation decision in 1954, the Supreme Court heard further arguments on the best way to implement its new policy. In 1955 it handed down its decision in *Brown v. Board of Education of Topeka II*.[7] In that case the Court was faced with two major questions: (1) How soon are the public schools to start desegregating? and (2) How much time should they be given to complete the process? Federal district judges given the task of enforcing the High Court's ruling were told that the public schools were to make a prompt and reasonable start and then proceed with all deliberate speed to bring about desegregation. What constitutes a prompt and reasonable start? How rapidly must a school district proceed to be moving with all deliberate speed? Because the Supreme Court justices did not provide specific answers to these questions, many lower-court judges were faced with school districts that continued to drag their feet while at the same time claiming they were acting within the High Court's guidelines.

A second example concerns the Supreme Court's decision in the 1962 reapportionment case *Baker v. Carr*.[8] The Court held that allegations of malapportioned state legislative districts in Tennessee presented a justiciable, not a political, question; that is, apportionment cases could properly be litigated in the courts. The case was remanded (sent back down) to the federal court for the middle district of Tennessee in Nashville for implementation. Justice William J. Brennan Jr.'s opinion for the Court concluded with the statement, "The cause is remanded for further proceedings consistent with this opinion." No guidelines were provided; the federal district judge was not told how rapidly to proceed or what methods to use. Justice Thomas C. Clark, in a concurring opinion, pointed out that the Court "fails to give the District any guidance whatever."[9]

Therefore, federal district judges implementing either of the policies described above could exercise a high degree of freedom and still legitimately say that they were in compliance with the Supreme Court's mandate. Although not all High

Court decisions allow such discretion, a good number of them do. Opinions that are ambiguous or poorly written are almost certain to encounter problems during the implementation process.

A court's decision may be unclear for several reasons. Sometimes the issue or subject matter may be so complex that it is difficult to fashion a clear policy. In obscenity cases, for instance, the Supreme Court has had little difficulty in deciding that pornographic material is not entitled to constitutional protection. Defining obscenity has proven to be another matter. Phrases such as "prurient interest," "patently offensive," "contemporary community standards," and "lacks serious literary, artistic, political, or scientific value" have become commonplace in obscenity opinions. These terms leave considerable room for subjective interpretation. It is little wonder that a Supreme Court justice admitted that he could not define obscenity but added that "I know it when I see it."[10]

Policies established by collegial courts are often ambiguous because the majority opinion is written to accommodate several judges. At times such opinions read more like committee reports than forceful, decisive statements. The majority opinion may also be accompanied by several concurring opinions. When this happens, lower-court judges are left without a clear-cut precedent to follow. Death penalty cases serve as an example. In 1972 the Supreme Court struck down the death penalty in several states, but for a variety of reasons. Some justices opposed the death penalty per se, on the ground that it constituted cruel and unusual punishment in violation of the Eighth Amendment to the Constitution. Others voted to strike down the state laws because they were applied in a discriminatory manner.[11] The uncertainty created by the 1972 decision affected not only lower-court judges but also state legislatures. The states passed a rash of widely divergent death penalty statutes and caused a considerable amount of new litigation.

A lower-court judge's discretion in the implementation process may also be affected by the manner in which a higher court's policy is communicated. The first step in implementing a judicial policy is to learn of the new appellate court ruling. Presumably, lower-court judges automatically are made aware of a higher court's decision, but that is not always so. Certainly the court from which a case has been appealed will be informed of the decision. The federal district court for the middle district of Tennessee was told of the Supreme Court's decision in *Baker v. Carr* because its earlier decision was reversed, and the case was remanded to it for further action. However, systematic, formal efforts are not made to inform other courts of the decision or to see that lower-court judges have access to a copy of the opinion.

The decisions that contain the new judicial policy are simply made available to the public in printed form or on the Internet, and judges are expected to read them if they have the time and inclination.

Opinions of the Supreme Court, lower federal courts, and state appellate courts are available in a large number of courthouse, law school, and university libraries. They are also increasingly available on the Internet. Today, some court opinions can be read the same day they are handed down or within a matter of just a few days. This widespread availability does not guarantee that they will be read and clearly understood, however. One complication is that many lower-level state judges, such as justices of the peace and juvenile court judges, are nonlawyers who have little interest or skill in reading complex judicial decisions.[12] Finally, even those judges who have an interest in higher-court decisions and the ability to understand them do not have adequate time to keep abreast of all the new opinions.

Given these problems, how do judges become aware of upper-court decisions? One way is to hear of them through lawyers presenting cases in the lower courts. It is generally assumed that the opposing attorneys will present relevant precedents in their arguments before the judge. Those judges who are fortunate enough to have law clerks may also rely upon them to search out recent decisions from higher courts.

Thus some higher-court policies are not quickly and strictly enforced because lower-court judges are not aware of them. Even those of which they are aware may not be as clear as a lower-court judge might like. Either reason contributes to the discretion exercised by lower-court judges placed in the position of having to implement judicial policies.

Interpretation by Lower Courts

One study noted that "important policy announcements almost always require interpretation by someone other than the policy maker."[13] This is certainly true in the case of judicial policies established by appellate courts. The first exercise of a lower-court judge's discretion may be to interpret what the higher court's decision means.

Consider an example from a famous Supreme Court decision concerning what types of speech are protected by the Constitution. In that 1919 case the Court announced that "the question in every case is whether the words used are used in such circumstances and are of such a nature as to create a clear and present danger that they will bring about the substantive evils that Congress has a right to prevent."[14] With that statement the Court announced what is known as the clear-and-present-danger doctrine. Although it may seem simple in the abstract to say that a person's right to speak is protected unless the words create a clear and present danger, lower-court judges do not decide cases in the abstract. They must fit higher-court policy decisions to the concrete facts of an actual case. Place yourself in the position of a lower-court judge deciding a case shortly after the announcement of the clear-and-present-danger policy. Assume that you were presiding over the trial of an individual who, in the course of a speech to a group of onlookers on a busy street corner in a large city, advocated violent overthrow of the U.S. government. You might well have had to answer one or more of the following questions in your own mind as you tried to interpret the clear-and-present-danger doctrine: (1) How well defined must the danger be for it to be clear? (2) How imminent must the danger be for it to be present? (3) Is the danger in question one the government has a right to prevent? (4) Did the speech bring about any danger? (5) At what point is the government allowed to intervene or stop the speech? Interpreting what is meant by the clear-and-present-danger policy is no simple task. Modern courts grapple with the free speech question just as did the courts in 1919.

The manner in which a lower-court judge interprets a policy established by a higher court depends upon a number of factors. Many policies are not clearly stated. Thus reasonable people may disagree over the proper interpretation. Even policy pronouncements that do not suffer from ambiguity, however, are sometimes interpreted differently by different judges.

A judge's own personal policy preferences will also have an effect upon the interpretation he or she gives to a higher-court policy. Judges come to the courts with their own unique background characteristics. Some are Republican, others are Democrat; one judge may be liberal, another conservative. They come from different regions of the country. Some have been prosecutors; others have been primarily defense lawyers or corporate lawyers. In short, their backgrounds may influence their own particular policy preferences. Thus the lower-court judges, given their wide latitude anyway, may read their own ideas into a higher-court policy. The result is that a policy may be enthusiastically embraced by some judges yet totally rejected by others.

Strategies Employed by Lower Courts

Appellate court policies are open to different interpretations. Those who favor and accept a higher court's policy will naturally try to enforce it and perhaps even expand upon it. Those who do not like a higher court's policy decision may implement it sparingly or only under duress.

A judge who basically disagrees with a policy established by a higher court can employ a number of strategies. One rarely used strategy is defiance, whereby a judge simply does not apply the higher court's policy in a case before a lower court. One study of judicial implementation offers this example:

Desegregation brought out considerable trial court defiance; in one extreme case, a Birmingham, Alabama, municipal judge not only refused to follow Supreme Court decisions desegregating municipal facilities but also declared the Fourteenth Amendment unconstitutional.[15]

Such outright defiance is highly unusual. Other strategies are not so extreme. A study of the libel decisions of the U.S. courts of appeals between 1964 and 1974 did not find a single case of noncompliance with Supreme Court mandates.[16] Another study, focusing on compliance with the Supreme Court's *Miranda v. Arizona* decision, found only one instance of possible noncompliance and twelve decisions that could be classified as narrow compliance among the 250 cases studied.[17]

Another strategy often employed by judges not favorably inclined toward a higher-court policy is to avoid having to apply the policy. Sometimes a case may be disposed of on technical or procedural grounds so that the judge does not have to rule on the merits of the case. It may be determined, for example, that the plaintiff does not have standing to sue or that the case has become moot because the issue was resolved before the trial commenced. Lower-court judges sometimes avoid accepting a policy by declaring a portion of the higher-court decision to be dicta. Dicta refers to the part of the opinion that does not contribute to the central logic of the decision. It may be useful as guidance but is not seen as binding. What constitutes dicta is open to varying interpretations.

Yet another strategy often employed by judges who are in basic disagreement with a judicial policy is to apply it as narrowly as possible. One method is for the lower-court judge to rule that a precedent is not controlling because factual differences exist between the higher-court case and the case before the lower courts. That is, because the two cases may be distinguished, the precedent does not have to be followed. Two good examples are provided by lower-court applications of the Supreme Court's decisions in *Escobedo v. Illinois* and *Miranda v. Arizona.*

The *Escobedo* decision held that a suspect being interrogated had to be allowed access to his lawyer. *Miranda* went a step further and declared that suspects taken into custody must be advised of their constitutional rights and that any confession made by a suspect who had not been so advised is invalid. A leading judicial scholar explains how these two landmark decisions were treated by some lower-court judges:

Lower court judges who did not like the *Escobedo* ruling . . . refused to apply *Escobedo* to anyone who did not already have a lawyer. Similarly, judges who did not like the *Miranda* ruling did not require warnings to be given to those not in custody, and then defined "in custody" as narrowly as possible.[18]

State court judges faced with interpreting or implementing civil liberties policies often rely on what is termed "new judicial federalism."[19] This idea originated in the early 1970s, primarily as a result of Warren E. Burger's appointment as chief justice of the U.S. Supreme Court. Many civil libertarians, fearful that the new Burger Court would erode or overturn major Warren Court decisions, began to look to state bills of rights as alternative bases for their court claims. The Burger Court encouraged a return to state constitutions by pointing out that the states could offer greater protection under their own bills of rights than was available under the federal Bill of Rights.

In the beginning, only the supreme courts of California and New Jersey showed much interest in new judicial federalism. Initially, courts used this approach to circumvent specific Burger Court decisions. However, over the past twenty-five years "state courts have undertaken major initiatives involving school finance, exclusionary zoning, the rights of defendants, and the right to privacy."[20]

Recent studies, however, have cautioned against too much optimism among those who advocate reliance on state constitutions as a way to avoid conservative precedents espoused by the Burger and Rehnquist Courts. In separate examinations of criminal justice decisions from all fifty state high courts, both Barry Latzer and Michael Esler concluded that state supreme courts continue to rely on federal law in the vast majority of their decisions.[21]

Not all lower-court judges are opposed to a policy announced by a higher court. Some judges have risked social ostracism and various kinds of harassment to implement policies they believed in but that were not popular in their communities.[22]

A judge who is in basic agreement with a higher-court policy is likely to give that policy as broad an application as possible. The precedent might be expanded to apply to other areas.

For example, in *Griswold v. Connecticut* the Supreme Court held that a Connecticut statute forbidding the use of birth control devices was unconstitutional because it infringed upon a married couple's constitutional right to privacy.[23] In other words, the Court said that a decision whether to use birth control devices was a personal one to be made without interference from the state. Five years later, a three-judge federal district court expanded the *Griswold* precedent to justify its finding that the Texas abortion statute was unconstitutional.[24] The court ruled that the law infringed upon the right of privacy of an unmarried woman to decide, at least during the first trimester of pregnancy, whether to obtain an abortion. Thus the lower court went further than the Supreme Court in striking down state involvement in such matters.

Influences on Lower-Court Judges

Lower courts are not slaves of the higher courts when implementing judicial policies. They have a high degree of independence and discretion. At times the lower courts must decide cases for which no precise standards have been provided by the higher courts. Whenever this occurs, lower-court judges must turn elsewhere for guidance in deciding a case before them.

One study notes that lower-court judges in such a position "may take their cues on how to decide a particular case from a wide variety of factors including their party affiliation, their ideology, or their regional norms." [25] Several analyses, for example, point out that differences between Democratic and Republican lower-court judges are especially pronounced when Supreme Court rulings are ambiguous, when there is a transition from one Supreme Court period to another, or when the issue area is so new and controversial that more definite standards have not yet been formulated.[26]

Regional norms have also been mentioned prominently in the literature as having an influence on lower-court judges when they interpret and apply higher-court decisions.[27] One study found, for example, that "federal judges tend to be more vigilant in enforcing national desegregation standards in remote areas than when similar issues arise within the judge's immediate work/residence locale." The prevailing local norms may mean that "when faced with desegregating his own community a judge may be more concerned with public reaction than when dealing with an outlying area."[28]

Congressional Influences on the Implementation Process

Once a federal judicial decision is made, Congress can offer a variety of responses.[29] It may aid or hinder the implementation of a decision. In addition, it can alter a court's interpretation of the law. Finally, Congress can mount an attack on individual judges. Naturally, the actions of individual members of Congress will be influenced by their partisan and ideological leanings.

In the course of deciding cases, the courts are often called upon to interpret federal statutes. On occasion the judicial interpretation may differ from what a majority in Congress intended. When that situation occurs, the statute can be changed in new legislation that in effect overrules the court's initial interpretation. A good example of this occurred in March 1988, when Congress effectively overruled the Supreme Court's decision in *Grove City College v. Bell*.[30] At issue in the case was the scope of Title IX of the 1972 Education Act Amendments, which forbids sex discrimination in education programs. In the *Grove City* case, which involved a small Pennsylvania college, the Court ruled that only the specific "program or activity" receiving federal aid was covered by Title IX. According to that interpretation only Grove City College's financial aid office was affected by the law. Many in Congress interpreted Title IX to mean that the entire college was subject to the act's prohibitions.

To overturn the Court's decision and restore the interpretation favored by many legislators, Congress passed the Civil Rights Restoration Act. The bill was vetoed by President Ronald Reagan. However, on March 22, 1988, the House and Senate mustered the necessary two-thirds vote to override the president's veto. In this way Congress established its view that if one part of an entity receives federal funds, the entire entity is covered by Title IX of the Education Act.[31] Still, the vast majority of the federal judiciary's statutory decisions are not touched by Congress. A study focusing on the Supreme Court's labor and antitrust decisions in the period 1950–1972 found that only 27 of the 222 decisions were the objects of reversal attempts in Congress, and that only 9 of those attempts were successful.[32]

Besides ruling on statutes, the federal courts interpret the Constitution. Congress has two methods to reverse or alter the effects of a constitutional interpretation it does not like. First, Congress can respond with another statute. On June 21, 1989, in *Texas v. Johnson*, the Supreme Court overturned a Texas flag desecration statute that made it illegal to "cast contempt" on the flag by "publicly mutilating, defacing, burning, or trampling" it. Gregory Lee Johnson had been found guilty of violating the law when he burned an American flag at the 1984 Republican National Convention in Dallas.[33] Although President George Bush and some legislators argued in favor of a constitutional amendment to overturn the Court's decision, others preferred not to tinker with the Constitution. Instead, Congress enacted a statute that was designed to avoid the constitutional problems of the Texas law by eliminating any reference to the motives of the person who damages an American flag. The Flag Protection Act of 1989 was passed by Congress on October 12, 1989, and became effective on October 28 after President Bush allowed it to become law without his signature.[34] The new law was immediately challenged in several flag-burning exhibitions that were held in various parts of the country on October

28–30. In one of these exhibitions, held on the steps of the Capitol on October 30, 1989, Gregory Lee Johnson joined several others in igniting an American flag. However, he was not among those charged with violating the new federal statute.[35] In 1990 the Supreme Court declared the Flag Protection Act unconstitutional.[36]

Second, a constitutional decision can be overturned directly by an amendment to the U.S. Constitution. Although many such amendments have been introduced over the years, it is not easy to obtain the necessary two-thirds vote in each house of Congress to propose the amendment and then achieve ratification by three-fourths of the states. The attempt to overturn the Supreme Court's 1989 flag-burning decision by a constitutional amendment provides an excellent example of this difficulty. Although the amendment was strongly supported by President Bush, it was rejected in the Senate on October 19, 1989, by a 51–48 vote, fifteen votes short of the required two-thirds of those present and voting.[37]

Only four Supreme Court decisions in the history of the Court have been overturned by constitutional amendments. The Eleventh Amendment overturned *Chisholm v. Georgia* (dealing with suits against a state in federal court); the Thirteenth Amendment overturned *Scott v. Sandford* (dealing with the legality of slavery); the Sixteenth Amendment overturned *Pollock v. Farmer's Loan and Trust Co.* (pertaining to the constitutionality of the income tax); and the Twenty-sixth Amendment overturned *Oregon v. Mitchell* (giving eighteen-year-olds the right to vote in state elections).[38]

Congressional attacks on the federal courts in general and on certain judges in particular are another method of responding to judicial decisions. Sometimes these attacks are in the form of verbal denouncements that allow a member of Congress to let off steam over a decision or series of decisions. Throughout 1997, for example, a number of Republican members of the U.S. House and Senate criticized several federal judges for their purported judicial activism. There were also threats of impeachment of sitting judges and more thorough investigations of the judicial philosophies of potential nominees to the federal bench.[39]

Federal judges may be impeached and removed from office by Congress. Although the congressional bark may be worse than its bite in the use of this weapon, it is still a part of its overall arsenal, and the impeachments of several federal judges in recent years serve as a reminder of that fact.

Finally, the confirmation process offers a chance for an attack on the courts. As a new federal judicial appointee goes through hearings in the Senate, individual senators sometimes use the opportunity to denounce individual judges or specific decisions. Without doubt, the best example was President Reagan's nomination of

Judge Robert H. Bork (of the D.C. Circuit Court of Appeals) as an associate justice of the Supreme Court. A number of senators on the Judiciary Committee took Judge Bork to task for opinions he had written in specific cases, his writings while he served as a law professor at Yale University, and his views on several controversial Supreme Court decisions (notably *Roe v. Wade*).[40]

However, Congress and the federal courts are not natural adversaries even though it occasionally may appear that way. Retaliations against the federal judiciary are fairly rare, and often the two branches work in harmony toward similar policy goals. For example, Congress played a key role in implementing the Supreme Court's school desegregation policy by enacting the Civil Rights Act of 1964, which empowered the Justice Department to initiate suits against school districts. Title VI of the act also provided a potent weapon in the desegregation struggle by threatening the denial of federal funds to schools guilty of segregation. In 1965 Congress further solidified its support for a policy of desegregated public schools by passing the Elementary and Secondary Education Act. This act gave the federal government a much larger role in financing public education and thus made the threat to cut off federal funds a most serious problem for many segregated school districts.[41] Such support from Congress was significant because the likelihood of compliance with a policy is increased when there is unity between branches of government.[42]

Executive Branch Influences on the Implementation Process

At times the president may be called upon directly to implement a judicial decision. An example is the famous Nixon tapes case.[43] The Senate committee investigation into the cover-up of the 1973 break-in at the Democratic Party headquarters in the Watergate Hotel led directly to high government officials working close to the president. It was also revealed during the investigation that President Richard M. Nixon had installed an automatic taping system in the Oval Office. Leon Jaworski, who had been appointed special prosecutor to investigate the Watergate affair, subpoenaed certain tapes that he felt might provide evidence needed in his prosecutions of high-ranking officials. President Nixon refused voluntarily to turn over the tapes on grounds of executive privilege and the need for confidentiality. The Supreme Court's decision—which, ironically, was announced on the day that the Judiciary Committee of the House of Representatives began holding hearings on whether to impeach Nixon—instructed the president to surrender the subpoenaed tapes to Judge John J. Sirica, who was handling the trials of the government officials. President Nixon eventually did comply with the High Court's directive and thus a decision was implemented that led to his downfall. Within two weeks he resigned from the presidency, in August 1974.

Even when not directly involved in the enforcement of a judicial policy, the president may still be able to influence its impact. Because of the status and visibility of the position, a president, simply by words and actions, may encourage support for, or resistance to, a new judicial policy. For instance, it has been argued that President Dwight D. Eisenhower's lack of enthusiasm for the *Brown v. Board of Education* decision and "his unwillingness to support it in more than a pro forma fashion encouraged southern resistance."[44] As a consequence, Eisenhower later had to send federal troops to Little Rock, Arkansas, to enforce the district court's integration order. Sending in troops made President Eisenhower's participation in the implementation process more direct.

A president can propose legislation aimed at retaliating against the courts. President Franklin D. Roosevelt, for instance, urged Congress to increase the size of the Supreme Court so he could "pack" it with justices who supported New Deal legislation. President Reagan used this tactic in another way. He was a consistently strong supporter of constitutional amendments to overturn the Supreme Court's school prayer and abortion decisions.

The appointment power also gives the president an opportunity to influence federal judicial policies. Although the White House shares the power to appoint federal judges with the Senate, evidence points to the fact that the president dominates the process at the Supreme Court and courts of appeals levels. (Senatorial courtesy is a major consideration in the appointment of federal district judges.)

During his campaign for the presidency in 1968, Richard Nixon made the Supreme Court an issue by criticizing the Warren Court for its liberal decisions and activist approach. He promised that, if elected, he would appoint "strict constructionists" to the Supreme Court and lower federal courts. In his first year in office, Nixon appointed Warren Burger as chief justice and Harry A. Blackmun as an associate justice. Two years later, Nixon was able to appoint another pair of justices—Lewis F. Powell Jr. and William H. Rehnquist.

How successful was President Nixon in accomplishing his goal of altering the policy direction of the Supreme Court? One student of the transition from the Warren Court to the Burger Court said that

on the whole the Court's decisions demonstrated considerable withdrawal from and undercutting of Warren Court policies affecting the entire range of civil liberties policies.[45]

Thus Nixon was generally able to accomplish his goal for the Supreme Court. Also, the uncertainty and ambiguity in Court precedents brought about by the transition from the Warren to the Burger Court left the lower federal courts with more discretion.[46]

Presidents have long realized that lower federal judges are important in the judicial policy-making process. For this reason, many chief executives have shown an interest in appointing lower-court judges who share their basic ideologies and values.[47]

A president can also influence judicial policy making through the activities of the Justice Department. The attorney general and staff subordinates can emphasize specific issues according to the overall policy goals of the president. For example, the 1964 Civil Rights Act authorized the Justice Department to file school desegregation suits. This allowed the executive branch to become more actively involved in implementing the policy goal of racial equality. The other side of the coin, however, is that the Justice Department may, at its discretion, deemphasize specific policies by not pursuing them vigorously in the courts.

Another official who is in a position to influence judicial policy making is the solicitor general. Historically, this official has been seen as having dual responsibility, to both the judicial and executive branches. Because of the solicitor general's close relationship with the Supreme Court, this official is sometimes referred to as the "tenth justice."[48] The solicitor general is often seen as a counselor who advises the Court about the meaning of federal statutes and the Constitution. The solicitor general also determines which of the cases involving the federal government as a party will be appealed to the Supreme Court. Furthermore, he or she may file an amicus curiae brief urging the Court to grant or deny another litigant's certiorari petition or supporting or opposing a particular policy being urged upon the High Court. The solicitor general thus reacts to the policy decisions of the Supreme Court.

Many judicial decisions are implemented by the various departments, agencies, bureaus, and commissions that abound in the executive branch. The Supreme Court decision in *Frontiero v. Richardson* called upon the U.S. Air Force to play the major implementation role.[49] The *Frontiero* case called into question congressional statutes that provided benefits for married male members of the Air Force but did not provide similar benefits for married female members. Under the laws, a married Air Force serviceman who lived off the base was entitled to an allowance for living quarters regardless of whether his wife was employed or how much she earned. Married female members of the Air Force, however, were not entitled to such an allowance unless their husbands were physically or mentally incapable of self-support and dependent on their wives for more than half their support. Lieutenant Sharron Frontiero challenged the policy on the ground that it constituted sexual discrimination in violation of the Fifth Amendment. Her suit was filed in a federal district court in Alabama on December 23, 1970. It was not until April 5, 1972, that the three-judge district court announced its decision upholding the Air Force policy. Lieutenant Frontiero appealed to the Supreme Court, which overturned the lower-court decision on May 14, 1973. The Air Force was then required to implement a policy it had fought for nearly three years.

Other Implementers

Besides lower-court judges, Congress, the president, and others in the executive branch, many other actors are involved in the interpretation and implementation of judicial policies.[50]

Although the focus thus far has been primarily on various federal officials, implementation of judicial policies is often performed by state officials as well. Many of the Supreme Court's criminal due process decisions, such as *Gideon v. Wainwright* and *Miranda v. Arizona,* have been enforced by state court judges and other state officials. State and local police officers, for instance, have played a major role in implementing the *Miranda* requirement that criminal suspects must be advised of their rights. The *Gideon* ruling that an attorney must be provided at state expense for indigent defendants in felony trials has been implemented by public defenders, local bar associations, and individual court-appointed lawyers.

State legislators and executives are also frequently drawn into the implementation process, often as unwilling participants. A judge who determines that a wrong has been committed may use the power to issue an equitable decree as a way of remedying the wrong. The range of remedies available is broad because cases vary in the issues they raise and the types of relief sought. Among the more common affirmative remedy options from which a judge may choose are process remedies, performance standards, and specified remedial actions.[51] Process remedies provide for such things as advisory committees, citizen participation, educational programs, evaluation committees, dispute resolution procedures, and special masters. The remedies do not specify a particular form of action. Performance standards call for specific remedies—a certain number of housing units or schools or a certain level of staffing in a prison or mental health facility. The specific means of attaining these goals are left to the discretion of the officials named in the suit. Examples of specified remedial actions are school busing, altered school attendance zones, and changes in the size and condition of prison cells or hospital rooms. This type of remedy provides the defendant with no flexibility concerning the specific remedy or the means of attaining it.

Implementation of these remedial decrees often devolves, at least partially, to the state legislatures. An order calling for a certain number of prison cells or a certain number of guards in the prison system might require new state expenditures, which the legislature would have to fund. Similarly, an order to construct more modern mental health facilities or provide more modern equipment would mean an increase in state expenditures. Governors would also naturally be involved in carrying out these types of remedial decrees because they typically are heavily involved in state budgeting procedures. Also, they may sign or veto laws. Some even have an item veto power, which permits them to veto certain budget items while approving others.

Sometimes judges appoint certain individuals to assist in carrying out the remedial decree. Special masters are usually given some decision-making authority. Court-appointed monitors are also used in some situations, but they do not relieve the judge of decision-making responsibilities. Instead, the monitor is an information gatherer who reports on the defendant's progress in complying with the remedial decree. When orders are not implemented or when barriers of one kind or another block progress in providing a remedy, a judge may name someone as a receiver. A good example occurred in the 1970s when the fights within Alabama's mental health agencies and facilities made it virtually impossible to obtain the action Judge Frank Johnson wanted. Finally, Judge Johnson ordered the governor to take over as receiver and empowered him to disregard normal organizational barriers.[52]

Space does not permit discussion of every state and local public official in the implementation process, but one group of individuals has been so deeply involved in implementing judicial policies that we feel compelled to deal with them here, if only briefly. These implementers are the thousands of men and women who constitute school boards throughout the country.

Two major policy areas stand out as having embroiled school board members in considerable controversy as they faced the inevitable task of trying to carry out Supreme Court policy. First, when the High Court ruled in 1954 that segregation has no place in the public schools, school boards and school superintendents, along with federal district judges, bore the brunt of implementing that decision.[53] Their role in this process has affected the lives of millions of schoolchildren, parents, and taxpayers all over America.

The second area that has involved school boards is the Supreme Court's policies on religion in the public schools. In *Engel v. Vitale* (1962), the Court held unconstitutional a New York requirement that a state-written prayer be recited daily in the public schools.[54] Some school districts responded to the decision by requiring instead the recitation of a Bible verse or the Lord's Prayer. Their reasoning was that because the state did not write the Lord's Prayer or the Bible, they were not violating the Court's policy. A year later, the Supreme Court struck down these new practices, pointing out that the constitutional violation lay in endorsing the religious activity and its determination did not depend on whether the state had written the prayer.[55] Some school districts continued to seek ways to provide religious activities for the students. *Santa Fe Independent School District v. Doe*, decided by the U.S. Supreme Court in 2000, provides a good example.[56] In that case the school district implemented a policy of allowing two student elections: one to determine whether "invocations" should be delivered over the public address system at varsity football games and a second to select the spokesperson to deliver the "invocation." By a 6–3 vote the High Court held that this policy also violates the Constitution's establishment clause.

Both of these policy areas involve basically private citizens—school board officials—in implementing controversial, emotion-charged policies. Furthermore, the school board officials may neither understand nor agree with the policies they are directed to enforce.

The Impact of Judicial Policies

Thus far, the focus here has primarily been on the implementation of judicial policies by various government officials, which is entirely appropriate because court decisions are often specifically directed at other public policy makers. However, as a recent study of the Supreme Court shows, the ultimate importance of the Court's decisions "depends primarily on their impact outside government, on American society as a whole."[57] Some argue that American courts may be too heavily involved in making decisions that affect society. They say that courts in the United States may be too involved in policy making, or too activist. This is not the case in all countries. For example, a recent study of Canadian judges concluded:

Clearly, judicial activism is more common and more accepted among American judges. Although the level of judicial activism may be increasing in Canada, Canadian judges still seem uncomfortable with the concept of judicial policy making.[58]

A few policies have had significant effects on society as a whole: the courts' role in developing a policy of racial equality, criminal due process, and abortion.

Racial Equality

Many point to the Supreme Court's *Brown* decision as the impetus for the drive for racial equality in the United States. However, Congress and the executive branch were also involved in the process of ensuring implementation of the decision's desegregation policy. Still, the courts initiated the pursuit for a national policy of racial equality with the *Brown* ruling. Thus one of the most important ways the federal judiciary can influence policy is to place issues on the national political agenda.

In the beginning, the court decisions were often vague, leading to evasion of the new policy. The Supreme Court justices and many lower federal judges were persistent in decisions following *Brown* and, in this way, kept the policy of racial equality on the national political agenda. Their persistence paid off with passage of the 1964 Civil Rights Act, ten years after *Brown*. That act, which had the strong support of Presidents John F. Kennedy and Lyndon B. Johnson, squarely placed Congress and the president on record as being supportive of racial equality in America.

One other aspect of the federal judiciary's importance in the policy-making process is illustrated by *Brown* and the cases that followed it. Although the courts stood virtually alone in the quest for racial equality for several years, their decisions did not go unnoticed. The *Brown* decision, as one team of judicial impact scholars puts it,

was a highly visible Court decision, a judicial attempt to generate one of the greatest social reforms in American history. And certainly in the years that followed, African Americans and their allies brought considerable pressures on other governmental bodies to desegregate the schools. Indeed, the pressures soon went far beyond schools to demand integration of all aspects of American life.[59]

Some debate has arisen, however, over whether *Brown* was a major cause of this mobilization of effort. One judicial impact scholar empirically examined the causal linkage between *Brown* and civil rights mobilization by studying periodical coverage of civil rights from 1940 to 1965.[60] He concluded that no evidence exists that *Brown*'s "influence was widespread or of much importance to the battle for civil rights."[61] Other scholars, however, attribute much greater influence to *Brown* in the mobilization process.[62]

Although no one would argue that the United States has achieved complete racial equality, some gains have been made. The federal courts are not totally responsible for those gains, but they have played a major role in their achievement.

Criminal Due Process

Judicial policy making in the area of criminal due process is most closely associated with the Warren Court period. Speaking of this era, a former solicitor general said, "Never has there been such a thorough-going reform of criminal procedure within so short a time."[63] The Warren Court decisions were aimed primarily at changing the procedures followed by the states in dealing with criminal defendants. By the time Warren left the Supreme Court, new policies had been established to deal with a wide range of activities. While a complete list of the Court's decisions is too lengthy to discuss here, among the more far-reaching were *Mapp v. Ohio, Gideon v. Wainwright,* and *Miranda v. Arizona.*[64]

The *Mapp* decision extended the exclusionary rule, which had applied to the national government for a number of years, to the states. This rule required state courts to exclude from trial evidence that had been illegally seized by the police. Although some police departments, especially in major urban areas, have tried to establish specific guidelines for their officers to follow in obtaining evidence, such efforts have not been universal. Because of variations in police practices and differing lower-court interpretations of what constitutes a valid search and seizure, implementation of *Mapp* has not been consistent throughout the country.

Perhaps even more important in reducing the originally perceived impact of *Mapp* has been the lack of solid support for the exclusionary rule among the Supreme Court justices. The decision was not a unanimous one to begin with, and over the years some of the justices, notably Chief Justice Warren Burger, have been openly critical of the exclusionary rule. Not surprisingly, then, some Burger and Rehnquist Court decisions have somewhat curtailed the application of the exclusionary rule. In 1984 the Burger Court adopted a limited good-faith exception to the exclusionary rule where officers seize evidence in good faith, relying on search warrants later held to be defective.[65] The Rehnquist Court reaffirmed the good-faith exception in 1995 in *Arizona v. Evans.*[66] Furthermore, Burger and Rehnquist decisions have broadened the scope of legal searches, thus limiting the applicability of the rule.[67]

The *Gideon v. Wainwright* decision held that indigent defendants must be provided attorneys when they go to trial in a felony case in the state courts. Many states routinely provided attorneys in such trials even before the Court's decision. The other states began to comply in a variety of ways. Public defender programs were established in many regions. In other areas, local bar associations cooperated with judges to implement some method of complying with the Supreme Court's new policy.

The impact of *Gideon* is clearer and more consistent than that of *Mapp*. One reason, no doubt, is that many states had already implemented the policy called for by *Gideon*. It was simply more widely accepted than the policy established by *Mapp*. The policy announced in *Gideon* was also more sharply defined than the one in *Mapp*. Although the Court did not specify whether a public defender or a court-appointed lawyer must be provided, it is still clear that the indigent defendant must have the help of an attorney. The Burger Court did not retreat from the Warren Court's policy of providing an attorney for indigent defendants as it did in the search and seizure area addressed by *Mapp*. All these factors add up to a more recognizable impact for the policy announced in *Gideon*.

In *Miranda v. Arizona* the Supreme Court went a step further and ruled that police officers must advise suspects taken into custody of their constitutional rights, one of which is to have an attorney present during questioning. Suspects must also be advised that they have a right to remain silent and that any statement they make may be used in court; that if they cannot afford an attorney, one will be provided at state expense; and that they have the right to stop answering questions at any time. These requirements are so clearly stated that police departments have copied them down on cards for officers to carry in their shirt pockets. Then, when suspects are taken into custody, the police officers read the suspects their rights.

If compliance is measured simply in terms of whether police officers read the *Miranda* rights to persons they arrest, then there has been a high level of compliance with the Supreme Court policy. Some researchers, however, have questioned the impact of *Miranda* because of the method by which suspects may be advised of their rights. It is one thing to read to a person from a card; it is another to explain what is meant by the High Court's requirements and then try to make the suspect understand them. Looked at in this manner, the impact of the policy announced in *Miranda* is not as clear.

The Burger Court did not show an inclination to lend its solid support to the Warren Court's *Miranda* policy. Although *Miranda* was not overruled, its impact was limited somewhat. In *Harris v. New York*, for example, the Burger Court ruled that statements made by an individual who had not been given the *Miranda* warning could be used to challenge the credibility of his or her testimony at trial.[68] Then, the Rehnquist Court, in a five-to-four decision, ruled that police are not required to stop questioning a suspect who makes an ambiguous request to have an attorney present.[69]

Congress reacted to *Miranda*, two years after the decision, by enacting a statute that in essence made the admissibility of a suspect's statements turn solely on whether they were made voluntarily. The statute received little attention until 1999 when the Fourth Circuit Court of Appeals, in a case involving an alleged bank robber who moved to suppress a statement he made to the FBI on the ground that he had not received "*Miranda* warnings" before being interrogated, held that the statute was satisfied because his statement was voluntary. The court of appeals decision raised the question whether the congressional statute or the High Court's *Miranda* decision should be followed. On June 26, 2000, the U.S. Supreme Court held that *Miranda*, being a constitutional decision of the Court, could not in effect be overruled by an act of Congress.[70] In other words, *Miranda* still governs the admissibility of statements made during custodial interrogation in state and federal courts.

In sum, the impact of the Supreme Court's criminal justice policies has been mixed, for several reasons. In some instances ambiguity is a problem. In other cases less than solid support for the policy may be evident among justices or support erodes when one Court replaces another. All these variables translate into greater discretion for the implementers.

Abortion

In *Roe v. Wade* the Supreme Court ruled (1) that a woman has an absolute right to an abortion during the first trimester of pregnancy; (2) that a state may regulate the abortion procedure during the second trimester to protect the mother's health; and (3) that, during the third trimester, the state may regulate or even prohibit abortions, except where the life or health of the mother is endangered.[71]

The reaction to this decision was immediate, and primarily negative.[72] It came in the form of letters to individual justices, public speeches, the introduction of resolutions in Congress, and the advocacy of "right to life" amendments in Congress. As might be expected, given the controversial nature of the Court's decision, hospitals did not wholeheartedly offer to support the decision by changing their abortion policies.

Reaction to the Court's abortion policy has not only continued but also has moved into new areas. Recent presidential elections have seen the two major party platforms and candidates take opposing stands on the abortion issue. Democratic platforms and nominees have generally expressed support for *Roe v. Wade,* whereas the Republican platforms and contenders have noted opposition to the Supreme Court's decision.

Congress has also been a hotbed of activity in response to the Supreme Court's abortion decision. Unable to secure passage of a constitutional amendment to overturn *Roe v. Wade*, anti-abortion forces used another approach. For several years they successfully obtained amendments to appropriations bills preventing the expenditure of federal funds for elective abortions. In 1980 the Supreme Court, in a five-to-four vote, upheld the constitutionality of such a prohibition.[73]

Most of the legislation in the aftermath of *Roe* has been at the state level. One study reports that within two years of the decision thirty-two states had passed sixty-two laws relating to abortion, most aimed at limiting access to abortions, regulating abortion procedures, or prohibiting abortions under certain conditions.[74]

Interest group activity increased dramatically after the *Roe* decision. Groups opposing the decision often organized public demonstrations against the decision and later began to picket clinics. Interest groups that support the *Roe v. Wade* decision have been more likely to focus their efforts on the courts.

The difference in strategies was clearly evident when the Supreme Court heard *Webster v. Reproductive Health Services* in 1989.[75] This case attracted widespread attention because the U.S. Department of Justice explicitly asked the Court to overturn *Roe v. Wade* (only four justices went on record as saying they favored doing so). A record seventy-eight amicus curiae briefs supported by more than three hundred organizations were filed in the case with pro-choice groups' filings or signings outnumbering those of pro-life groups by a five-to-one margin.[76]

The Supreme Court's latest opportunity to overrule *Roe v. Wade* came in the 1999–2000 term when it decided *Sternberg v. Carhart*.[77] By one vote, the Court reaffirmed the *Roe* decision and struck down a Nebraska law criminalizing dilation and extraction (termed "partial birth abortion" by opponents) because the law placed an undue burden on the woman seeking an abortion by limiting her options to less safe procedures.[78]

While battles over the abortion issue were being fought in the courts, political campaigns, and legislative arenas, others preferred a more direct approach, demonstrating at and blockading abortion centers. The Supreme Court has ruled, however, that reasonable time, place, and manner restrictions may be placed on such demonstrations. That position was reaffirmed on June 28, 2000, when the Court upheld a Colorado statute making it unlawful for a person to knowingly approach another person without that person's consent to hand out a leaflet, display a sign, or orally protest within one hundred feet of a health care facility.[79]

Conclusions

Some judicial policies have a greater impact on society than others. The judiciary plays a greater role in developing the nation's policies than the constitutional framers envisioned. However,

American courts are not all-powerful institutions. They were designed with severe limitations and placed in a political system of divided powers. To ask them to produce significant social reforms is to forget their history and ignore their constraints.[80]

Within this complex framework of competing political and social demands and expectations is a policy-making role for the courts. Because the other two branches of government are sometimes not receptive to the demands of certain segments of society, the only alternative for those individuals or groups is to turn to the courts. Civil rights organizations, for example, made no real headway until they found the Supreme Court to be a supportive forum for their school desegregation efforts. They were then able to use *Brown* and other decisions as a springboard to attack a variety of areas of discrimination. Thus a champion at a high government level may offer hope to individuals and interest groups.

As civil rights groups attained some success in the federal courts, others were encouraged to employ litigation as a strategy. For example, several scholars found that women's rights supporters followed a pattern established by minority groups when they began taking their grievances to the courts.[81] What began as a more narrow pursuit for racial equality was thus broadened to a quest for equality for other disadvantaged groups in society.

Clearly, then, the courts can announce policy decisions that attract national attention and perhaps stress that other policy makers have failed to act. In this way the judiciary may invite the other branches to exercise their policy-making powers. Follow-up decisions indicate the judiciary's determination to pursue a particular policy and help keep alive the invitation for other policy makers to join in the endeavor.

All things considered, the courts seem best equipped to develop and implement narrow policies that are less controversial in nature. The policy established in the *Gideon* case provides a good example. The decision that indigent defendants in state criminal trials must be provided with an attorney did not meet any strong outcries of protest. Furthermore, it was a policy that primarily required the support of judges and lawyers; action by Congress and the president was not necessary. A policy of equality for all segments of society, however, is so broad and controversy-laden that it must move beyond the judiciary. As it does so, the courts become simply one part, albeit an important part, of the policy-making process.

Summary

We began this chapter by pointing out that judicial decisions are not self-executing. The courts depend upon a variety of individuals, both inside and outside the judicial branch, to carry out their rulings.

Lower-court judges are prominent in the implementation process. Our discussion of their role in carrying out decisions of higher courts emphasized the discretion they exercise. Factors that account for the flexibility that rests with the lower-court judge include the decentralization of the judicial system and ambiguity of higher-court rulings. We examined, as well, the strategies that lower-court judges may employ in resisting appellate court decisions they dislike.

Congress and the president may also be involved in the implementation process. Each of these two branches can react either positively or negatively to a court decision. The wide range of influences the president and Congress exert in enforcing a judicial decision was described in some detail.

We also noted that some policies call upon state officials to take part in the implementation process. State court judges, for example, played the major role in enforcing the Warren Court's criminal due process decisions. Local school boards have also been called upon to carry out Supreme Court policies.

We concluded the chapter with a discussion of the impact on society of several important federal court policies. Explanations were offered as to why some policies have a greater impact on society than others. Most important, perhaps, is that if a ruling—such as the Supreme Court's original decision on abortion— faces opposition, Congress and other implementers are likely to drag their feet. A final section of the chapter offered some thoughts on the role of courts in bringing about changes in society. In it we noted that the judiciary can act as a kind of beacon for traditionally underrepresented groups seeking to achieve their goals.

NOTES

1. *Gideon v. Wainwright*, 372 U.S. 335 (1963).

2. For a good description of the bureaucratic theory, see Walter F. Murphy, "Chief Justice Taft and the Lower Court Bureaucracy: A Study in Judicial Administration," *Journal of Politics* 24 (1962): 453–476.

3. Richard J. Richardson and Kenneth N. Vines, *The Politics of Federal Courts* (Boston: Little, Brown, 1970), 144.

4. Lawrence Baum, "Implementation of Judicial Decisions: An Organizational Analysis," *American Politics Quarterly* 4 (1976): 91.

5. The desegregation policy was announced in *Brown v. Board of Education of Topeka*, 347 U.S. 483 (1954). For a study of the lower federal courts involved in implementing *Brown*, see Jack W. Peltason, *Fifty-Eight Lonely Men* (New York: Harcourt, Brace and World, 1961).

6. For an excellent account of the school desegregation struggle in Georgia, see Harrell R. Rodgers Jr. and Charles S. Bullock III, *Coercion to Compliance* (Lexington, Mass.: Lexington Books, 1976).

7. *Brown v. Board of Education of Topeka II*, 349 U.S. 294 (1955).

8. *Baker v. Carr*, 369 U.S. 186 (1962).

9. Ibid., 237, 251.

10. The statement was made by Justice Potter Stewart in *Jacobellis v. Ohio*, 378 U.S. 184 (1964).

11. *Furman v. Georgia*, 408 U.S. 238 (1972). A good account of the various views held by the justices, as well as the behind-the-scenes events leading to the final decision, may be found in Bob Woodward and Scott Armstrong, *The Brethren: Inside the Supreme Court* (New York: Simon and Schuster, 1979), 205–220.

12. For a good discussion of this point with pertinent examples, see Bradley C. Canon and Charles A. Johnson, *Judicial Policies: Implementation and Impact*, 2d ed. (Washington, D.C.: CQ Press, 1999), 49–50.

13. Ibid., 29.

14. *Schenck v. United States*, 249 U.S. 47 (1919).

15. Canon and Johnson, *Judicial Policies*, 38.

16. See John Gruhl, "The Supreme Court's Impact on the Law of Libel: Compliance by Lower Federal Courts," *Western Political Quarterly* 33 (1980): 517.

17. See Donald R. Songer and Reginald S. Sheehan, "Supreme Court Impact on Compliance and Outcomes: *Miranda* and *New York Times* in the United States Courts of Appeals," *Western Political Quarterly* 43 (1990): 307.

18. Stephen L. Wasby, *The Supreme Court in the Federal Judicial System*, 4th ed. (Chicago: Nelson-Hall, 1993), 376.

19. See G. Alan Tarr, *Understanding State Constitutions* (Princeton, N.J.: Princeton University Press, 1998), 161–170.

20. Ibid., 166.

21. See Barry Latzer, "The Hidden Conservatism of the State Court Revolution," *Judicature* 74 (1991): 190–197; and Michael Esler, "State Supreme Court Commitment to State Law," *Judicature* 78 (1994): 25–32.

22. See Peltason, *Fifty-Eight Lonely Men*; and Richardson and Vines, *The Politics of Federal Courts*, 98–99.

23. *Griswold v. Connecticut*, 381 U.S. 479 (1965).

24. *Roe v. Wade*, 314 F. Supp. 1217 (1970).

25. Ronald Stidham and Robert A. Carp, "U.S. Trial Court Reactions to Changes in Civil Rights and Civil Liberties Policies," *Southeastern Political Review* 12 (1984): 7.

26. See, for example, Kathleen L. Barber, "Partisan Values in the Lower Courts: Reapportionment in Ohio and Michigan," *Case Western Reserve Law Review* 20 (1969): 406–407; Robert A. Carp and C. K. Rowland, *Policymaking and Politics in the Federal District Courts* (Knoxville: University of Tennessee Press, 1983), chap. 2; C. K. Rowland and Robert A. Carp, "A Longitudinal Study of Party Effects on Federal District Court Policy Propensities," *American Journal of Political Science* 24 (1980): 301; and Ronald Stidham, Robert A. Carp, and C. K. Rowland, "Women's Rights before the Federal District Courts, 1971–1977," *American Politics Quarterly* 11 (1983): 214.

27. See, for example, Peltason, *Fifty-Eight Lonely Men*; Kenneth N. Vines, "Federal District Judges and Race Relations Cases in the South," *Journal of Politics* 26 (1964): 338–357; Richardson and Vines, *The Politics of Federal Courts*, 93–100; and Michael W. Giles and Thomas G. Walker, "Judicial Policy-Making and Southern School Segregation," *Journal of Politics* 37 (1975): 917–936.

28. Giles and Walker, "Judicial Policy-Making and Southern School Segregation," 931.

29. For a good study of the relationship between Congress and the Supreme Court, see John R. Schmidhauser and Larry L. Berg, *The Supreme Court and Congress: Conflict and Interaction, 1945–1968* (New York: Free Press, 1972).

30. 465 U.S. 555 (1984).

31. For accounts of the hearings, see Nadine Cohodas, "Echoes from the Past Punctuate *Grove City* Debate," *Congressional Quarterly Weekly Report*, March 12, 1988, 677; and Mark Willen, "Congress Overrides Reagan's *Grove City* Veto," *Congressional Quarterly Weekly Report*, March 26, 1988, 774.

32. Beth M. Henschen, "Statutory Interpretations of the Supreme Court: Congressional Response," *American Politics Quarterly* 11 (1983): 441–458.

33. *Texas v. Johnson*, 491 U.S. 397 (1989).

34. "D.C. Flag Burning Tests New Law," *Congressional Quarterly Weekly Report*, November 4, 1989, 2952.

35. Ibid.

36. *United States v. Eichman*, 496 U.S. 310 (1990).

37. Joan Biskupic, "Anti-Flag Burning Amendment Falls Far Short in Senate," *Congressional Quarterly Weekly Report*, October 21, 1989, 2803.

38. 2 Dallas 419 (1793); 19 Howard 393 (1857); 158 U.S. 601 (1896); and 400 U.S. 112 (1970), respectively.

39. See Harvey Barkman, "Spiking Judges for Rulings," *National Law Journal*, June 30, 1997, A1, A11.

40. See Nadine Cohodas, "For Robert Bork, The Real Test Begins Now," *Congressional Quarterly Weekly Report*, September 12, 1987, 2159–2163; Nadine Cohodas and Mark Willen, "Who Is Bork?" *Congressional Quarterly Weekly Report*, September 12, 1987, 2164–2168; Ronald V. Elving, "The Supreme Court: How Much Difference Would Justice Bork Make?" *Congressional Quarterly Weekly Report*, September 12, 1987, 2169–2171; and Nadine Cohodas, "Reagan's Judiciary," *Congressional Quarterly Weekly Report*, September 12, 1987, 2176–2177.

41. See James E. Anderson, David W. Brady, and Charles S. Bullock III, *Public Policy and Politics in America* (North Scituate, Mass.: Duxbury Press, 1978), 291–292; and Charles S. Bullock III, "Equal Education Opportunity," in *Implementation of Civil Rights Policy*, eds. Charles S. Bullock III and Charles M. Lamb (Monterey, Calif.: Brooks/Cole, 1984), 57–58.

42. Wasby, *The Supreme Court in the Federal Judicial System*, 256.

43. *United States v. Nixon*, 418 U.S. 683 (1974).

44. Canon and Johnson, *Judicial Policies*, 129.

45. Wasby, *The Supreme Court in the Federal Judicial System*, 16.

46. See Carp and Rowland, *Policymaking and Politics in the Federal District Courts*, 43.

47. For a discussion of this point, see Ronald Stidham, Robert A. Carp, and C. K. Rowland, "Patterns of Presidential Influence on the Federal District Courts: An Analysis of the Appointment Process," *Presidential Studies Quarterly* 14 (1984): 548–560.

48. See Lincoln Caplan, "Annals of Law: The Tenth Justice," pt. 1, *The New Yorker*, August 10, 1987, 32. Also see Lincoln Caplan, *The Tenth Justice: The Solicitor General and the Rule of Law* (New York: Knopf, 1988).

49. *Frontiero v. Richardson*, 411 U.S. 677 (1973).

50. One study, for example, analyzed judicial implementation and impact from the standpoint of the roles of four populations: an interpreting population, an implementing population, a consumer population, and a secondary population. See Canon and Johnson, *Judicial Policies*.

51. Our discussion of the use of powers to provide equitable remedial decrees is largely drawn from Phillip J. Cooper, *Hard Judicial Choices* (New York: Oxford University Press, 1988), 12–14, 342, 348–349.

52. Ibid., 348–349.

53. See Rodgers and Bullock, *Coercion to Compliance*; and Giles and Walker, "Judicial Policy-Making and Southern School Segregation."

54. *Engel v. Vitale,* 370 U.S. 421 (1962).

55. See *Abington School District v. Schempp,* 374 U.S. 203 (1963).

56. No. 99–62, http://supct.law.cornell.edu/supct/html/99-62.ZS.html.

57. Lawrence Baum, *The Supreme Court,* 6th ed. (Washington, D.C.: CQ Press, 1998), 261.

58. Mark C. Miller, "Judicial Activism in Canada and the United States," *Judicature* 81 (1998): 265.

59. Canon and Johnson, *Judicial Policies,* 206.

60. See Gerald N. Rosenberg, *The Hollow Hope: Can Courts Bring About Social Change?* (Chicago: University of Chicago Press, 1991).

61. Ibid., 156.

62. See, for example, Canon and Johnson, *Judicial Policies*; Doug McAdam, *Political Process and the Development of Black Insurgency* (Chicago: University of Chicago Press, 1982); and Aldon Morris, *The Origins of the Civil Rights Movement* (New York: Free Press, 1984).

63. Archibald Cox, *The Warren Court* (Cambridge, Mass.: Harvard University Press, 1968), 74.

64. *Mapp v. Ohio,* 367 U.S. 643 (1961); *Gideon v. Wainwright,* 372 U.S. 335 (1963); and *Miranda v. Arizona,* 384 U.S. 436 (1966).

65. See *United States v. Leon,* 468 U.S. 897 (1984); and *Massachusetts v. Sheppard,* 488 U.S. 981 (1984).

66. 514 U.S. 1 (1995).

67. See the discussion of search and seizure in Otis H. Stephens Jr. and John M. Scheb II, *American Constitutional Law,* 2d ed. (Belmont, Calif.: West/Wadsworth, 1999), 587-594.

68. *Harris v. New York,* 401 U.S. 222 (1971).

69. See *Davis v. United States,* 114 S. Ct. 2350 (1994).

70. *Dickerson v. United States,* No. 99-5525, http://supct.law.cornell.edu/supct/html/99-5525.ZS.html (2000).

71. *Roe v. Wade,* 410 U.S. 113 (1973).

72. For a good case study of the impact of *Roe v. Wade,* including reactions to the decision, see Canon and Johnson, *Judicial Policies,* 5-16. Our discussion is drawn largely from this study.

73. See *Harris v. McRae,* 448 U.S. 297 (1980).

74. See Eva Rubin, *Abortion, Politics, and the Courts:* Roe v. Wade *and Its Aftermath* (New York: Greenwood Press, 1987), 127.

75. 492 U.S. 490.

76. See Canon and Johnson, *Judicial Policies,* 14; and Barbara H. Craig and David O'Brien, *Abortion and American Politics* (Chatham, N.J.: Chatham House, 1988), 204 and 214-218.

77. No. 99-830, http://supct.law.cornell.edu/supct/html/99-830.ZS.html (June 28, 2000).

78. See "Highlights of the Supreme Court's 1999-2000 Term," http://supct.law.cornell.edu/supct/00highlts.html.

79. See Ibid. The case is *Hill v. Colorado,* No. 98-1856, http://supct.law.cornell.edu/supct/html/98-1856.ZS.html.

80. Rosenberg, *Hollow Hope,* 343.

81. See Richard C. Cortner, "Strategies and Tactics of Litigants in Constitutional Cases," *Journal of Public Law* 17 (1968): 287-307; Jo Freeman, *The Politics of Women's Liberation* (New York: David McKay, 1975); Leslie Friedman Goldstein, "Sex and the Burger Court: Recent Judicial Policy Making toward Women," in *Race, Sex, and Policy Problems,* eds. Marian Lief Palley and Michael B. Preston (Lexington, Mass.: Lexington Books, 1979), 103-113; and Karen O'Connor, *Women's Organizations' Use of the Courts* (Lexington, Mass.: Heath, 1980).

SUGGESTED READINGS

Bullock, Charles S. III, and Charles M. Lamb, eds. *Implementation of Civil Rights Policy.* Monterey, Calif.: Brooks/Cole, 1984. A collection of articles that focus on how civil rights policies are carried out.

Canon, Bradley C., and Charles A. Johnson. *Judicial Policies: Implementation and Impact,* 2d ed. Washington, D.C.: CQ Press, 1999. A good study of the process and actors involved in carrying out and enforcing judicial decisions.

Cooper, Phillip J. *Hard Judicial Choices.* New York: Oxford University Press, 1988. The book focuses on the use of remedial decrees in carrying out judicial decisions.

Craig, Barbara H., and David M. O'Brien. *Abortion and American Politics.* Chatham, N.J.: Chatham House, 1993. A good study of the response to the Supreme Court's abortion decisions.

Legal Information Institute's Supreme Court Collection. Available online at: http://supct.law.cornell.edu/supct/. An excellent source of information about the U.S. Supreme Court's history, justices, and opinions.

Peltason, Jack W. *Fifty-Eight Lonely Men.* New York: Harcourt, Brace and World, 1961. An excellent study of the southern federal judges who were given the task of implementing the U.S. Supreme Court's *Brown v. Board of Education* decision.

Rodgers, Harrell R., Jr., and Charles S. Bullock III. *Coercion to Compliance.* Lexington, Mass.: Lexington Books, 1976. A good study of the implementation of school desegregation policies in Georgia.

Rosenberg, Gerald N. *Hollow Hope: Can Courts Bring About Social Change?* Chicago: University of Chicago Press, 1991. The book focuses on the ability of courts to effect social change.

Wasby, Stephen L. *The Impact of the United States Supreme Court: Some Perspectives.* Homewood, Ill.: Dorsey, 1970. The author discusses the various actors involved in the process of implementing decisions of the U.S. Supreme Court.

CHAPTER 7

Policy Making by American Judges:
A Synthesis

How exactly the courts should interpret broad terms in the U.S. Constitution is an issue of enduring controversy. Here the Founders of the Republic take turns signing their names.

"AN EDUCATION," THE SAYING GOES, "is what you have left after you've forgotten what you've learned." This text has presented many facts, theories, statistics, and examples about the federal and state court systems. But as time goes on and the myriad of facts and illustrations are largely forgotten, what education ought you to have about the operation and policy making of American courts? It is the purpose of this chapter to pull out of the previous twelve chapters certain key ideas and significant themes that we would like you to remember long after most factual tidbits have faded from memory.

The decisions of federal and state judges and justices affect the lives of all Americans. Whether it be the norm enforcement rulings or the broader policy-making decisions, the output of federal and state courts permeates the warp and woof of the body politic in the United States. No one can have a full and accurate understanding of the American political system without being cognizant of the work of the men and women who wear the black robe. In examining decision making by the judiciary, two basic questions are worthy of consideration. First, what are the conditions that cause judges to engage in policy making and to do so boldly? Second, does the literature give any clues as to the substantive direction of this policy making; that is, will it be conservative or liberal, supportive of or antagonistic toward the status quo? In seeking answers to these two basic questions, we have synthesized four sets of variables that shed some light in this area: (1) the nature of the case or issue presented to the court, (2) the values and orientations of the judges, (3) the nature of the judicial decision-making process, and (4) extraneous influences that serve to implement and sustain judicial decisions.

The Nature of the Case or Issue

One critical variable that clearly affects the degree to which (and sometimes the direction in which) American jurists influence citizens' lives is the type of controversy that might serve as grist for the judicial mills. If it is the sort of issue that judges can resolve with room for significant maneuver, the impact of the case on public policy may be impressive. Conversely, if American jurists are forbidden to enter a certain decision-making realm or enter with only limited options, the policy impact will be nil. There are several aspects of this general proposition.

Jurisdiction

In Chapter 2 we outlined the jurisdiction of the three levels of the federal judiciary. A knowledge of the topic is important in and of itself, but it takes on a second meaning in the context of this discussion—namely, that judges may not make policy in subject areas over which they have no legal authority. The controversy between the United States and Russia over whether it is legitimate for the United States to go ahead with the development of an antimissile defense system is of great significance to the American people—and national security may be dependent on it. However, U.S. judges will not affect the situation because they have no jurisdiction over U.S. defense policy and security matters between the United States and other nations. Conversely, the courts will have considerable policy impact in matters of racial segregation and damage awards against the tobacco companies because such disputes fall squarely within the legal jurisdiction of the U.S. judiciary.

Although the courts do have some leeway in determining whether they have jurisdiction over a particular subject, for the most part jurisdictional boundaries are set forth in the U.S. and state constitutions and by acts of Congress and the state legislatures. In the same context, a legislative body's power to create and restrict the courts' jurisdiction can often greatly affect the direction of judicial decision making.

For example, Congress, by virtue of the Voting Rights Act, has granted citizens the right to sue local governments in federal courts if those governments alter the contours of electoral districts so as to dilute significantly the voting strength of minorities. By giving courts jurisdiction in this area and by telling judges in effect how to decide the cases (by establishing the decision-making goals), Congress has had a major impact on judicial policy making. Likewise, the current threat by some members of Congress to remove certain matters from federal court jurisdiction, such as the power to use busing as a tool of desegregation, has policy-making potential of equal magnitude.

Judicial Self-Restraint

The nature-of-the-case variable is also related to whether a controversy falls into one of those forbidden realms into which the "good judge" ought not set foot. One judge might like to rule on a particular matter that is crying for adjudication, but if the litigant has not yet exhausted all legal or administrative remedies, the jurist will have to stay his hand. Another judge might like to overturn a particular presidential action because she thinks it "smacks of fascism," but if no specific portion of the Constitution has been violated, she will have to express her displeasure in the voting booth—not in the courtroom. The enormous emphasis that the judicial system places on respecting past precedents (that is, the doctrine of stare decisis) further restrains jurists from giving reign to impulsive decision making. The various maxims of judicial self-restraint may come from a variety of sources, including the Constitution, tradition, and acts of Congress and state legislatures; some have been imposed by the judges themselves. But whatever their source, they serve to channel the potential areas of judicial policy making. Judges would have little success in attempting to adjudicate matters if doing so would soon bring reversal, censure, or organized opposition from those who are in a position to "correct" a judge who has strayed from the accepted pathway of judicial behavior.

Norm Enforcement versus Policy Making

Throughout this book we have discussed judicial behavior as including both norm enforcement and significant policy making. Most cases fall into the former category—particularly for the lower judiciary. That is, in the majority of cases, judges routinely cite the applicable precedents, yield to the side with the weightiest evidence, and apply the statutes that clearly control the given fact situation. Discretion is at a minimum. In these routine cases, judges are not so much making policy as they are applying and enforcing existing norms and policy. In addition to norm enforcement, however, judges are presented with cases in which their room to maneuver—their potential to make policy—is much greater. Such opportunities exist at all levels of the judiciary, but appellate judges and justices probably have more options for significant policy making than do their colleagues on the trial court bench. Since the late 1930s, Bill of Rights issues, not labor and economic questions, have provided judges with the greatest opportunities for significant policy making.

In exploring this subject, we identified several situations (or case characteristics) that greatly enhance the judge's capacity to make policy rather than merely to enforce existing policy. One such opportunity occurs when the legal evidence is contradictory or is equally strong on both sides. It is not uncommon for judges to preside over a case for which the facts and evidence are about equally compelling for both sides or for which about an equal number of precedents would sustain a finding for either party. Being pulled in several directions at once may not be an entirely comfortable position, but it does allow the jurists freer rein to strike out on their own than if prevailing facts and law impelled them toward one position.

Likewise, judicial policy making can flower when jurists are asked to resolve new types of controversies for which statutory law and past judicial precedents are virtually absent. For example, when the federal courts were asked whether artificially created life forms could be patented, they could not avoid making policy. (Even the refusal to decide is a decision, as the existentialists have long argued.) Thus some cases by their very nature invite judicial policy making, whereas others carry with them no such invitation. Judges differ in their perceptions of whether there is an opportunity in a given case for creative, innovative decision making. To some extent such differences are a function of the judges themselves. But our contention here is that whether a case calls for garden-variety norm enforcement or whether it invites major judicial policy making depends to a large degree on the nature of the controversy itself.

Summary

In considering whether and in what direction judges' decisions will significantly affect people's lives, we can say this: The nature of the case is a vital component in this line of inquiry. Judges can make policy only in those areas over which the U.S. and state constitutions and the legislative branches have granted them jurisdiction and only in a manner consistent with the norms of judicial self-restraint. Also, if the controversies presented to the judges provide them with some room to maneuver—as many current civil rights and liberties issues do—more policy making likely will occur than if the cases were tightly circumscribed by clearly controlling precedents and law.

The Values and Orientations of the Judges

A second set of variables to be considered if an understanding is to be reached about judicial policy making and the direction it will take concerns the judges themselves. What are their background characteristics? How were they appointed (or elected) and by whom? How do they conceive of their judicial role? By learning something about the values and orientations of the men and women who are tapped for judicial service, people are better able to explain and predict what they will do on the bench. (Also recall from previous chapters that the attitudes and values of other actors in the judicial process—for example, police officers, prosecutors, and the solicitor general—affect the content and direction of their important duties.)

We have looked at judicial background characteristics in a variety of contexts in this book. Here we shall examine several that have particular relevance vis-à-vis judicial policy making and its direction.

Judges as a Socioeconomic Elite

In Chapter 3 we made much of the fact that America's jurists come from a narrow segment of the social and economic strata. To an overwhelming degree they are offspring of upper- and upper-middle-class parents and come from families with a tradition of political, and often judicial, service. They are the men and women to whom the U.S. system has been good, who fit in, and who have succeeded. The mavericks, malcontents, and ideological extremists are discreetly weeded out by the judicial recruitment process.

What does all this suggest about judicial policy making and its direction? Given the striking similarity of the jurists and the backgrounds from which they come, their overall policy making is generally going to be fairly modest, conventional, and ideologically moderate. Although many judges have a commitment to reform and will use their policy-making opportunities to this end, it is to adjust and enhance a way of life that they basically believe in. Seldom bitten is the hand of the socioeconomic system that feeds them. Although an occasional maverick may slip in or develop within the judicial ranks, most judges are basically conservative in that they hold dear the traditional institutions and rules of the game that have brought success to them and their families. America's elite has its fair share of both liberals and conservatives, but it does not have many who would use their discretionary opportunities to alter radically the basic social and political system.

Judges as Representatives of Their Political Parties

Although the nature of the judicial recruitment process gives virtually all U.S. judges a similar and fairly conventional cast, there are differences. The prior political party affiliation of jurists does alter the way they exercise their policy-making discretion when the circumstances of a case give them room to maneuver. Judges and justices who come from the ranks of the Democratic Party have been somewhat more liberal than their colleagues from Republican ranks. This has meant, for one thing, that Democrats on the bench are more likely to favor government regulation of the economy—particularly when such regulation appears to benefit the underdog or the worker in disputes with management. In criminal justice matters, Democratic jurists are more disposed toward the motions made by defendants. Finally, in questions concerning civil rights and liberties, the Democrat on the bench tends to establish policies that favor a broadening position.

In the same context, we stress the important policy link between the partisan choice made by voters in a presidential election, the judges whom the chief executive appoints, and the subsequent policy decisions of these jurists. When voters make a policy choice in electing a conservative or a liberal to the presidency, they have a discernible impact upon the judiciary as well. We have noted that this phenomenon is not unique to the United States but is true in many other nations as well, including Canada, Germany, and Japan. Despite the many participants in the judicial selection process and the variety of forces that would thwart policy-oriented presidents (and governors) from getting "their kind of people" on the bench, it is still fair to say that, to an impressive degree, chief executives tend to get the type of men and women they want in the judiciary.

In a speech made just prior to the 1984 presidential election, conservative Supreme Court justice William H. Rehnquist discussed this phenomenon with unusual candor. Although he was speaking primarily about the Supreme Court, his remarks pertain to the entire U.S. judiciary. There is "no reason in the world," said Rehnquist, why President Ronald Reagan should not attempt to "pack" the federal courts. The institution has been constructed in such a way that the public will, in the person of the president, have something to say about the membership of the Court and thereby indirectly about its decisions. Thus, Rehnquist felt, presidents may seek to appoint people who are sympathetic to their political and philosophical principles. After calling new judicial appointments "indirect infusions of the popular will," Rehnquist added that it "should come as no surprise" that presidents attempt to pack the courts with people of similar policy values, but "like murder suspects in a detective novel, they must have motive and opportunity."[1]

Judges as Manifestations of Localism

Another aspect of the values and orientations of the judges themselves has an impact upon their policy-making process: the attributes and mores that the judges carry with them from the region in which they grew up or in which they hold court. We have documented a wide variety of geographic variations in the way both trial and appellate jurists view the world and react to its demands. For example, we noted that on many policy issues Northern jurists have been more liberal than their colleagues in the South. Likewise, regional variations in judicial decision making are not unique with the United States. For example, conscientious objector cases in Norway were decided differently depending on which region of the country the case was heard (see Chapter 10).

Not only does judicial policy making vary from one region of the land to another, but studies reveal that each of the circuits tends to be unique in the way its appellate and trial court judges administer the law and make decisions. The presence of significant state-by-state differences in U.S. trial judge behavior is further evidence that judges bring with them to the bench certain local values and orientations that subsequently affect their policy-making patterns.

Judges' Conceptions of Their Judicial Roles

We noted three basic ways in which judges conceive of their roles vis-à-vis the policy-making process. At one end of the spectrum are the lawmakers, who take a broad view of the judicial role. These jurists, often referred to as activists or innovators, contend that they can and sometimes must make significant public policy when they render many of their decisions. At the other end of the spectrum are the law interpreters, who take a narrow view of the judicial function. Sometimes called strict constructionists, they believe that norm enforcement is the only proper role of the judge. In between are the pragmatists, or realists, who contend that judging is primarily a matter of enforcing norms but that on occasion they can and must formulate new judicial policy.

Understanding the role conception that a judge brings to the bench (or develops on the bench) will not reveal much about the substantive direction of his or her policy making. It is possible to be a conservative activist as well as a liberal activist. One can go out on a judicial limb and give the benefit of the doubt to the economic giant or to the underdog, to the criminal defendant claiming police brutality or to the police officer urging renewed emphasis on law and order. But a knowledge of the judges' role conceptions will indicate a good deal about whether they are more inclined to defer to the norms and policies set by others or to strike out occasionally and make policy on their own.

Summary

In attempting to learn about policy making by judges and its substantive direction, we have set forth a second factor that helps channel our thinking—namely, the values and orientations that the judges bring with them to the bench. Four items are particularly relevant: (1) America's judges come from the establishment's elite, a fact that serves to discourage radical policy making; (2) judges' policy making is reflective of their partisan orientations and of the executive who nominated them; (3) policy decisions manifest the local values and attitudes that judges possess when they first put on the black robe; and (4) judges will engage in more policy making if they bring to the bench a belief that it is right and proper for judges to act in this manner.

The Nature of the Judicial Decision-Making Process

Knowing how judges think and reason, how they are influenced in their decision making, provides a good clue about policy making by U.S. judges. Although this factor is inexorably intertwined with the first two we have outlined here, it is distinct enough to warrant a separate discussion. In the section about the legal subculture in Chapter 4, we examined the nature of the legal reasoning process that is at the heart of the system of jurisprudence in America. We noted that this is essentially a three-step process described by the doctrine of precedent as follows: (1) similarity is seen between cases, (2) the rule of law inherent in the first case is announced, and (3) the rule of law is made applicable to the second case. Adherence to past precedents is also part and parcel of the legal reasoning process. Skillfully shaping and crafting the wisdom of the past, as found in previous court rulings, and applying it to contemporary problems is what this time-honored process is all about.

Decision making by collegial courts has some dimensions not inherent in the behavior of trial judges sitting alone. In Chapter 5 we examined several approaches that judicial scholars have used to get a theoretical handle on the way appellate court judges and justices think and act. One of these is small-group dynamics, an approach that sees the output of the appellate judiciary as being strongly influenced by three general phenomena: persuasion on the merits, bargaining, and the threat of sanctions.

Persuasion lies at the heart of small-group dynamics. It means that because of their training and values, judges are receptive to arguments based on sound legal reasoning, often spiced with relevant legal precedents. Both hard and anecdotal evidence indicates that judicial policies are influenced in the refining furnace of the judicial conference room.

Bargaining, too, molds the content and direction of judicial policy outputs. The compromises that are made among jurists—during the decision-making conference and while an opinion is being drafted—to satisfy the majority judges are almost always the product of bargaining. It is not that judges say to one another: "If you vote for my favorite judicial policy position, I'll vote for yours." Instead, a justice might phrase a bargaining offer—say, in a case dealing with the right of students to appeal adverse disciplinary rulings from a state university to the federal courts—more like this: "I don't agree with your opinion as it now stands permitting students to appeal all adverse disciplinary decisions to the local federal district court. That's just too liberal for me, and I don't approve of interfering in university affairs to that degree. However, I could go along with a majority opinion that permitted appeals in really serious disciplinary matters that might result in the permanent suspension of a student." The first justice must then decide how badly the colleague's vote is needed—badly enough to water down the opinion to include only cases dealing with permanent suspension instead of all cases, as in the original opinion? Such is how judicial policies are generated through bargaining.

The sanctions that we discussed include a variety of items in the genteel arsenal of judicial weaponry. A judge's threat to take a vote away from the majority and to dissent may cause the majority judges to alter the content of a policy decision. A judge's willingness to write a strong, biting dissent is another sanction that occasionally causes a unity-conscious majority to consider policy changes in an opinion. The threat to "go public" is a third tactic that judges in collegial courts use to alter the policy course of other jurists. Public exposure of an objectionable internal court practice or stance is probably the least pleasant of the sanctions. Finally, we noted that chief justices of the U.S. and state supreme courts and their counterparts at the appellate and trial court levels all have singular opportunities to guide and shape the policy decisions of the courts. The status and options that are part of their unique leadership positions provide them an opportunity for crafting court policy if they have the desire and innate ability to make the most of it.

Besides small-group dynamics, we also looked at an approach to appellate court decision making known as attitude theory. This school of thought sees judges as possessing a stable set of attitudes that guide their policy choices. Such attitudes exist on civil rights and liberties issues, social issues (matters of voting and ethnic status), and economic questions dealing with the equal distribution of wealth. Justices with similar attitudes on these questions tend to vote in a similar manner on cases and thus form voting blocs. Research in this realm has borne some impressive fruit because it has been possible to demonstrate that members of the appellate judiciary do decide cases in accordance with consistent underlying value dimensions and that voting blocs do form and behave according to predictable patterns. Attitude theory has been used successfully to explain and predict the voting patterns of appellate court jurists in many other nations, such as Australia, Canada, India, Japan, and the Philippines.

Besides the attitudinal model we discussed an approach that has been gaining many new adherents in recent years—rational choice theory. This model does not reject the assumptions of attitude theory, but it contends that the attitudinal model is simplistic and shortsighted. Rational choice theorists argue that goal-directed justices operate in what they call strategic or interdependent decision-making contexts. The justices understand that the outcome of their policy goals depends on the values of other decision makers, such as Congress, the president, and other justices on the Court. When making decisions, the justices must consider not only how they want the case to be decided but also how such an outcome might be affected by the decisions of these other actors. Rational choice theorists have been able to marshal some impressive data to sustain their theoretical contentions.

What does this third general factor—the nature of the judicial decision-making process—say about judicial policy making and its substantive direction? We would offer two observations. First, most policy making by judges is likely to be slow and incremental. This is exactly what one would expect from a reasoning process that relies so heavily on respecting precedents and that places such emphasis on stability and continuity. The decision-making process of American judges does not lend itself to radical and abrupt departures from precedents and past behavior. Yet change does occur and new policies are made. But legal history suggests that American jurists have often "reformed to preserve," and that is a principle often associated with conservatism.

Second, an understanding of the judicial thought process and of the small-group dynamics of collegial courts does not in itself reveal anything about the substantive direction of a court's policy making. However, knowing which judges and justices are masters at persuasion, bargaining, and the use of sanctions does provide some insight into explaining and predicting the content of judicial policy decisions. If, on a given court, the conservatives have developed a mastery of these tactics, then the bettor would do well to wager a few dollars on more conservative judicial decisions.

The Impact of Extraneous Influences

The making and implementation of judicial policy decisions undoubtedly are influenced by a variety of actors and forces outside the courtroom. It is not just judges and law clerks with leather-bound casebooks and arguments by silver-tongued lawyers that affect the shaping and carrying out of judicial decisions. Into the calculus must also go such unwieldy variables as the values and ability of the chief executive, the will of Congress or the legislature, the temper of public opinion, the strength and ideological orientation of key interest groups, and the attitudes and good will of those called on to implement judicial decisions in the real world.

The executive input into the making and implementation of key judicial decisions is considerable. As the policy choice of the citizenry in the past election, the chief executive has the opportunity to fill the courts with men and women who share the basic political and judicial philosophies of the administration. Once on the court, judges may be encouraged or discouraged in their policy making by the words and deeds emanating from the White House or the governor's mansion. For instance, the willingness of Presidents Dwight D. Eisenhower and John F. Kennedy to use federal troops to help enforce judicial integration orders must have encouraged subsequent policy decisions regarding presidents' use of armed force to achieve this goal. Conversely, President George Bush's vocal opposition to the use of racial or gender quotas in employers' hiring practices or in the awarding of government contracts may have caused many federal judges to think at least twice before ordering or condoning the use of such quotas. The overall role of the chief executive in implementing judicial policy decisions was examined in Chapter 6.

Congress has an impact on the creation and nurturing of judicial policy decisions, just as the legislature does at the state level. In its power to establish most of the original and appellate jurisdiction of the federal judiciary, it has the capacity to determine the subject matter arenas where judicial policy battles are fought. In its capacity to establish the number of courts and determine the financial support they will have, Congress can show its approval or displeasure regarding the third branch of government. By accepting or rejecting presidential nominees to the courts, the Senate helps to determine who the judicial decision makers will be and hence their value orientations. Finally, the implementation of many key judicial policy decisions is dependent on legislation that Congress must pass to make the ruling a meaningful reality for those affected by it. Had not Congress passed several key bills to implement the courts' desegregation orders (discussed in Chapter 6), integration of the public schools would be little more than a nice idea for those whom the rulings were intended to benefit.

Public opinion also has a role to play in this policy-making process—not an outrageous prospect for a nation that calls itself a democracy. In rendering key policy decisions, judges can hardly be oblivious to the mood and values of the citizenry of which they themselves are a part. In many policy areas (such as obscenity, desegregation, and legislative apportionment), judges have been ordered by the Supreme Court to take the local political and social climate into consideration when they tender their rulings. The support or opposition of the public is often a key variable in determining whether a judge's orders are carried out in the spirit as well as the letter of the law.

Interest group activity is another thread in the tapestry of judicial policy making. Such organizations often provide the president (or a state governor) with the names of individuals whom they support for judicial office, and they lobby against those whose judicial values they consider suspect. They often provide the vehicle for key judicial decisions by instigating legislation, by sponsoring test cases, and by giving legal and financial aid to those litigants whose cases they favor. They can thwart implementation of judicial decisions or help carry them out more effectively (see Chapter 6).

The final group of extraneous forces consists of those individuals and organizations that are expected to implement the judicial policy decision on a day-by-day basis out on the street: the police officer who is asked to be sure that the accused understand their legal rights; the physician who must certify that a requested abortion is truly in the mental health interests of the pregnant woman; the personnel officer at a state institution who could readily find some technicality for refusing to hire a minority applicant; or the censor on the town's movie review board who is told that nudity and obscenity are not synonymous but who does not want to believe it. It is the values, motivations, and actions of such individuals that must be considered to fully understand the judicial policy-making process. Their good-faith support of a judicial policy decision is vital to making it work; their indifference or opposition may cause the judge's ruling to die aborning.

Our intention in this chapter is to get some grip on the slippery handle of policy making by American judges. Although many more questions have been raised than answered, perhaps a little better understanding has been reached as to where to search for some answers. To learn the conditions that allow for bold policy making, and to predict the direction that policy making will take, attention must be focused on the nature of the case or controversy that can properly be brought into court; on the values and orientations of the jurists who preside over these courts; on the precise nature of the decision-making process of American judges; and, finally, on a variety of extraneous actors and forces whose values and effects filter into the American judicial process from beginning to end.

NOTE

1. "Rehnquist Says It's OK for a President to Pack High Court," *Houston Chronicle*, October 19, 1984, A3.

Glossary

Activism (judicial). The willingness of a judge to inject into a case his or her own personal values about what is good and bad public policy.

Adversarial process. The process used in American courtrooms where the trial is seen as a battle between two opposing sides, and the role of the judge is to act as a sort of passive referee.

Advisory opinions. Rendering a decision on an abstract or hypothetical question (something that American courts are not supposed to do).

Amicus curiae. ("Friend of the court.") A person (or group), not a party to a case, who submits views (usually in the form of written briefs) about how the case should be decided.

Appellate jurisdiction. The authority of a higher court to review the decision of a lower court.

Attitude theory. The theory of appellate judge behavior that holds that once the researcher learns the judges' basic set of attitudes, he or she can explain and predict how those judges will vote in the cases that come before them.

Bench trial. Trial without a jury in which the judge decides which party prevails.

Blue slip. The device that senators use to invoke the practice of senatorial courtesy when they are objecting to a president's nomination to a district judgeship.

Certification. The procedure by which one of the U.S. appeals courts asks the U.S. Supreme Court for instructions or clarification about a particular legal matter. Either the justices may choose to honor this request or not, or they may request that the entire record of the case be sent to the Supreme Court for review and final judgment.

Class action. A suit brought by persons having similar grievances against a common entity; for example, a group of smokers with lung cancer suing a tobacco company.

Collegial courts. Courts having more than one judge, which are almost always appellate courts.

Concurrent jurisdiction. A situation in which two courts have a legal right to hear the same case. For example, both the U.S. Supreme Court and U.S. trial courts have concurrent jurisdiction in certain cases brought by or against ambassadors or counsels.

Concurring opinion. An opinion by a member of a court that agrees with the result reached in the case but offers its own rationale for the decision.

Conservative. For judges this means support for the prosecution in criminal cases, support for the government in its attempts to restrict freedom of expression, and support for the individual (or corporation) that is being regulated by the government.

Corpus juris. The entire body of law for a particular legal entity.

Court of appeals. A court that is higher than an ordinary trial court and has the function of reviewing or correcting the decisions of trial judges.

Cue theory. The theory that Supreme Court justices do not have the time to carefully review all cases that are appealed to them, so they develop short-hand methods of seeking out easy-to-find cues to help them determine whether they want to review a particular case.

Declaratory judgment. When a court outlines the rights of the parties under a statute, a will, or a contract.

Dissenting opinion. An opinion by a member of a court that disagrees with the result reached in the case by the court.

Diversity of citizenship suit. A civil legal proceeding brought by a citizen of one state against a citizen of another state.

En banc. ("In the bench" or "as a full bench.") Court sessions with the entire membership of a court participating, not just a smaller panel of judges.

Federal question. If a court case centers around the interpretation of a federal law, the U.S. Constitution, or a treaty, then it contains a federal question and the case may be heard by a U.S. court.

Fluidity. The degree that appellate court judges change their opinions between the time a conference vote is taken and the vote is announced in open court.

Grand jury. A body of sixteen to twenty-three citizens who listen to evidence of criminal allegations, which is presented by the prosecutors, and determine whether probable cause exists to believe an individual committed an offense.

Habeas corpus. A writ (court order) that is usually used to bring a prisoner before the court to determine the legality of his or her imprisonment.

Impeachment. The only way in which a federal judge may be removed from office. The House of Representatives brings the charge(s), and the Senate, following trial, convicts by a two-thirds vote of the membership.

Judicial realist. One who believes that judges, like other human beings, are influenced by the values and attitudes learned in childhood.

Judicial review. The power of the judicial branch to declare acts of the executive and legislative branches unconstitutional.

Jurisdiction. The authority of a court to hear and decide legal disputes and to enforce its rulings.

Justiciability. Whether a judge ought to hear or refrain from hearing certain types of cases. It differs from jurisdiction, which pertains to the technical right of a judge to hear a case. For example, lawsuits dealing with political questions are considered nonjusticiable.

Law. A social norm that is sanctioned in threat or in fact by the application of physical force. The party that exercises such physical force is recognized by society as legitimately having this kind of authority, such as a police officer.

Liberal. For judges this means support for the defendant in criminal cases, support for a broadening position for freedom of expression, and support for the government in its attempt to economically regulate individuals and corporations.

Moot. Describes a case when the basic facts or the status of the parties have significantly changed in the interim between when the suit was filed and when it comes before the judge.

Opinion of the court. A judge's written explanation of the court's decision. Because the case may be heard by a panel of judges in an appellate court, the opinion can take two forms. If all the judges completely agree with the result, one judge will write the opinion for all. If all the judges do not agree, the formal decision will be based on the view of the majority, and one member of the majority will write the decision.

Oral argument. An opportunity for lawyers to summarize their position before the court and to answer the judges' questions.

Original jurisdiction. The court that by law must be the first to hear a particular type of case. For example, in suits with at least $75,000 at stake between citizens from different states, the federal district courts are the courts of original jurisdiction.

Per curiam. ("By the court.") An unsigned opinion of the court, often brief.

Petit jury (or trial jury). A group of citizens who hear the evidence presented by both sides at trial and determine the facts in dispute.

Plaintiff. The person who files the complaint in a civil lawsuit.

Political question. When the courts refuse to rule because they believe that under the U.S. Constitution the founders meant that the matter at hand should be dealt with by Congress or the president, the courts are refusing to rule on a political question.

Private law. This deals with the rights and obligations that private individuals and institutions have when they relate to one another.

Public law. The relationships that individuals have with the state as a sovereign entity; for example, the tax code, criminal laws, and Social Security legislation.

Rational choice theory. The theory that appellate judges' votes may be explained by knowing more than just their basic attitudes. Judges realize that the fate of their policy goals often depends on the values of other decision makers, such as their colleagues on the bench, the president, and members of Congress.

Recess appointment. An appointment made by the president when Congress is in recess. Persons appointed in this manner may hold office only until Congress reconvenes.

Reversible error. An error committed at the trial court level that is so serious that it requires the appellate court to reverse the decision of the trial judge.

Role (judicial). How judges view themselves as jurists and the degree to which they believe in judicial activism or judicial self-restraint.

Rule of four. On the Supreme Court at least four justices must agree to take a case before the Court as a whole will consider it.

Rule of eighty. When the sum of a judge's age and number of years on the bench is eighty, Congress permits the individual to retire with full pay and benefits.

Self-restraint (judicial). The reluctance of a judge to inject into a case his or her own personal ideas of what is good or bad public policy.

Senatorial courtesy. Under this practice senators of the president's political party who object to a candidate that the president wishes to appoint to a district judgeship in their home state have a virtual veto over the nomination.

Small-group analysis. The theory that appellate court behavior may be explained in part from what social scientists know generally about the decision-making process of small groups of any kind.

Social leadership (on appellate courts). A judge performing this role attends to the emotional needs of his or her associates by affirming their values as individuals and as court members, especially when their views are rejected by the majority.

Socialization (judicial). The process by which a new judge is formally and informally trained to perform the specific tasks of the judgeship.

Standing. The status of someone who wishes to bring a lawsuit. To have standing the person must have suffered (or be immediately about to suffer) a direct and significant injury.

Stare decisis, the doctrine of. ("Stand by what has been decided.") In effect, the tradition of honoring and following previous decisions of the courts and established points of law.

Statutory law. The type of law enacted by a legislative body, such as Congress, a state legislature, or a city council.

Task leadership (on appellate courts). A judge performing this role is the intellectual force behind the conference deliberations, focusing on the actual decision and trying to keep the court consistent with itself.

Three-judge district courts. With some types of important cases Congress has mandated that the case cannot be heard by a U.S. trial judge acting alone but has to be decided by a panel of three judges, one of whom must be an appeals court judge.

Three-judge panels (of appellate courts). Most decisions of the U.S. courts of appeals are not made by the entire court sitting together but by three judges, often selected at random, to hear any given case.

Venue. The geographical location in which a case is tried.

Writ of certiorari. An order issued by the U.S. Supreme Court directing the lower court to transfer records for a case that it will hear on appeal.

Writ of mandamus. A court order compelling a public official to perform his or her duty.

Subject Index

Case Index